HUNTER'S POINT

HUNTER'S POINT

A Black Ghetto

ARTHUR E. HIPPLER

BASIC BOOKS, INC., PUBLISHERS

NEW YORK

To Mango,
who helped me feel my way through;
to Joan,
who aided in many ways;
and to Sheelik,
whose memory will always be with me.

CONTENTS

III
The Community   135

PREFACE

BETWEEN the time the field work for this study was completed and the present, a number of works by social scientists and others have been published which are on the surface not only different in perspective from this one but appear to present a reality greatly at variance with the one described here.

Four works, in particular, are of special interest to me, and I will take this opportunity to comment on them and their relationship to this study of Hunter's Point. One of the most important is Grier and Cobbs's *Black Rage* (1968), the basic thesis of which is that black American life is permeated by an anger rooted in the fact of white oppression. I have no argument with Grier and Cobbs that at bottom the historical experience of black Americans has predisposed them toward anger within and at American society. My basic difference with Grier and Cobbs stems from my observation that the present familial structure of lower-class blacks — abetted and supported, as I note, by racial prejudice against them — creates a negative feedback system in which the same pathology is reproduced in each generation and which has taken on the characteristics of a self-perpetuating dynamic. Grier and Cobbs's description of socialization practices, personality traits, and the meaning of manhood and womanhood, I believe, supports this idea. Thus, there is no fundamental disagreement about observed data;

Grier and Cobbs simply interpret differently the data they observe.

Hendin (1969) in discussing black suicide notes the importance of self-hate which I find to be such an integral part of urban black American life. Hendin shows the relationship between socialization and self-loathing in the overall context of racial prejudice more directly than do Grier and Cobbs. The very defensive postures I have observed in black lower-class men and women are the ones whose failure leads, as Hendin points out, to suicide.

Liebow's *Tally's Corner* (1967) describes in great detail the kinds of posturings that men use as defenses against feelings of insecurity and as weapons in the continually perceived warfare between men and women, which is one of the cornerstones of my own work. My work differs from Liebow's, however, in that I attempt to relate these behaviors to their psychological underpinnings.

The collection of essays edited by Katz and Gurin (1969) is an attempt to provide an overview of the social science studies of black Americans. These works are critical to understanding the present state of such research, but they are, I believe, collectively marred by a particular myopia. The main thrust of these works aims at supporting the notion that whatever individual personality problems exist in lower-class black Americans are a function of racial derogation by whites, and that solutions to this problem can be found by viewing it as essentially structural.

At one time, before my own field work among black Americans and other depressed ethnic minorities (American Indians and Eskimos), I might also have accepted this thesis (see the Epilogue). I no longer believe this to be an accurate description of reality. It is my belief that there are fundamental differences among human groups in their ability to achieve and create. I do not propose, nor do I have any evidence, that these differences are due to in-born intelligence. Within any group, individuals exist who, because of differential socialization or innate ability, seem able to overcome nearly any adversity. Apart from such individuals, however, the modal differences among groups remain.

The aims of this work are not immediately ameliorative. My principal concern has been to show the way in which the convergence of many factors in lower-class black experience produces its unique life style. If this presentation seems essentially negative, I can only submit that these are the circumstances as I find them. Being neither an economist nor a politician, I do not profess to know how to ameliorate such a situation. I can only hope, therefore, that I have contributed to the solution of one of the overriding problems of our age by helping to define it.

ACKNOWLEDGMENTS

THERE are many people to whom I owe a debt of gratitude for their assistance in this work. Overall I was guided in this work by George A. DeVos, professor of anthropology at the University of California in Berkeley. I am also grateful for the assistance of Dr. L. Bryce Boyer who materially assisted me in the use of psychoanalytic theory. The interpretations in this work however are entirely my own and I bear the responsibility for them.

I am further grateful for the moral support of Dr. Arlon Tussing and Dr. Thomas Morehouse, friends and colleagues, and for the substantial support of the Institute of Social, Economic, and Government Research, University of Alaska, and its director, Victor Fischer, who made such support available, without which the completion of the manuscript would have been difficult. I am further indebted to Dr. Robert King for his editorial advice and to Joan Gedney for manuscript preparation.

Finally I am deeply grateful to the people of Hunter's Point, without whose cooperation and friendship I could not have completed this study.

Introduction

THIS study is an attempt to show the interrelationship of the social, cultural, and psychological dimensions of life in a black ghetto in San Francisco. Aside from the fortuitous reasons which guide most research — those of contiguity, adequate funding, and the like — there seemed a particular reason to investigate this group.

While there are at present some 20 million blacks in the United States, about half of whom live in major urban areas in the northern part of the country, at the time of my field work there was astonishingly little significant participant observation and anthropological research concerning them. Although there exists a vast array of literary and popular treatments of black American life and numerous demographic, sociological, and quasi-anthropological works, the particular integrated and holistic anthropological approach which attempts to uncover the personal, social-structural, and subcultural aspects of such life has been relatively neglected.[1]

There are a number of possible reasons for this neglect. It may well be that anthropology has not yet (and perhaps cannot) escape its original reputation as the study of man primarily through "primitive" cultures. The study of Euro-American and especially industrial societies, apart from the peasantry, has been popularly conceded to be the prerogative of sociology, while the study of more "colorful" and "exotic" communities belongs in anthropology. There is, moreover, the more cogent argument that some kind of "distantiation" is necessary for objectivity. Thus it has been considered easier to study communities very "different" from that of the observer. Yet another problem with such studies is the identification of the units to be studied. In a large heterogeneous population it is quite difficult to isolate not only the group to be studied but to clarify with any precision the varying weights of the impact of social forces on individuals of a specific ethnic background. In addition, there is the unmentioned but quite real fact that most anthropologists are white. The unique tensions between blacks and whites in the United States have produced both conscious and unconscious guilt in many well-intentioned scholars. This guilt, combined with the tensions that produce it, usually precludes easy or comfortable entry into the life of a black community.

Finally, this tension and guilt may have been in part responsible for the general belief held by members of the white majority in the United States that the larger society is actually a "melting pot" and that subcultural differences within that society are therefore minimal and irrelevant to its social development. Few serious observers of the American scene really believe this any longer.[2] There is an increasing need, both in theoretical academic terms and in a practical sense, to understand better the interrelationship of the relatively distinct racial and subcultural groups which comprise American society. To do so at all, it is necessary first to describe the dimensions of life for such subcultural groups and the dynamics which maintain those life styles.

Various social scientists have made theoretical statements about the quality of black American life and the personality structure modally associated with it in the past. However, at this point in time, the civil rights movement and its aftermath of the 1960s and early 1970s created new structural dynamics and new social movements among black Americans. Thus, this study in part will indicate whether there have been changes of any substantial type from the findings of previous scholars, such as Karon (1958), Kardiner and Ovesey (1951), and Davis and Havighurst (1948). But much beyond this, it is an attempt to show the present-day manner of integration of (a) the social situation in which black Americans find themselves; (b) their economic and political position; and (c) the family structure common in black American households in large urban areas. By doing so, I hope to clarify the attitudes, values, and behaviors which inevitably follow from this interpenetration of the social and the personal.

Finally, I shall describe the manner in which the two communities, the dominant white and the subordinate black, contact and confront each other, the way in which these contacts reinforce and/or change their perceptions of one another, and the resultant behavior of each toward the other.

4

To do this, I investigated the community itself, its family and social structure, work, and amusements, and its relationships with the larger community. Central to this investigation is an attempt to evaluate, through the medium of life histories and TATs (Thematic Apperception Tests), some aspects of the personalities of selected individuals in this community illustrative of its particular cultural configurations.

The group chosen for this investigation is the population of some fourteen hundred families living in the "permanent housing" (sometimes called the "new housing") in the San Francisco Housing Authority's Hunter's Point housing project. This group is probably *not* typical of San Francisco blacks — perhaps not even of all Hunter's Point residents. But there are vital reasons for investigating it. Here, I suggest, taken to its most extreme development, is the explication of all those pathological forces (social, familial, and personal) which act on black American populations. Here also, then, exist in extreme form the reactions, personal defenses, and institutionalized techniques that black Americans have developed for coping with these forces. And here in microcosm is the response (in part unique to San Francisco, in part ubiquitously American) of the white community to this embedded subculture. In discussing the black American, Kardiner and Ovesey (1951) analyze something which they call the "mark of oppression." This destructive self-hate and self-denigration they view as central to the lives of black Americans. A significant aspect of black American life was the existence of the matrifocal family, itself a product of slavery and productive of certain negative psychodynamics in black American life. In a further explication of this phenomenon, several years later and in part based upon the earlier Kardiner and Ovesey work, the Moynihan report (1965*a*) indicates, both directly and obliquely, the causes and effects of what Moynihan sees as this devastatingly destructive, increasingly matrifocal and absent-father pattern in black American life.

The introduction of the concept of matrifocality and its meaning to the populations in which it exists is not a new phenomenon in anthropology. A series of anthropological investigations have indicated the effect, in a variety of cultural and structural situations, of the matrifocal family (Boyer, 1964; Smith, 1956; Lewis, 1959, 1961; Cohen; 1955; Young and Wilmott, 1957; Burton and Whiting, 1960, 1961). All of these studies and a host of others have indicated in one way or another the effects of matrifocality and the absent-father pattern on

5

the development of individual personality and social institutions. Matrifocality, as a number of writers (including Kardiner and Ovesey) have noted, is a central aspect of the black American family situation. Thus, any investigation of black American urban populations must investigate the status of this matrifocal family pattern if changes are to be discerned.

What I believe to have discerned is that the interaction of social structure and personality factors in this population has combined to produce a relatively stable modal family structure almost entirely matrifocal in structure, with fathers commonly absent either physically or psychologically.

The structural position of the black population in the macrosociety is that blacks are essentially uneducated, hold low-paying jobs, and are ordinarily either severely harassed or completely neglected by the police. This situation has created feelings of social impotence that are reinforced by fears of sexual impotence on the part of males and by distorted ideation about sexuality by members of both sexes. Thematic Apperception Test responses support this. Additionally, the generalized acceptance, among blacks, of stereotyped concepts of their own inadequacy has led to a defensive posture consisting of aggressive and manipulative acts directed primarily at peers, denial of what appears to be the reality, and fantasized achievement. Further, a value system stressing a present-time orientation and the elevation of expressive values over those of work and achievement has decreased the likelihood of social mobility for members of this population.

Exacerbating these tensions is the fact that almost all formal and informal leadership in this community, as well as organizational power, is in the hands of women. Thus, one of the most important functions of the 1966 civil disturbances (the "riots") in Hunter's Point, I suggest, was to enhance the self-esteem of otherwise almost totally powerless young males.

I further suggest that though this is a select population, the experiences are similar enough to those of a significant number of urban black Americans to constitute a fairly accurate picture of the condition of much of America's black population. I conclude, therefore, that there has been no significant change either in the structural or personal psychological aspects of this population since Kardiner Ovesey's 1951 study.

SHORT NOTE ON METHODOLOGY

My original investigations of Hunter's Point began with a limited short-term (four-month) field evaluation of a community organization project funded through the Department of Criminology of the University of California at Berkeley. During the course of this study, it became immediately apparent that the forms of social and personal pathology described by Kardiner and Ovesey (1951) and Moynihan (1965a) existed in Hunter's Point to a high degree. During the following year and a half my further investigations in this community convinced me that the interplay of social, economic, political, and personality forces in this community made it an excellent example of the interaction and inter-relatedness of all of these aspects of the life of northern urban black Americans in the context of American racial discrimination.

To do such research, friendly personal relationships were established with a dozen families, more superficial relationships with a larger number, and close personal ties with four particular families. Eventually, life histories, personal sketches, and TATs were elicited from individuals whom I judged to be representative of the residents of Hunter's Point. Such a sample is not, strictly speaking, scientific. Unfortunately, however, there would be no way of assuring that people selected truly at random would be amenable to the lengthy close relationship which participant observation requires (or vice versa). This is partially a function of methodology. No questionnaires were ever used with this population because, quite simply, I distrust questionnaire responses.

Having made myself a part of the community by virtue of my constant presence, I learned much that no questionnaire can elicit. I seldom asked questions. It was generally thought that I was doing some (unspecified) work with the "Community Organization Program," simply visiting in a friendly fashion those people whom I liked, night or day. The exact nature of my work was unclear to most, but with one exception no one seemed to mind.[3]

It must be stated, though, that I do not feel I truly became a part of the community. I was accepted and adapted to in the way that people come to learn to accept and adapt to other inevitable and somewhat inexplicable phenomena. I made no pretense of somehow truly "understanding" the quality and meaning of life in Hunter's Point as it is felt and experienced by its inhabitants, and my aims here are similarly modest.

I feel it important, however, to discuss at least in passing what was done and how, since many individuals have expressed surprise that a white person could get certain kinds of information from blacks. First of all, some techniques cannot be described for reasons which will be clear to any professional ethnographer. But the core of such research is the establishment of intense and intimate personal relationships. Some information is obtainable only through the intimacy of friendship and its extension to being privy not only to conversation but also to intimate social situations in which many of the social relationships described occurred. In such situations, the *participant* aspects of participant observation become central.

Another technique, one borrowed from the black American himself, is one Ralph Ellison (1952) speaks of in *The Invisible Man.* Many, if not all, blacks are accustomed to experiencing social invisibility in the presence of whites. A variation on this technique, which has permitted actual survival for many blacks, provided a most powerful tool for research. I simply became "invisible." Two kinds of "invisibility" were used in this research: the invisibility of the high status person and the "invisibility" of the low status person. The most provocative stance, that of ambiguous status, elicited few responses of significance. Inhabitants of Hunter's Point were less concerned with resolving ambiguities than in withdrawing from and ignoring them.

High-status techniques involved such tactics as appearing to be so involved in talking with the "important" people at places such as the Youth Opportunity Center or the Bayview Community Center that "ordinary" people could afford to ignore one's presence. Obviously, someone like that, so involved in complicated discussions, could not be paying much attention to what was going on around him or to social interactions of which he was not a part.

On the other hand, a drunken bum sprawled out in a doorway or sleeping in a bar is nobody to present the "special" self to. In early stages of my work, and especially on Third Avenue, I often wore very old clothing and in fact did present myself in these situations as a non-communicative and uninvolved "bum." Similarly, someone who spends hours, days, or weeks on end in a record shop doing nothing but listening to records can after a while be ignored. If he is that wrapped up in his own world, he is obviously not interested in yours. Or someone who is busily examining every square inch of a playground fence for "structural defects" clearly can be considered uninterested in the interaction of the children in the yard. These and numerous other approaches were used.

Finally, with some few people, I was able to make clear that I was an ethnographer and to explain what I was about.

Such research, however, cannot be done without creating ambivalent feelings for the researcher. Friendships are made which the researcher knows have an all-too-obvious instrumental basis — on both sides (for example, many in the community knew I had contacts with people who could furnish them jobs). Yet personal friendships of a real kind did develop, eventually, untainted by overtones of manipulation or the treatment of other human beings as objects. Describing the lives and times, personal limitations, individual pathologies and the defenses raised against them, and the successes of human spirit of these people, some of whom were very close to the investigator, is not an easy task for me. I have used only pseudonyms. Such pseudonyms may not, in some cases, mislead anyone really familiar with the community. Some facts cannot be disguised by changing names. Only distortions so gross as to limit their use as examples could do that. Thus, I have chosen not to distort incidents or cases at all, and have relied only on anonymity to protect the individuals involved.

An additional point must be made. My investigations were essentially in the area of uncovering dynamics and personal and social structure which, by and large, appeared to me to be pathological. In part this is a reflection of the objective situation as I found it, in part a reflection of the poverty of conceptualization that motivates much personality and culture research in anthropology. The entire terminology of cross-cultural, psychiatric, quasi-psychiatric, and anthropological research lends itself more easily to descriptions of states of pathology and inadequate defense systems, on the one hand, or to steady-state "functional analysis" of a Pollyannaish bent on the other, than to any real understanding of how humans truly manage to live with pathos and yet find joy and meaningfulness in their lives.[4]

Such an understanding must await further theoretical work and field research. The present work must thus content itself with indicating some of the institutionalized and personal techniques of adaptation. But this should not blind us to the fact that despite the apparent continuing failure of the group there is evidence of individual success in resisting pathology and achieving positive personal integration. How such success is achieved, I do not know.

A final note: this book is written in the "ethnographic present"; that is, although the field work covered the years 1966-1967, it is presented in the present tense except where there is need to indicate the actual date to avoid confusion or for clarification.

NOTES

[1] In fact, a survey of literature on black Americans (Miller, 1966) does not disclose a single actual ethnographic study in participant-observation style.

[2] Nathan Glazer and Daniel Patrick Moynihan (1963) *Beyond the Melting Pot: Negroes, Puerto Ricans, Jews, Italians and Irish of New York City.* Cambridge, Mass.: M.I.T. Press.

[3] Mango expressed anger at sociologists and others who made a living off Hunter's Point. I thus felt constrained eventually to tell him what I was doing. At the end of my work, I discussed my investigations and their implications with him. Our personal friendship sufficed to offset his hostility toward my research.

[4] Dr. Robert Coles, who has investigated black American populations in the southern United States, has similarly indicated how strongly he felt this poverty of conceptualization, which prevents one from being able to describe as dramatically how people are "making it" in the face of difficulty as how they are succumbing. (Personal communication.)

I

The Background

1

THE PHYSICAL
SETTING

THE Hunter's Point-Bayview district, defined by tracts L4, L5A, and L5B of the 1960 census and in which the Hunter's Point housing project is located, is a twenty-one-square-mile area in the southeastern portion of the city of San Francisco. The 1960 census showed this area to have 10,224 dwelling units housing approximately fifty thousand people.

Hunter's Point itself is a peninsula extending into San Francisco Bay. The tip of the peninsula is owned by the federal government and is the site of a United States Navy shipyard. On the high hill in the center of the peninsula is the large housing project named after the area and commonly referred to as Hunter's Point.

Prior to World War II, the hill was a sparsely populated, relatively wild area. A dramatic change came about in World War II with the development and rise in importance of the naval shipyard. The influx of vast numbers of industrial and shipyard workers, many of them black immigrants from the states of the Old South, compelled the navy to erect "temporary housing," which eventually became public housing in the postwar period. The presence of thousands of semiskilled and unskilled black shipyard workers who had been laid off immediately after the war and who stayed on in San Francisco represented what city officials considered a "civic problem" — hopefully soluble through cheap public housing and welfare. Thus, many of the black shipyard workers and their families stayed on in Hunter's Point as public assistance cases in this postwar "public housing area" leased from the navy.

Many of these new residents lacked economic resources and the skills necessary to remain employed during the recession period which immediately followed the war. Furthermore, discriminatory housing and job-hiring policies in the rest of the city discouraged the majority from leaving Hunter's Point and intensified the rapid deterioration of this area into an almost uniracial semislum.

Of interest is the fact that the forced removal of Japanese Americans from those areas of the city now called the Western Addition and the Fillmore district provided the only other real "openings" in the city for blacks. The Fillmore district — though still by 1967 not entirely black in population and still lacking rigid boundaries defining it as a ghetto — took on the definite configuration of a black neighborhood during this World War II and postwar period. Thus, the "openness" of San Francisco (relative to other cities) to black immigrants, which helped create the Fillmore district and the other major black neighborhood in the city, was a direct result of the federal government's racist policy, in response to wartime hysteria, regarding West Coast Japanese Americans.

The public housing in Hunter's Point consists of units defined as "permanent" and "temporary" dwellings. The older, temporary housing, built of lathe and plasterboard, consists of long, barracks-type structures each comprising eight two-bedroom apartments. The more recent buildings, while built of more durable construction materials, exhibit the same multidwelling style. Although there are many physical similarities in the superficial appearance of the new and old structures, the more important distinction between them (for our present purposes) is associated with relatively distinct social groupings. Newer housing tends to contain a much higher proportion of fatherless families, and its inhabitants reflect a distinctly different social organization, a difference primarily due to the income criteria for tenancy. (It is these matrifocal, poverty-stricken families that are the specific subject of the investigation.) The apparent paradox of the poorer families in the newer housing simply reflects the fact that as new housing was built, those people already settled in Hunter's Point often did not wish to be relocated. Additionally, the demand for new Public Housing was a function of new families becoming eligible. It apparently was far easier to locate the newer families in the newer housing than to undergo the massive shuffle of relocation of two families for each new unit.

Although differences exist, in part due to the length of stay and the relative poverty of the two factions, these are differences of degree and not of kind. In fact I believe that the primary difference is one of the age of the occupants and the number of young dependent children. Though my principal effort was directed toward these newer families, I also observed numbers of people who lived in the older housing units.

In this physical setting, isolated as it is from the rest of the city as a result of the concentration of poverty-stricken families, an intense "ghettoization"[1] has developed. A community has been created based on income[2] which is almost perfectly correlated with race and with a distinct style of life.

The population of Hunter's Point, as I have intimated, is predominantly black: San Francisco Housing Authority (SFHA) data identify 95 percent of the inhabitants as "Negro" and 5 percent as "Caucasian" and "Samoan."[3]

The population is also predominantly poor. While some of the residents have well-paying jobs, most receive low (even poverty-level) incomes — partly because of the general structural position which blacks occupy in American society (Moynihan, 1965b) and partly because of SFHA residency criteria, which both select for such families and discourages them from raising their income level. While some thirteen hundred Hunter's Point men are employed by the three largest employers in Hunter's Point (this 1961 figure had probably been reduced to around a thousand by late 1967), some nine hundred families in the area receive some form of public assistance (Old Age Service, Aid to Dependent Children, etc.). Regarding absent-parent statistics, the best estimate obtainable in conjunction with evaluations from the Office of the State Department of Welfare, locally called "the welfare office," and other field workers is that in roughly 40 percent of the families in Hunter's Point either the father or mother is absent — in the vast majority of cases the father.[4]

The SFHA's 1963 figures indicate that the median income for the total area was $4,800 per year; 1967 figures indicate that some 37 percent of the families were in the "poverty class" as defined by the federal government's Office of Economic Opportunity — i.e., received under $4,000 annual income.[5]

15

The population, moreover, does not consist primarily of recent migrants. A reasonable estimate would be that very few of the Hunter's Point residents (10 to 20 percent at most) under the age of twenty were born outside the state. A substantial proportion, perhaps approaching 50 percent, were born either in Hunter's Point or some other part of San Francisco. Even of the population over forty, very few have not resided on some part of the West Coast for over twenty years. There are very few recent immigrants from the Old South.[6]

Further, the bulk of the Hunter's Point population lives in the new housing units. In spring 1967 Hunter's Point housed the following groupings of families:

Fourteen hundred families in "permanent housing."

Eight hundred families in "temporary housing."

One hundred families in housing on federal property in the Hunter's Point naval shipyard.[7]

The "permanent housing" is characterized not only by the greater solidity of the structures, but much more importantly (in terms of this study) by the fact that there are income limits on the occupants. Occupants whose income rises above a certain level (which fluctuates depending upon the criteria used to determine "poverty levels" by the United States government) are forced to move out or to pay higher rents. "Temporary housing," however, has no such income limits or rent adjustments — i.e., one's rent is not raised when one's income goes up. This is a fact of political importance in Hunter's Point, as many of the "temporary housing" residents would like to keep their housing from being destroyed for a number of reasons. Low rents have obvious advantages in tenants' eyes, not the least of which for many residents has been the opportunity to save money in order eventually to move to "better neighborhoods."

Control of many major dimensions of life in the Hunter's Point housing project area is not in the hands of its occupants. This public housing tract, like twenty-two similar tracts throughout the city of San Francisco, is under the direct supervision and control of the San Francisco Housing Authority, the "landlord" to the Hunter's Point tenants. The SFHA is a five-member commission appointed by the mayor under the mayor's office but subject to federal audit and control. It exerts

16

direct authority over the residents of the Hunter's Point housing area through its area office in Hunter's Point.

The residents of Hunter's Point, then, are poor, mostly black tenants who are in a dependent position upon, as well as physically isolated from, the rest of the city and in only minimal contact with whites.

This physical isolation makes downtown shopping inconvenient for Hunter's Pointers, and makes Hunter's Point itself a place few whites ever visit and in which very few live. It is served by a single bus line, which does not run in Hunter's Point after 1:30 A.M. and is perhaps the only bus line in the city where time table inquiries can elicit conditional responses from the dispatcher's office of the Municipal Railway System. For example, it is common for a dispatcher to answer a phone inquiry by saying, "The next bus, barring disturbances or attacks on drivers, will arrive at Hunter's Point in twenty minutes."

In addition to its physical isolation, the population is essentially isolated emotionally from the rest of the city. It is only of concern to most San Franciscans through the periodic sensationalistic treatment of its problems in the *San Francisco Chronicle*. At times the paper has alleged the area to be a hotbed of juvenile delinquency and gang warfare, but more recently it has condemned the inaction of the city fathers to alleviate the poor living conditions there. Still, very few white residents of San Francisco have any accurate notion of the physical appearance of Hunter's Point, not to mention the attitudes, beliefs, and life styles of its inhabitants. On the other hand, the inhabitants of Hunter's Point believe the rest of the city despises them, and they themselves know very little about the workings or even the physical dimensions of the rest of the city.

The physical realities of Hunter's Point are easy to describe. The "temporary housing" has already been discussed. The "permanent" buildings inhabited by the "tenants" are concrete, six-unit apartment houses. The buildings are clumped into groups of three or four units placed side by side. The individual buildings are separated from each other by a space of about thirty yards. These three or four buildings share a common courtyard area where women wash clothes and small children play. The small amount of playground area in Hunter's Point is inadequate, and so children usually play in the wider parts of the streets. Although the apartments range from one to four bedrooms, most are one- and two-bedroom apartments. While the buildings are not considered by the residents to be beautiful, they are admittedly durable. Commonly they are set back some thirty feet from the street and have lawns in varying states of repair. The area is traversed by several inter-connected streets which wind around the contours of the ridge on which the buildings stand.

Hunter's Point residents have an excellent view of the rest of the city. From most parts of the hill one is treated to expansive, impressive panoramas of San Francisco and the entire Bay Area (including Oakland and Berkeley across the bay). It is warmer here than in most of the city and essentially smog-free due to its location upwind of the industrial area and downwind of the "spillways" in the San Francisco western hills through which a continual ocean breeze blows.

The hilltop itself (essentially the area bounded by Hilltop, North-ridge, and Southridge Roads) contains a semicircle of "temporary" buildings in the area labelled "hilltop" on the map, which once housed a variety of retail establishments, laundries, churches, and the like. Directly across from this semicircle of now-abandoned stores, on the southwest side of the hilltop, is the only church in Hunter's Point proper. Its young (thirty-five-year-old) white Protestant minister is quite active in social and community political organization in Hunter's Point.

On the northern edge of the hilltop is a large, wood frame and plasterboard structure also once used for commercial purposes. Until it was finally abandoned completely in the summer of 1967, part of it was used by the Youth Opportunity Center, the State Employment Service, various "outreach" organizations, and occasional individuals concerned with various aspects of community problems related to youth.

In the more or less enclosed space which these buildings form are two distinct areas. On the northern side near the Youth Opportunity Center and adjacent to the entry to the Jedediah Smith School yard is an area favored by younger teenagers who come up there especially on Friday afternoons to make dates — an area where boys and girls can meet each other. It is a lively spot — there are always several transistor radios playing music and a great deal of joking and laughter — but it is not primarily a place for entertainment. After meeting one another there, boys and girls either split up and go home or leave for Third Street and the record shops, barbecue stands, or "hot dog and shake" places which line it.

About two hundred feet to the southwest of this meeting place is a parking lot where middle-aged men, sitting in or near middle-aged cars, quietly drink alcoholic beverages and occasionally talk. Unlike the teenagers, these men can be found there almost any time of day — except perhaps dinnertime (around five-thirty). These are the unemployed and often unemployable social rejects of Hunter's Point. They are commonly scorned by the rest of the local population and referred to as those "useless old men," though none seems to be over fifty.

The physical distance between these two groups is, as we have noted, about two hundred feet. The emotional and social distance seems much farther, but I suggest that this is not so. There is a progression, inevitable for some, which takes young boys from the northern part of this hilltop and through a series of near-relentless pressures turns them into the old men who sit and drink on the southwest side of the hill. There is no overt communication between these groups. There is no need for it. The seeds that created the "old men's society" are already sprouting in the teenage boys.

On the other hand, no middle-aged women ever come to the top of the hill except to go to church there. The progression for women is in a different physical direction and with different results. The real indigenous power in the community lies down on Third Street in the Bayview Community Center and in the local OEO offices. This power is primarily in the hands of women. For our purposes, the manner in which these postures of power and impotence develop is best understood by examining the family, those groups which live in the houses scattered between the top of the hill — where young men and women meet and old men sit — and the bottom of the hill — where middle-aged women sit in control.

NOTES

[1]This term is used advisedly. The ghetto in European urban areas was characterized not only by the concentration of one racial or ethnic group, but by overt attempts by the dominant community to enforce the rigid boundaries of such areas. This has been the case in Hunter's Point.

[2]The actual figures on income in this area, if averaged for the entire Hunter's Point area, tend to belie this. If one averages incomes one obscures the great variation in the group and especially obscures the fact that very many people are quite poor.

[3]Reliable figures are difficult to obtain. The Redevelopment Agency of San Francisco, using the Hunter's Point Joint Housing Committee's investigations, boasted an estimated 91 percent return on their census figures and hoped-for accuracy through using "native information collectors."

This figure, however, covered only the old housing area, and the information was collected to strengthen the Redevelopment Agency's power to condemn and remove these "relatively wealthy" groups. If the SFHA could show that people were "wealthy," it could remove them to make room for "poor" people. (See Appendix A.)

Information on the new housing units is very poor considering the degree of control the SFHA has over the area.

[4] For the fourteen hundred families in the "permanent housing" the figures for matrifocality are extremely high: the best estimates that I was able to make through spot checks and depth interviews is from 50 to 80 percent. The wide range reflects the indecisiveness of the term *matrifocal*. Just what a "permanent" adult is, is open to a variety of interpretations.

[5] The proportion of families receiving various levels of income in the "temporary housing" units in Hunter's Point are given by the San Francisco Redevelopment Agency as follows:

Under $2,400 per year	16.2%
$2,400-4,200	19.9
$4,200-6,000	27.7
$6,000 and over	30.3
No report	5.9

It is difficult to evaluate this information, but the fact that it includes many double-wage earner families is stated by the agency. In the "permanent housing," however, all of the occupants are below the poverty level in income. But, of course, this is by definition and is a self-selected sample, as it were.

[6] Such impressionistic data is easily borne out by sample interviews and questioning. Sixty percent of the population sampled had lived in the San Francisco area for eighteen years or more.

[7] These are unofficial estimates obtained from the Housing Authority office in Hunter's Point.

2

SOCIALIZATION AND
THE LIFE CYCLE

THE FAMILY

THE family in the Hunter's Point "permanent housing" area is typically
headed by a woman. She may be a grandmother whose daughters and
grandchildren are living with her, or a mother who may simply not be
old enough to have married daughters (or daughters who have children).
Young men, as I shall show, are rarely found in the home and certainly are not part of its authority structure. Though they may sleep
there, they prefer to be absent as much as possible from the home. Random collections of young nieces and nephews, an occasional grandfather
and sometimes visiting relatives make up the ordinary cast of characters
of the family here. Very seldom (in perhaps only 20 percent of the
families) is there a father in the home.

Many authors (Strodtbeck, 1964; Schwartz, 1965; Karon, 1958)
have commented on the reasons for this absent-father pattern (Moynihan, 1965a, gives a good summary of the discussion), so I shall only
briefly recapitulate it here. The first absent-father families among
blacks in the United States were a direct by-product of slavery, when
slaveowners and -traders, seeking the most efficient use of their "prop-

erty," thought nothing of breaking up families, usually leaving younger children with their mothers. After Emancipation, female blacks consistently found it easier to get work (e.g., as domestics) than black males — especially after the tide of European immigration starting in the 1880s and 1890s. The resultant economic and social dependency of black men on their women inevitably produced a mutual antagonism, that survives to this day, based on this "unacceptable" set of conditions. The present structure of racial discrimination, which is the legacy of slavery — and more recently of the reaction to Reconstruction, culminating in the Supreme Court's 1896 pronouncement of the "separate but equal" doctrine — continues this pattern. "Last hired, first fired" is still an accurate way of describing black male employment opportunities in San Francisco (as in other U.S. cities). Thus, black mothers with small children are not usually in financially sound positions. Often dependent upon public assistance, they are forced to accept public housing. Thus, since nearly by definition the families here are poor and matrifocal,[1] they are continually selected as occupants of the housing and, for the reasons I shall show, tend to reproduce this pattern in succeeding generations.

The mother in the matrifocal family is obviously the core of the family, if only by definition. But to understand her importance — and, in fact, her own emotional orientation — it is necessary to consider her in terms of her effects on her husband, her sons, and her daughters, and to examine the mechanisms which perpetuate this form of family and social structure. It is through the socialization experience itself that the impact of this type of family is most deeply felt, and it is this experience that the present chapter treats.

BIRTH AND INFANCY

Babies are loved and desired in Hunter's Point. The information that a new baby is on the way is generally received with pleasure, and although there may be some recrimination against an unmarried expectant mother, it is minimal.[2] Having a child confers a certain degree of status on a young woman. It is a clear indication of biological maturity, and while biological functions are taken much more for granted here than in many white or black middle-class communities, pregnancy nevertheless establishes a girl's new status. All that is required to achieve a total rank as a woman is the title *"Mrs."*

Though the acquisition of this title is of value in Hunter's Point, young girls are rarely desperate for marriage. They will almost all eventually marry; they seem to feel that there is certainly no need to rush it in the teen years. In fact, many of the problems which would be associated with out-of-wedlock pregnancy among middle-class white girls simply don't exist here, further reducing the pressure for "emergency" marriages.

Since the household structure commonly includes more than one female past puberty — or at least one who can easily mobilize resources of other females, either friends or relatives, to help care for a new baby — the disruption of schedules and routines the arrival of an infant often causes in white middle-class homes does not exist here.

Even mothers with several children show active pride in a new addition. The child is joked about and playfully held and tickled by a series of mostly female relatives and friends, and for several weeks after the baby's arrival he (or she) is the social cynosure of the household.

There is about an equal amount of breast-feeding and bottle-feeding of babies to start with; that is, about half the mothers appeared to or claimed to start their babies on the breast. But even among those mothers who breast-feed there is a tendency toward early and rather abrupt weaning (after four months or so). Characteristically, weaning is accomplished by total substitution of bottle for breast. I saw no evidence to indicate the use of any bitter substances on the mother's breast, nor of any physical punishment of half-year-old children who cried a great deal as a result of weaning; pacifiers are often used to quiet an unhappy baby that is being weaned.

If weaning is abrupt, toilet-training tends to be rather mild. Severe censoring of a child for defecating in his clothes is rare prior to age two-and-a-half. However, in this as in other areas of child rearing, the range of variability is great. Generally, those individuals who tended to view themselves as upwardly mobile and who were most critical of "nigger ways" (a term used by blacks in Hunter's Point, not by me) both weaned and toilet-trained earliest. I saw no evidence of concern over toilet-training in any case with children under a year-and-a-half.[3]

When comparing residents of the old and new housing areas, though, some striking differences were observed in child rearing, as in other aspects of life styles. Children from the older housing areas tended to be better dressed on the average — that is, with clothes that were both newer and cleaner and additionally better fitting. The differences were not total, and could only be gauged impressionistically by me; however, the differences were clear and are, probably in part, the result of different economic levels.

Babies are fondled a great deal, touched and played with continuously, not only by their mothers, but by any female near them. Much pleasure is expressed by the adult female playing with an infant when she elicits a smile from him in the course of play. Happy babies are enjoyed as objects which bring pleasure to the observer. Unhappy, colicky infants under four to six months are almost nonexistent.

This comparatively nurturant childhood pattern, however, tends to give way to a rather severe rejection about the time the infant shows sufficient individuality to try to explore and manipulate his environment by walking and making verbal demands. Generally, about the time the child has reached the age of one year or so his mother is treating him quite differently than she has earlier. Often by this time there is another new infant in the home, and all the immediate attention is focused on him to the exclusion of the older child. Not only is the new infant now the nearly exclusive recipient of the mother's positive attention, but the older child is the direct recipient of all her negative attitudes. Comments directed at the older child in such situations, such as "Get out of here — You bother me," "You're nothin' but a lot of trouble," and "I'm gonna beat you if you don't quit botherin' me," are so common as to be almost completely interchangeable from family to family in Hunter's Point. The mother makes no attempt to hide from the older child the fact that she is much more interested in the new baby.

Children who react bitterly to the advent of a younger brother or sister (or niece or nephew), and who may even try to attack it, are beaten. However, this is not the first beating most children get. Physical means of coercion, especially by mothers, are common after or around the age of one year. Children then, even without a newborn around, become "a bother," "no fun," "always hangin' on you," "gettin' in the way." Children this age tend to withdraw, to exhibit a general lack of communicativeness.

Some children rebel against the withdrawal of attention by their mothers, aunts, and sisters. Especially violent rebelliousness is directed at older sisters, who have, as does any female relative, the prerogative of inflicting corporal punishment on small children. The reaction to the mother's lessened interest and the irritation of the mother either at the child's whining withdrawal or overt rebelliousness (or the alternation of both) usually provokes the mother to send the child outdoors to get him "out of her hair." It is at this age — eighteen to twenty-four months — that the child usually first experiences being locked out of the house except for mealtimes.[4] I observed no family in the new housing units (the primarily matrifocal dwellings which are the main object of our study) which did not lock children out at one time or another, regardless of the child's wishes in the matter. On the other hand, far fewer than half of the families observed in the older housing did the same.

Children of three or so are commonly locked out on their own, but a younger child is not usually left entirely alone. There is almost always an elder subteen sister, or some neighbor's older children to provide a nominal watch over the child. Further, because Hunter's Point is a small and rather isolated community with no heavy traffic pattern during most of the day, there is very little danger from cars associated with this "lockout." All the same, children universally dislike it. While most children show a definite preference for playing outside the house, they often cry bitterly to be let in when they are tired or not to be locked out when they do not want to go out at all. Sometimes such importunings work, at other times they do not. The rationale for either locking out or not locking out is apparently arbitrary. A sudden irritation with the child, the appearance of a visitor, or a particular television program — almost anything may trigger the desire to lock children out.

While children react to this with some hostility, parents (in this case, almost exclusively mothers) never seem to pay much attention to such reactions at all. That this is sometimes a conscious effort to exclude the child and sometimes an almost unconscious act only became apparent to me after I asked one woman why she had locked the door on the child who wanted to come in at the time. The woman denied that she had done so until confronted with the chained and locked door; seemingly only then did she become conscious of the demanding cries of the child to be let in. She then went to the door and opened it.

Two other incidents almost identical in character led me to hypothesize that mothers in this group develop mental techniques which permit them to be completely inattentive to those complaints of their children they do not wish to hear, and that some kinds of withdrawal of attention, such as locking children out, are only partially conscious acts.

Occasionally, mothers in Hunter's Point were defensive about physically punishing or locking out a child in my presence. This defensiveness, however, seemed to vary with the degree of sophistication on the

25

part of the mother regarding the differences between child-rearing practices acceptable in Hunter's Point and those acceptable in middle-class communities. The more knowledgeable mothers were more defensive with me.

Even more, though, maternal defensiveness seemed to reflect the degree of identification with white norms and general defensiveness about "all that nigger shit."

Specifically, physical punishment of children, withdrawal of food and affection, and locking out as a means of controlling children are all viewed ambivalently in Hunter's Point. Two kinds of child-rearing norms exist in Hunter's Point, the "white" and the "Negro" norms. Mothers give stronger lip service to the "white" norm (or what is perceived as such) and stronger behavioral commitment to the "Negro" norm. It is believed that white norms stress discipline, the inculcation of obedience and cleanliness, helping with schoolwork, and the like in child rearing. Mothers often state these as ideal norms, but only that aspect of white norms which stresses (or is felt to stress) corporal punishment is actually followed.

Corporal punishment for the purpose of disciplining children is apparently practiced, not because it is an aspect of white norms, but because it is an integral aspect of the overall ethos of Hunter's Point and accurately reflects the higher level of interpersonal violence there. Most mothers in Hunter's Point would claim (with as much justification as any middle-class mother) that they dearly love their children and take excellent care of them. Their ideas about such things, however, do diverge widely from middle-class norms.

The aims of child rearing in Hunter's Point also appear to be different from those of middle-class families. American middle-class families tend to stress discipline, reasoned obedience, nonaggressive actions, and personal independence. Childhood experiences in Hunter's Point, on the other hand, tend to produce a child who is emotionally dependent (and thus gratifying to the mother) but not underfoot too much – and with enough independence and physical mobility to achieve the latter aim.

While our description of "locking out" might suggest that the mother is striving to produce an independent child, we suggest as an alternative explanation that she is actually abandoning him because of what she sees as his refusal to remain gratifyingly tied to her, especially if she has a new completely dependent infant. All children have both dependency needs and independent exploratory urges. The child's independence in

Hunter's Point is, of course, in part furthered by permitting (or rather forcing) this degree of physical freedom. The mother, however, manipulates the child's dependency needs primarily by the manner in which she distributes food. The very young child, of course, is unable to see to his own feeding, but mothers tend to give food conditionally to children of all ages.

Meals generally tend to be taken at irregular intervals, but nearly always, for the younger child, only after his complaints have finally been acceded to by the mother. The conditional giving of food, contingent on the child's behavior, is perhaps the single most powerful socialization technique used by the Hunter's Point mother. A mother will often refuse to feed a child who has disobeyed or otherwise angered her and then some minutes later arbitrarily begin to feed him.

When children are old enough to fend for themselves — by getting food and preparing it themselves or by going to a neighbor for it (around eight years) — mothers tend to shift tactics. Children then are often not permitted to prepare food because they "make a mess" or "they don't know how." Additionally, since physical punishment is common and severe, interspersing it with arbitrary and spontaneous affection, both verbal and physical — hugging the child, telling him/her that he/she is handsome/beautiful and is a wonderful boy/girl and that he/she is loved more than anything or anyone — tends to keep children emotionally off-balance, but still in most cases emotionally tied to their mothers.

Infancy, then, is a period of early nurturance followed by rather precipitate weaning and withdrawal of affection as soon as the child develops physical mobility and the ability to make clear, independent verbal demands and/or is replaced by a new sibling.

CHILDHOOD

Childhood is a period during which the patterns of development of infancy are extended and some new ones introduced. In three quarters or more of the families in the new housing and at least a third of those in the old housing the child lives in a home without a father in residence. In addition to the psychodynamic factors which I shall explain and the structural factors associated with poverty there are yet other reasons which are based on realities. Some married men do not live in the same house as their wives because her Aid to Dependent Children payments may be suspended if an "employable" male is found to be in residence. That *employable* in this sense may have no relationship to the reality of hiring policies in the Bay Area or to the skills of black males there tends to be overlooked by welfare agencies. Such agencies, however, are reputed by many observers to be less unpleasant regarding this legal requirement in Hunter's Point than elsewhere in the Bay Area.[5]

Mothers or other females tend to be the sole socializing agents even in most homes with a resident husband or father. Males take a very inactive role in child rearing and by and large are either very loath to use corporal punishment or do not feel it to be their place to do so. Most men in the household either spend very little time there or remain emotionally uninvolved while in attendance. Those men who are at home during the day are usually sleeping or watching television. There is little concept of the father as a "pal" to a son as in middle-class communities, and father-son antagonisms are strong. These antagonisms, which on the surface might appear surprising due to the minimal contact between fathers and sons, is perhaps best explained by precisely that lack of contact. Sons need to believe that their somewhat passive and emotionally distant fathers are really strong, aggressive men. They thus tend to fantasize an aggressive father, since such a father is a better role model for a boy. The realities of family life are quite different.

Most important economic decisions, whether concerning food or furniture or getting a job, are made by women. In those households with a resident male his decision is more important in buying a car, but even in those cases where he is clearly the sole support of the family, most major decisions about spending money are usually made by the women. The child, then, is confronted by a pattern of female dominance in the home and ordinarily is presented with a passive and often self-acknowledgedly inadequate male image.

After the initial period of extrusion, around the age of seven or eight,[6] girls are allowed in the house more frequently, and appear to want more to be indoors, than boys. No doubt this is partly because mothers find girls of this age beginning to be useful for household chores, especially those surrounding the care of infants, and for such other help as errands to stores.

Outside the household, girls of this age tend either to associate with only one or two girl friends or to be part of the larger all-girl play groups. From age three or four to the onset of puberty, public play tends to be unisexual, although this does not imply a lack of contact between the sexes during these ages.

28

The child soon learns that the most significant adults in his life are women. Many women have several relatives — mother, sisters, aunts, cousins, and grandmothers — living nearby, often in the same building. These are the people, continually present, to whom he must respond and from whom he must learn about the world. Thus, the girl child learns that she is to be part of this dominant group and begins to learn its routines, and both boys and girls learn the sex roles they are expected to take in light of this particular female dominance.

One of the first lessons the girl child learns is that women cannot trust men, since all men are inherently worthless. It is carefully explained, overtly and covertly, directly and indirectly, that men get women pregnant and desert them. Mothers (and female relatives and friends) state openly that fathers do not love their children because they abandon them or refuse to make enough money to support them. It is made explicitly clear that the child can only rely on his mother, who (for some unstated reason) will continue to love him even though he is a male.

Abundant confirmation of what the women say is available to the Hunter's Point child. Men, during the short periods of time they are present in the home, are either sullenly indifferent to the women around them or try to impress them with braggadocio. The women, on their home ground, tend to berate men for their infidelity, perfidy, laziness, and general uselessness. Seeing men accept this kind of verbal abuse from women convinces the child that men agree with this definition of the situation. Only occasionally, and then only apparently out of desperation, do men respond with physical aggression against their female tormentors, which aggression only tends to convince the child even more that there is something evil about men. This perception of male "evil" leads the girl to develop defenses against males and gives the boy an image to try to turn to advantage, a tactic he learns in the youth group outside the home.

Thus, the child perceives women as dominant, though somehow "put upon" by "evil men," at the same time that he is aware of the reality of weak men trying to be dominant and being "put down" by women. For the boy in particular there is no easy way out. Either he will accept dominance by the "worthy" and "sinned-against" women or, by trying to assert himself, incur the guilt of being one of the "evil men" who aggresses against women. The solution to this dilemma is the burden of his youth.

YOUTH

It is in the period of youth (roughly ages seven to twelve) that the Hunter's Pointer begins to develop the subcultural responses to his (or her) social situation. The modal defense patterns and the expected behaviors are all learned in this period. By the age of eight or nine, the Hunter's Point youth is already exhibiting in rudimentary form the values and attitudes that he/she will have as an adult. Some of the most important influences on his/her thinking at this time are those exerted by his/her peer group, and one very important reason for the overwhelming power and importance of the peer group is the action of the mother. Her decision to force him (or, less often, her) out of doors is instrumental in accelerating the development of these far-reaching peer group ties. There is, however, for the Hunter's Point male youth a much more important reason for attaching himself deeply to a group of people his own age. In addition to his mother's almost forcing him out, and his own exploratory urges, the Hunter's Point male child is motivated by fear.

There is literally no one at home to protect the boy from his mother and his emotional reactions to her. Normal Oedipal attachments become distorted in the presence of no adequate male model to emulate. Dai (1948), Mussen and Distler (1959), Burton and Whiting (1961), and many others (see, e.g., DeVos and Hippler, 1969) have suggested that this lack of an adequate male model leads to the problem of cross-sex identity and resultant role confusion in absent-father families. The problem in simple terms is that children need some model to teach them how to become adults and what kind of adults to become. The adults in their own family are the models most children use, since they are most easily available for emulation. Where the father is absent (physically or even just emotionally), as he is in Hunter's Point, the male child tends to identify with the mother as the only relevant adult around; and she may also, because of emotional barrenness in her own life, turn to the child as a source of emotional gratification. Girls have an easier time of it in such a case. Their legitimate role model is present. However, their perception of the male role becomes distorted. They begin to perceive males as weak people who will abandon women and (sometimes enviably) go their own irresponsible way. The boy's problems are greater. He tends to identify with the mother and at a very young age to denigrate the male role. This essentially "regressive system"[7] leads either to effeminacy on the part of the boy (and its attendant overt or covert homosexuality) or, at best, to severe emotional difficulties for both sexes over social sex-role identity, often resolved by males in a defensively aggressive "supermale" pattern. Such is the case at Hunter's Point. The boy turns avidly toward a youth group both as a source of escape from his mother and as a source of learning "manly" skills such as fighting, cursing, and flaunting male sexuality. Under these circumstances, youth group experiences become extremely vital. It is also possible that while there seems to be no true "latency" period (in the sense of total sublimation of sexual interest), the latent homosexual aspects of male solidarity also play a part here.

Groupings, of course, are not limited to preadolescent males. Youth groupings are comprised of two types, preteen groupings of males and teenage groupings of both sexes. In the preteen group, the young Hunter's Point boy learns the basic rudiments of social interaction with his peers and, as we have noted, develops the value orientations he will carry into adulthood. The perceptions of reality most often conveyed indirectly within the family — that is, female dominance and desperate male demands for respect and independence — are defensively developed by the Hunter's Point male youth as patterns of life with all their ramifications in these preteen male youth groups.

While there is nothing unique about preteen fighting to establish dominance hierarchies in humans, and indeed in other primates,[8] there is a special emphasis placed on such behavior in Hunter's Point. The boy must learn to "fight and jive"; he must learn to be ready at all times to defend himself with his fists to gain the reputation of being a "bad motherfucker" and at the same time to learn the verbal skills which permit status victories without physical effort.

Fighting in Hunter's Point is of prime importance since it is one of the only roads to status open to the young boy. Achievement in school, for example, not only fails to confer positive status, but seems to be negatively correlated with peer status. Rank orderings in a male youth group which are primarily set according to fighting ability carry over into all other areas of social interaction. An individual once cast into a low position in the dominance hierarchy usually finds it almost impossible to rise. Fights between closely ranked individuals take on a very desperate character as they are symbolically life-and-death struggles to the Hunter's Point boy.

There also appears to be another possible basis for the intensity of these fights. Fighting is clearly a manly occupation in the eyes of the Hunter's Point male youth. The unconscious threats to his manhood generated by the absent-father family are in part overcome or at least subdued by his continually "proving" his manliness through fighting. Because he cannot count on having his masculinity reinforced by the way the adult females in and around his family treat him, his social identity as a male is almost totally determined by how well he does in this all-male world of subteen youths.

In a way which does not seem to be duplicated in middle-class neighborhoods, the Hunter's Point male youth makes a continual self-assertive demand to be recognized and treated as an adult male with all its implications of sexual potency. It is already clear in his mind that the treatment he receives from women is the greatest single threat he faces to his masculine self-image. There is no greater insult to a seven- or eight-year-old Hunter's Point male than for some adult woman to address him as "little boy."

_____

"I'se a man, woman, I'se a man, you hear? See what I got." [*Points to penis.*]

_____

The Hunter's Point boy seven to twelve years of age characteristically insists that women of all ages, but especially those young enough to be considered as sexual objects, address him as "man." Boys, however, are rarely successful in these demands, and sarcastic female reactions tend to drive boys deeper into their own unisexual group.

At this point, then, the Hunter's Point boy is not only learning to fight and jive, and to identify females as enemies, but is also in the same spirit of defensive masculine assertiveness being initiated into sexual activity. Not all Hunter's Point boys, however, are adequate to these intense peer group demands for fighting spirit and roosterlike self-admiration. Some boys spend most of their time at home. These are teased and taunted by other boys about their inadequate masculinity. Such boys appear to begin to take on certain effeminate characteristics — leading (we assume at least in some cases) to the adoption of a homosexual role, although only an intensive longitudinal study could ascertain this. It is clear, however, that these intense pressures to prove masculinity do push some boys "out of the game" at relatively early ages.

The intensity of this search for masculinity, as we have noted, is based in the inadequate adult male role models available to boys for emulation. Fathers who are psychologically distant or physically absent create a situation fraught with severe conflict for the young boy. Since his unconscious tendency is to identify with the mother, his hyper-aggressiveness and hypersexuality are ways in which he acts out roles of "maleness" in order to alleviate his anxiety about his identification with his mother.

Verbal dueling, learned as an adjunct to physical fighting in the pre-teen years, slowly begins to replace fighting in the teen years. In verbal dueling, which can vary from simple affronts to the complicated rhythmic and poetic structures of the "dirty dozens,"[9] one boy characteristically insults another's mother or sister as a means of attacking him.

"Your Mama got a pussy so big they call her a barn door."

"Yea, well your Mama give it away so much they call her Santa Claus."

"They only *call* my Mama Santa Claus — yours got a real prick — but I guess that's okay since your old man's got a cunt."

"Yea, that cunt he got is your sister."

Thus, verbal dueling exhibits the characteristic tensions arising from the particular family structure of Hunter's Point. The central concern is with the sexuality of the mother and sister (mother-surrogate). The desires and the fears connected with them are then worked out once again in this particular dueling pattern. It can also be said that the attribution of male sex organs to females and vice versa operates as a defense against anxieties about cross-sex identity (see Bettleheim, 1962).

Verbal dueling is also a secondary mobility route to status for the less adequate fighters. In fact, this may be its primary conscious motivation. Soon enough, it becomes clear that not every good fighter is correspondingly good at verbal dueling. On the other hand, inadequate physical fighters may out of necessity develop into accomplished verbal duelers. As one moves further into the teen years, physical aggression, which was at an earlier age occasionally enjoyable and relatively safe, becomes dangerous due to the increased physical strength of the combatants; thus, the tendency increases to use verbal dueling almost exclusively, albeit backed up by the threat of fists.

Hunter's Point boys moreover learn, not surprisingly, to aggress against women. During the prepubescent period, the male is also learning to fulfill his need to manipulate women. He is confirmed in his distrust of women by his peer group. Women, he learns both from the example of adult males around him and the confirmed beliefs of his peer group, must be manipulated or they will manipulate you. They are good for "fucking," but you can't trust them at all. After listening to the discussion of the sexual experiences of others, in which the cooperating girl is personally denigrated (even while her capabilities may be extolled), he quickly goes on to sexual experimentation.

He learns not only the mechanics of sexual activity, but begins to develop his own "strong line," a term used to describe a "potent" manipulative verbal attack on a woman designed to make her succumb to his sexual advances. Once again, we might note at least in part the underlying theme of maleness and toughness suggested by the term *strong line.* Sexual activity is already seen at this age as combat. In such a combat, the better the "weapons" the better the chance of victory.

At the same time the girl is learning that she must not trust boys. She comes to see sexuality as a key to popularity, but she also learns how to contend with "strong lines" so as to suggest that she cannot be manipulated or otherwise overcome by clever verbal assaults. A girl learns to denigrate sexual experience and to suggest that "it really didn't get to me" as a defense against male aggressiveness. Her best defense, however, lies in an attack on the male adequacy of her would-be seducer. Thus, while the boy is learning to view his sexuality as a weapon against women, the girl is learning to reduce the potency of that weapon by symbolic castrative acts.

Nonetheless, girls who can attract numbers of boys are considered to have proven themselves to be real women. Girls, therefore, try to attract boys and to manipulate them while never appearing to be deeply emotionally involved. All these patterns, of course, are being learned both by boys and girls by watching older youths act them out, and they are well understood and internalized by age eleven or twelve.

While sexual experiences and the learning of one's social sex role take place in the preteen grouping, it is at this time also, both in the gang grouping and in the home, that the Hunter's Point youth is learning about "telling it like it is." "Telling it like it is" is one of the experiences of this community which is perhaps most foreign to middle-class whites, but which is of vital importance to the developing child, and an integral part of life in Hunter's Point. Simply stated, "telling it like it is" implies the stripping off of all human pretensions and the cessation of all game playing. It is a favorite technique of informal socialization in the home, as well as other informal groupings. "Telling it like it is" specifically exposes some individual to the merciless glare of "realistic" portrayal by other members of the group. Much as in Synanon-type group therapy,[10] the individual is permitted no defense and no hiding. Every unsavory fact or attitude about him that is known or can be inferred is unearthed for public scrutiny.

An individual's private hopes and dreams, where they have been confided, will be mercilessly derided as unrealistic and childish. Personal sexual habits and habits of dress, speech, eating, and sleeping are dissected. No area is inviolable and no one is excepted from such attacks. Such discussions take on an especially brutal character when they stigmatize some personal relationship as inadequate or insane. Friendships and even budding love affairs are destroyed if individuals cannot continue them after having seen their motives (or supposed motives) so thoroughly dissected and attacked.

We suggest these interactions should be called attacks because, regardless of their other functions, they are in fact attempts to injure others.[11] One popular notion is that "telling it like it is" is related to the forced reality-orientation of the underdog. We suggest that not only is this formulation inadequate, but that it smacks of a kind of neopaternalistic racism.

"Telling it like it is," we suggest, is in actuality one aspect of black self-hate and internalized aggression. Oppressed groups often tend to accept, if only unconsciously, the denigrating stereotypes about themselves spread by the dominant group (Bettleheim and Janowitz, 1964). In such a situation, hatred which might be directed (more healthily) outward at the oppressor group may be internalized and directed against the self and similar objects. The mechanism appears to operate in the child-rearing situation itself. Adult males, unable to be economically meaningful because of racism (and because of its internalized results — i.e., feelings of personal inadequacy), provide an essentially negative model for a young child. Young girls similarly see themselves as representatives of a group (women) which cannot "hold their men." These personal attitudes, then, are apparently easily generalized into a racial context, and the result is black self-hate, which is then reinforced by many of the institutions of the dominant (and thus perceived as better) society.

The internalization of hate against the self rather than against the "oppressor" whites seems to have this brutal infighting as one of its manifestations. Just as most black violence is directed against other blacks (see Robins, 1968), so "telling it like it is" is one of the many forms of verbal abuse which Hunter's Point residents learn to use on each other. Perhaps one of the best-developed psychic defenses here is the way in which some Hunter's Pointers take pride in regarding "telling it like it is" as an aspect of black culture — an aspect, moreover, to be defended as a "good thing" instead of as a pathological response to a pathogenic situation (as we perceive it at least in part).

It is in this context of general self-hate and self-denigration and distrust of persons of the opposite sex that dating begins. Even so, as the Hunter's Point youth enters into his early teen years (thirteen, fourteen, fifteen) the first, perhaps the most meaningful, and for some what appear to be the only true love affairs in their lives are initiated.[12] While preteen boys and girls have been experimenting sexually and imitating adult sexual behavior, the quality of the relationship changes in the early teen years. Where the early pattern of sexual aggression — by males to prove both their masculinity and their ability to manipulate females, by females to insure popularity while denigrating the actual experience (perhaps their earliest attempts to be castrative[13]) — is the norm in the preteen years, what appears to be actual love occurs in the early teens. At least in part, this is clearly the result of the increased sexual maturity of the early teen years and the onset of the physical capacity for orgasm. During this period many individuals develop strong and exclusive feelings for others.

It might be speculated that these strong, exclusive heterosexual ties act as defenses against fears about social sex roles; however, there seems to be a more mature quality about such relationships than would be evident if it were mere defensive behavior. In any event, tenderness and depth of feeling are apparent on the part of both partners in these love affairs. However, both partners seem inevitably to be driven toward acts which will destroy the love relationship.

At any given point in a love affair one of the partners may well be a little "less involved" than the other. The "less involved" partner almost inevitably begins to take advantage of the situation along the lines of the sexual conflict which exists in Hunter's Point. Both boys and girls find an apparently irresistible desire to humiliate the partner for whom they also have a deep and tender feeling.

We postulate several reasons for this. First and perhaps most important is the overwhelming influence of the early family experience, in which distrust of the opposite sex is learned. Then, both in the family and outside it, the individual learns to perceive sexuality as a weapon and to distrust liking anyone too much for fear of being manipulated. Moreover, in the absence of adequate adult models, as we have noted, the peer group serves as an overwhelmingly important model for behavior — and the peer group's response to love affairs is generally negative.

Since at any given time many of the members of a boy's or girl's peer group will not be involved in a "love relation," their comments, couched as they are in terms of an aggressive and distrustful model of sexuality, may and do force similar responses from the "lover" about his beloved. When members of the group jokingly and maliciously inquire about the physical dimensions of the loved one's genitalia, or ask how easy it is to get her or him to perform acts commonly considered perversions in Hunter's Point (i.e., fellatio or cunnilingus), the pressure is on the lover to respond about his beloved in the same fashion at the risk of losing peer group esteem. He/she must also pretend he/she could not be seriously emotionally involved but is only manipulating the other. Tender feelings are naturally rapidly eroded by the corrosive quality of such evaluations. Constant warnings by one's peers not to get "sucked in" or "hooked" or "trapped" by the loved one eventually take their toll. Love affairs commonly disintegrate in the face of such pressure into a contest for dominance.

Later, teenage sexual relationships never seem to regain the tender aspect of these early love affairs, even though peer group pressure drops off rapidly in middle and late teens and sexual interests and relationships continue at a high level.[14] Never again does the same degree of trust appear to prevail. Distrust of the opposite sex becomes established and hardened as a pattern for life. Verbal attacks on members of the opposite sex and highly defensive verbal maneuvering seem to characterize these later interactions.

As we have noted, during both preteen and early teen years males are developing what they hope is a "strong line," a verbal attack aimed at seduction, while girls are learning to contend with a strong line in a manner which suggests that they cannot be sexually manipulated. At least in part, this means the girl develops methods of verbal counterattack which impugn the masculinity of the aggressor and suggest that sex with that particular male would be unrewarding in the extreme. The strong line and the response to it have many variations. Only usually in the event of a collapse of technique or a serious "putdown" will a boy interject openly hostile elements into the interaction. Such hostile elements usually center about the area of sexual inadequacy and fears of female domination. Girls, of course, respond in kind.

Perhaps the best way to illustrate such sexual combat is to present in detail a short approach which breaks down both because of its inadequacy and because of the girl's lack of interest:

Boy: Hey, sweet thing, you headin' on down? You sure are nice. [*Girl doesn't respond.*] Hey, you just as sweet as cake, baby.

Girl: It's all icing and the cake is real too. [*Muffled giggling.*]

Boy: Hey, baby, what you say you name is? I seen you down at _____[local record shop] . You must seen me too, babe — they all notice me.

Girl: I seen you. You ain't heard me sayin' nothin' to you yet, have you?

Boy: Hey, sweet stuff, that's no way to be carryin' on, I'll give you a lift.

Girl: What you talkin' 'bout man, that ain't you car.

Boy: Come on, baby, I'll take you an' show you a good time.

Girl: [*Laughs loudly and contemptuously.*] That's all you'll show.

Boy: What you mean, baby, you couldn't take two inches.

Girl: Yea, you ain't got two inches, man.

Boy: Yea, baby? Well, I don't talk to girls with glass in their crotch.

Concern with preservation of self-image, denigration of the sexual partner, and actual fear of intercourse as potentially castrating are all evident in this interaction. While an interaction in reality rarely breaks down so thoroughly or blatantly, the emotional pattern revealed by this exchange continues in male-female relations for many years.

Nonetheless, teenagers and young adults continue to seek out stable sexual relationships. Such relationships, however, are ideally expected to involve a nondemanding, technically perfect, and extremely responsive sexual partner who can be manipulated but will not seek to manipulate. These goals not only reinforce the notion of controlling the sex partner but also raise the continued problem of potency and adequacy.

Correspondingly, such attitudes also lead to a kind of paradoxical puritanism about sex. One "liberal" kind of attitude toward sex in American society today suggests that if two people are in love, any means of sexual expression that does not hurt or degrade either partner is permissible. This is *not* the attitude of the Hunter's Pointer. Conversations and expressed attitudes suggest that any form of coitus other than the rather narrowly defined "missionary postures" is seen as manipulative. Oral-genital contact is likewise seen as degrading to the performing partner.

The humiliation-control technique seems to reflect patterns learned in preteen sex contacts and the basic distrust men and women feel for each other. It is important to recognize that in the sexually permissive atmosphere of Hunter's Point, it is not merely the sex act itself which is important. Sexual activity is common enough to be taken more or less for granted in Hunter's Point. One of its most important aspects, then, is the way in which sexual activity here is symbolic of conquest and dominance. What is important for a man or a woman is to get the other "tied to you."

"Man, that chick couldn't live without me."

It is with this attitude that young boys learn to use sexuality as a weapon against girls. They also learn, as do girls, to use and manipulate expressions of tenderness from the other party. Soon, all such expressions of tenderness become thoroughly suspect. At the same time that boys are aggressing against girls sexually, they are seeking girls out for gratification of dependency needs. The original gratification of these needs, in the earliest true "love affairs," gives way in the girl to a sense of triumph if she has a boy "tied to her." In many cases, her success only inspires her contempt for the "conquered" boy.

On the other hand, girls, whose needs to attract and punish boys are equal to analogous needs in boys, will often find that fear makes them sexually responsive. Often, girls can be "made" by threats more easily than by "sweet talk." The pattern is too unreliable to be depended upon, for while violence works one time, sweet talk may work another, and nothing works a third time with the same girl. At any rate, this lack of predictability also operates to confuse the meaning of sexual activity and seems to further a search for impersonal sexual involvements with the "technically perfect," impersonal, compliant partner.

Finally, while the Hunter's Point male is evolving his sexual attitudes in the direction of impersonal promiscuity (because he sees long-lasting relationships as threats and traps), and is developing his own sexuality as a weapon for use against women, he is also moving toward noninvolvement and a kind of floating detachment in order to avoid aggressive contact with his peers. The Hunter's Point male teenager acts as if he believed that aggression against or submission to another were the only possible normal responses of men toward each other. His fear of the dangers involved in either aggression or submission leads him to a general dissociation from intense personal contact of any kind. The open aggressiveness of the preteen years gives way to verbal dueling — then to mere sullenness. The verbal dueling with its insults of another male's mother and sister gives way finally in the late teens to a nondueling noninvolvement.

"I don't fight and I don't play."

This common statement can be explicated thus: "I've grown past fighting, and I will not involve myself in verbal dueling with you as a test of wits or manhood. I have withdrawn my feeling."

This withdrawal comes about because the Hunter's Point male distrusts not only females, but also other males (probably as a defensive response to covert homosexual fears). There is, however, another powerful emotional element which enters into this. By his late teens, regardless of what he wants to think, the Hunter's Point male has come to think of himself as negative in most respects. Distrust and dislike of whites, even denigration of certain aspects of "white culture," do not make up for the reality of his structural position. He is modally a "dropout" (see the discussion of education in Chapter 7), he is unemployed, and he is despised by both society at large and himself. Very little in his life has given him any positive feelings about himself. The overt and covert discrimination he feels in interaction with whites, his generalized fears of "the man," his "poverty pocket" level of living and lack of stable emotional life or adequate material goods to buttress himself against such feelings have all taken their toll. By his very early twenties at the latest, he has become "cool."

Cool as a descriptive term for a floating noninvolvement has been made popular by both blacks and unsophisticated whites (in much the same way as "telling it like it is") into a virtue associated with black life styles. If the apparent ontogenesis of it in Hunter's Point bears any resemblance to the causes of "cool" elsewhere it is, rather than a spontaneous positive expression, a defense against a world which has not and will not permit deep emotional realtionships. It is an admission of defeat, personal inadequacy, and fear.

"You can never get to my cool."

"I got cool [that] makes icebergs [seem] warm."

"Baby, you can't touch me; I've got cool I ain't used yet."

Cool is the withdrawal and refusal to interact or to be moved, the inability to be riled, to be touched by any sort of misfortune. There is thus little difference between the foot-shuffling, handkerchief-headed Uncle Tom and the more modern cool, except the style. The aggressiveness which could not be openly expressed through fear but which was implied in the slave's (feigned) clumsiness and stupidity while doing the white man's tasks was one expression of an emotionally destructive situation, the unexpressed and repressed aggressiveness of the nonviolent, noninvolved cool yet another.

What differences exist are the differences between aggression turned toward whites (even if passively) and aggression turned inward. The slave at least had his inefficiency as a weapon, however limited, against his obvious oppressors. The black in Hunter's Point, faced with a more diffuse, "sophisticated" racism and the intolerable social and familial results of it has very few such options. (We shall see one such option in discussing the "riots" in Chapter 10.)

The value of such defenses as cool[15] seen in this context is at once obvious. When aggressive acts toward whites (or toward other blacks) may be ineffective, counterproductive, or even deadly to the individual, when one's armor is being continually searched for chinks by one's peers, when one's sex role is insecure and social prospects minimal, and when even that personal safeguard of the middle class, the family, into which one might wish to retreat from an unpleasant world, is to a large extent denied, emotional withdrawal has a sheer survival value for the Hunter's Point black.

MARRIAGE AND ADULT RELATIONSHIPS

Adult behavior in Hunter's Point is essentially continuous with what has gone on before, as there are few crises in adult life which do not seem to have been foreshadowed in the earlier socialization experiences. Adult behavior differs only in degree, not in kind, from that of teenagers. The need for deep relationships, the impossibility of achieving them, unisexual groupings as defenses against the fear of the other sex, and the male retreat from the home all echo earlier patterns.

The problems of sex identity, for example, continue into adulthood. The pattern of male-female relations both in familial interaction and outside the family remains manipulative, distrusting, hesitant, and fearful, and is characterized either by emotional distancing or aggressive attack. The female denigration of male sexuality which starts in preteen and early teen years as a female defense against the submission implied in her own sexual responses continues also into adult life. It must be remembered that this denigration of male sexuality and the sexual act does *not* imply a lack of enjoyment of sex among Hunter's Point females. Such denigration is merely a way of refusing to admit that such obviously worthless creatures as men could ever have any real emotional meaning to a woman, and, further, is a way of simply denying the sexual aggressiveness of males which might make women unable to see men as useless and passive. Men, then, may be seen as pathetic, impotent, and nonthreatening, and thus unnecessary to take seriously. Sometimes, actual impotence is induced to maintain dominance.

Mrs. Sincero, a thirty-five-year-old woman with four children, was discussing her married life with me:

"I'm trying to get a divorce. My old man, he beats me too much. He's always calling me uppity and saying I'm claiming I'm better than him. It ain't true. I can't help it that I'm part French.

"I had to go to a psychiatrist once, cause I'm a very sensitive person, and he said to me, 'I don't see how you put up with it, Mrs. Sincero.' But if I leave him I'm afraid he'll keep my kids and say I'm crazy so I can't have them. But I make like I'm using herbs [witchcraft] on him in secret, just enough so he suspects. Then I act real innocent. I make him weak [i.e., impotent] and I laugh when he can't do it. He's scared of me, but I'm afraid he'll kill me. That's why I got to get legal aid. How am I gonna get legal aid?"

Mrs. Sincero's personal pathology is of interest only because she exhibits in a more overt manner and with fairly transparent defenses many of the same destructive impulses that are found in many of the families studied. In reality, Mr. Sincero is a rather quiet, passive man who can be goaded into physical violence only on occasion. Mrs. Sincero does not seem to be aware that she apparently solicits the physical beatings she gets and yet uses them and her own manipulative efforts to thwart her husband sexually. Such sexual frustrations drive Mr. Sincero deeper and deeper into passivity and apathy, relieved only by periodic aggressive outbursts against his wife who uses his sexual failure – which she has helped to induce, or at least to reelicit – as an excuse to despise him.

This pattern, albeit in less overtly pathological forms, is so common as to be a major mode of behavior among the families studied. Men do marry, and many often try to create a home which will be stable, and there is little doubt of the sincerity of women in many such attempts as well. But the role of expectations that each brings to marriage, combined with the social sex-role confusion inculcated by both the child-rearing pattern and the position of the adult in the larger (white) society, dooms many marriages to complete failure.

Many Hunter's Point men, though they by and large have internalized "white" norms of proper male behavior and "white" consumption patterns and job expectations, find that they are personally often unsuited to a routine eight-hours-a-day, five-days-a-week, fifty-weeks-a-year job. Even if they are inclined and able to do steady work, they usually find that jobs in the "desirable" categories (either through prejudice of the employer or through their own lack of formal education – also caused, as we shall see, in large part by prejudice) are not available. Jobs when available tend to be in low-paying, low-status categories, often with poor prospects not only for advancement, but even for long tenure. Thus, the overall structural position of the Hunter's Point black man in a prejudiced dominant white community substantially reduces his ability to support a family.

This inability (and partly lack of desire) to support a family makes a man's authority position in the family tenuous. Hunter's Point women typically, as we have noted, despise men for their weakness and hate them because, though they deny it, they are physiologically and psychologically in need of them. Such women also envy the irresponsibility of men. Typically, marriages here tend to "fall apart" after a man has been unemployed for about six months. Unless the man has completely adjusted to having his wife support him – and to withstanding the concomitant emotional abuse – he leaves.[16] Typically, he and other men in the same position, as do young unmarried men in their early twenties or late teens, live together five or six to a room in some small, cheap place in the Bayview or Fillmore districts. Pooling clothes and money, they are able to maintain a semblance of independence from women.

Men may and do come home, for differing periods of time, to "visit" either their wives or their mothers. While both wives and mothers will berate them for their absences and uselessness, typically they have been in some sort of contact all along. Wives very often refuse their husbands admittance, especially if they are currently having another man "live in." This leads to arguments which often culminate in fights and even bloodshed, depending on how seriously the husband allows himself to be injured. Rarely do real reconciliations occur.

Women often have one or two "friends" who in return for sexual favors act as substitute fathers for the children, taking them to the zoo, giving them pocket money, and the like. But because such men very often attempt to maintain similar relationships with several women, frequently getting money from them, the hostilities engendered make even these informal affairs brittle. The comments of various women indicate this, as well as their general disparagement of marriage.

"I don't need no man."

"Sheeit, nigger, you ain't gonna sweet talk me into none of that [i.e., marriage] ."

"I've been married twice, ain't never gonna do that no more. Who needs it?"

"They just come around a-sniffin' and a-scratchin', and they done with you — they off like a hound sniffin' and scratchin' someone else."

The fact that women can get welfare support and Aid to Dependent Children, as well as the fact that women have an easier time getting jobs, means that even those men who are in attendance as husbands, unless they have very secure jobs, have no position of power from which to determine the life pattern of their family. This may take such extreme forms as not being able to interfere with the wife's extramarital affairs. Sometimes, such situations are accepted with good grace, and sometimes husbands even acquiesce in their wife's occasional prostitution activities, justifying them in economic terms.[17]

Since a night's work in the Fillmore district, the Tenderloin district, or downtown, where many prostitutes from Hunter's Point work, may

44

net between fifty and one hundred fifty dollars, the rationale has a reality-oriented basis. While the number of professional prostitutes who make their home in Hunter's Point seems to be very small, occasional prostitutes or amateurs who turn a few tricks to supplement their income are numerous.

Ruby M.: I got five kids, two of them by Johnny there [*Johnny acknowledges this with a shy, diffident smile*] , and three by another cat. He sends me money now and then, but I get food stamps from welfare. I make more than him [*nods toward Johnny*] any time I want to work.

You know, I needed this money for the kid's clothes, you know, so this guy from "the welfare" [*with that sort of emphasis*] , he comes over here and asks me where I got the stove and refrigerator from, you know, cause what they furnish you here and what they say you supposed to have, it ain't much, and you can't have no freezer, and you stove is just as tiny as it can be. I tell him, "What you care — what you care if I tricked for the money, least you don't have to pay me none for it, I'm payin' for it myself."

While some women make a virtue of their forced independence, and while many use this independence as a weapon against their husbands or consorts, others deeply feel the lack of a man in the family. There is no one to talk to "the man" when some contact with authority or the public agencies occurs.

Joan B.: They broke my window the other night, and I called the project cops. They said to me, "What do you want us to do?!" Well, hell, I don't know, ain't they supposed to do something to find out who does it and stop them?

They come around with this bill for five dollars for letting me in when I got locked out. Five dollars just for lettin' me in. And that cop he say I just like a dumbbell and got no sense. They don't talk to you like that you got a man with you. And I got a ticket, I got no man to fight back. When you poor, you just gotta take it. But if I had a man here — they'd probably shoot him though.

While the absence of secure, strong males takes its toll, even among women who claim not to need men, the personal cost in degradation

and humility reaches apocalyptic proportions among the older population of males. While the denigration of males continues throughout the
entire age cycle, by the time a man reaches late middle age he has become so accustomed to this pattern of life that he will accept most
attacks, and most physical and verbal abuse by women, with a degree of
apparent calmness and resignation.

Mr. and Mrs. Blasingame are a couple in their mid-sixties. Mr. Blasingame is partially blind and has not been able to work for five years
because of this. This is upsetting to him because he has been accustomed to an active life and to financially providing for his family. Mrs.
Blasingame has been employed as a maid for the last ten years and for
the last five has been the sole support of the family (Mr. Blasingame
never having paid into Social Security). They live in the older housing
section and have furnishings comparable to most working-class families
in white America (inexpensive but sound furniture, television, etc.).

Mr. B.: Yeah, I worked thirty-five years, most I could, then I get
blind, but I always . . .

Mrs. B.: Shut up, he [*referring to me*] don't care nothin' about your
old aches and pains. We're a God-fearing family, not like some I
could say, all this dancin' and carryin' on late at night, they never
stay at home — leave their kids — out with all kinds of men — got
no proper husbands — all they want is that welfare check.

Not only was Mrs. Blasingame dismissing her husband as being of too
low a status to interest me, but also, by adopting an attitude of black
self-denigration and at the same time distinguishing herself from such
"low-class" types, she was establishing her own status with me. Of
course, Mrs. Blasingame, a devout Baptist, was not only speaking for
effect; she appeared to believe what she said.

When community organization was mentioned, Mr. Blasingame
attempted again to reenter the conversation.

Mr. B.: Yeah, I'm kinda hopin' we'd get organized, do somethin',
anyway. What we need to do —

Mrs. B.: What you talkin' 'bout, man? — they ain't nothing you got to
say, you ain't no workin' man.

Mr. B.: I used to —

Mrs. B.: You ain't no more. I'm goin' to work now [*meaning*: "I must leave for my job or I'll be late"] . I can't stay here no longer just talkin' to you [*addressing her husband, with whom, of course, she had not really been talking*] , I gonna be late. [*She did, however, stay and talk to me for another forty-five minutes.*]

Mrs. Blasingame then went on to discuss how much she disliked people living off "the welfare" and how she especially despised men who lived off women, pointedly looking at her husband, who continued to watch television, saying nothing.

NOTES

[1]I am using *matrifocality* here not only in its narrowest denotative sense, but in the broader connotative focus which implies not only that the mother is the sole financial support and emotional center of the family, but that she focuses all of the family's needs around her, and that even as adults her children either directly or indirectly come under her general authority. Specifically we are describing families in which an adult female (or two or more lineally related adult females) lives without the permanent presence of an adult male consort. Variants include the sporadic residence of unemployed males who contribute little to the structure of the family. Though *matrifocality* is a structural term, its implications are emotional, as I shall show.

[2]This is a pattern commented on by Frazier (1957), Dai (1948), Pettigrew (1964), and others.

[3]It might be important to note at this time that information about weaning and toilet-training is presented merely to indicate general attitudes; such information, as many writers have noted, is meaningless out of context of the entire child-rearing situation, and I do not propose to initiate some simple "trauma" explanation of adult behavior through patterns of child rearing in weaning and toilet-training. To borrow a phrase from Barnouw (1963), we are attempting a "total situational analysis utilizing child training as one aspect of the etiology of adult behavior."

[4]Naturally this leads to a certain amount of relatively public defecation and urination by young children, which is often interpreted by biased or untrained observers as being additional evidence of black people's "animality" (and is commonly commented on in this way by local whites).

[5]Alameda County across the Bay, for example, was noted in the mid 1960s for its "bed check" night raids and its somewhat Neanderthaloid notions about welfare recipients, the purpose of its night raids being to uncover men who were "illegitimately" living in the home of an AFDC mother.

[6]Since it was much more difficult for me to get information concerning the activities and style of life of prepubescent girls than of boys, the following statements about girls will have to be taken as tentative to a much greater degree than those for boys.

[7]Parsons (1964) analyzes the social-structural implications of this system and describes it as "regressive," since it does not lead easily to emotional maturation.

[8]Indeed, Sherwood L. Washburn (private communication 1965) suggests that the establishment of dominance hierarchies is a vital evolutionary survival mechanism among primates.

[9]Eddington (1968) discusses this form also while relating some aspects of it to the behavior of pimps.

[10]Synanon is a privately run social therapy grouping which concentrates its efforts on alcoholics and drug users. It uses a characteristically brutal type of personal-defense stripping as one of its techniques.

[11]That this same technique used against the white world may be a technique of release from unbearable tensions we do not deny. On the other hand, it is rarely used this way. Malcolm X, however, made great headway using this technique on fellow blacks.

[12]I am aware that such decisions about the quality of human emotional experience are fraught with the danger of ethnocentrism and may also result from projection and other forms of psychic defense on my part. I have only suggested this after long consideration. If the Midtown Manhattan Survey (Strole et al., 1962) could indicate 80 percent personal pathology of some type and the D. Leighton et al. (1963) work in Canada 57 to 69 percent personal pathology, it is not irrational to accept similar rates for Hunter's Point, at least as a working hypothesis. This might explain why even with increased personal maturity, adults facing so many psychological problems are modally unable to recapture the particular freedom and emotional lability which apparently characterizes these early love affairs.

[13]Symbolic castrative activities in females most likely arise here from young girls' disappointment at the inadequacy of the father.

[14]Illegitimacy levels in Hunter's Point are considered to be as high as those in any lower-class ghetto in the United States by social workers who have case loads in Hunter's Point, although specific rates are hard to determine.

[15]Claude Brown in his *Manchild in the Promised Land* indicates another extremely effective defense technique which began to appear in Harlem in the '50s: men began to call one another "baby." Brown suggests that this epithet arose from the desire of the black man to show others that he wasn't "uptight" about homosexuality, that he really felt that he was a real man — enough of a man to be able to afford the looseness of affect implied by treating other men with a degree of emotional familiarity ordinarily reserved for women.

This is a very interesting and sophisticated defense. It is, in fact, the verbal acting out of the feeling which exists, removing the negative affect from it. On the other hand, the problems of having such a release without having clearly defined the problem or understanding the meaning of the release may lead to displacement of the tension into other areas.

[16]One "adjustment" is to develop the defensive attitude of claiming that one likes to be supported by women, that it is only right that men live off of them.

[17]On the other hand, the actual psychic pain is probably immense. Much of the physical abuse of women by men here is related to real or imagined infidelity.

48

II

Four Families

ALTHOUGH the sociocultural framework in which the family in Hunter's Point exists is crucial to understanding the overwhelming role it plays in the molding of the lives of its members, the actual quality of the family life can only truly be shown by a direct look at the family itself. The family is both cause and effect, the creator and the product, the shaping cauldron and the result of that shaping. It is the core of life in Hunter's Point as it is elsewhere in all human societies. To describe more accurately the families in Hunter's Point I have selected key individuals from four families broadly representative of those in the new, "permanent housing," described them and their families, and let them tell their life histories in their own words. In addition, Thematic Apperception Test (TAT) responses were elicited from these same individuals.

My approach was to ask individuals whom I had known for at least a year to give me, usually after about a week's notice, their life histories and, when they had completed them, to ask them if they would help me to get their responses to the Thematic Apperception Test. I attempted to capture both the life histories and the TAT responses verbatim. Rena Lea's, Jerry's, and Mary Ellen's life histories were taken down in notes, the others on tape. Seemingly by chance, those on tape were more extensive and often much more revealing. In retrospect I believe this to be in part due to the limitations of memory in reconstructing conversation from scribbled notes. Nonetheless, the three life histories taken down in notes *were* in fact shorter and their content more restricted. This in part appears to reflect the personal responses of these individuals to me.

The families very broadly represent a kind of cross section of the community, as shown below:

	More Stable	Less Stable
Father absent	Babalona	Mary Ellen
Father present	Mango and Adelaide	Rena Lea and Jerry

(In the family designations in the following chapters the dominant member's name appears first, e.g., "Rena Lea and Jerry," and "Mango and Adelaide.")

Babalona's and Rena Lea and Jerry's families are probably illustrative of the bulk of families in Hunter's Point. In Rena Lea and Jerry's family, Rena Lea is dominant even though Jerry is employed. Jerry's employment is sporadic and ill-paying, and without the support which Rena receives from a prior husband for her children by that husband, life would be economically quite difficult for them. Their relationship is less stable than that of Mango and Adelaide, yet there is no overt evidence that their marriage is in difficulty or that the family unit faces immediate disruption. The reasons for this will become clear if the reader keeps in mind our analysis of the structure of that kind of family.

Babalona's family represents perhaps as many as one-quarter to one-third or more of the families I studied in Hunter's Point. Her family unit, held together with the help of sisters and a nearby mother, and supported by her sporadic paychecks and continuing welfare payments, is truly a stable family, albeit not in the white middle-class sense. Together, families like Babalona's and Rena Lea and Jerry's make up over 50 percent of the families studied in Hunter's Point.

The families of Mary Ellen and of Mango and Adelaide deviate from the above patterns, but in their general dimensions probably represent something like 20-25 percent and 10-15 percent, respectively, of the families of Hunter's Point. Mary Ellen is personally more disorganized and less responsible than most mothers in Hunter's Point, but her poorly integrated family with few supporting relatives and no father and little supervision of children is nonetheless one of the representative modes of living in the project.

Mango is somewhat unique. The fact that he resides in the family home, holds a permanent, reasonably well-paying job, and seems to be the dominant member of his family makes him representative of a fairly small but important group of families in Hunter's Point.

Other kinds of family units in Hunter's Point — young married couples without children, older couples who are retired or retiring, and single individuals, as well as a few absent-mother families — are rare at this time in the new housing area.

One group we have made no attempt to represent significantly here are the young unmarried men and women, teenagers, and "young hoods" (in Rena Lea's words). Such individuals by and large are outside the focus of this study.

THE THEMATIC APPERCEPTION TEST

The Thematic Apperception Test was devised as a projective test by Henry A. Murray. It is a simple device. Twenty pictures that were derived from popular magazine illustrations, mostly involving people in ambiguous situations, are presented to the person taking the test. The individual is instructed to make up a story about what he sees.

The test elicits responses assumedly based upon the unconscious dynamics that motivate the individual in interpersonal strategies in life and upon his orientation toward the world. Scoring may be done in a variety of ways. The reader may turn to any of a number of books and articles on the subject, starting with Murray (1950) himself.

Essentially, scoring approaches stress either quantitative analyses or qualitative analyses, or a combination of both. Quantitative analyses stress the number of *kinds* of responses coded in various ways and then scored in terms of the general presence or absence of traits indicative of various psychodynamic processes. Qualitative analyses stress the similarity of the responses to those of a psychiatric interview, in which the *order* of the responses is considered important because of the eliciting effect of one response upon the following one and the perseveration of themes.

While doubts have been raised by some researchers concerning the validity of this test, especially when applied to other than white, middle-class respondents, I believe it has great validity. (See DeVos and Hippler, 1969 for a fuller discussion of cross-cultural uses of projective tests.) I have found, in a number of research projects in different cultures, that the kinds of stories people develop when presented with the picture cards do reflect what I am able to determine through other kinds of observations to be central to their lives. The emotional dynamics laid bare by the cards are in fact projective. That is, they show that individuals project onto the cards motivations, emotional drives, anxieties, and defenses with which they are most familiar themselves.

I could argue indefinitely about the use and validity of the technique. I feel, however, that presenting the responses in their entirety will either convince the reader or not. The reader is free to make up his own mind in light of what else I have asserted about the community and the extant literature on similar populations.

I have included the TAT responses in detail even though they are to some extent repetitious. The very repetitiveness of certain themes, I believe, confirms the significance of the core emotional organization which I view as characterizing Hunter's Point residents. In analyzing TAT responses I have relied less upon a comparative analysis of quantitative responses with those of other groups which have been similarly tested, because it is my belief that it is in the qualitative analysis that the relevant dynamics more clearly reveal themselves. Further, the intimate contacts I established with the families under discussion allowed me to make qualitative observations that might have been questionable had they been attempted "cold," that is, without knowing the respondents.

My emphasis upon the pathic aspects of the responses is dictated in part by what I believe actually exists in the records and in the lives of the respondents. It is not that the kind of emotional concerns expressed are unique to this population. All human beings possess the same kinds of basic emotional needs. The particular "mix" of these needs and defenses, however, is characteristic of this population. Those needs and defenses that continually resurface in the TAT responses are, I believe, the very ones which are continually in the forefront of the emotional organization of Hunter's Point residents.

3

RENA LEA
AND JERRY'S FAMILY

RENA LEA, twenty-six, has been married twice and divorced once.
(Divorce is a little unusual among Hunter's Pointers, but not strikingly
so.) She has six children, three by her former husband and three by her
present husband. She is an attractive woman, a tidy housekeeper, and
pleasant and friendly in her relations with others.

Jerry, her husband, works nights as a janitor in a downtown San
Francisco office building. A passive, dark brown man, he gives the
appearance of being quite athletic and graceful. Generally noncommuni-
cative, he is nevertheless quite friendly and open when successfully
engaged in conversation. His ambition, which he shares with Rena, is to
own his own home "on the Peninsula" (i.e., the area south of San Francisco, toward Menlo Park).

Rena was born in San Francisco ("That's where I met my first husband"), and except for short periods of time spent in Oakland (across
the bay from San Francisco) and in Los Angeles ("I think they's more
for colored to do there"), she has lived in San Francisco all her life.

Jerry, from Alabama, is thirty-three. His family came to San Francisco when he was six years old.

Rena Lea was for a short time a member of one of the Hunter's

Point "block clubs" — organizations usually formed around living groups for the purpose of dealing with local authorities and agencies through collective organization, petition, and demands. (See the discussion of block clubs in Part III.) Jerry has refused to join. "I just ain't got the time." Rena says, "He don't like all that women stuff," an argument with which Jerry essentially agrees. The clubs' business is in fact by and large "women's stuff": nearly all social and political groups are woman-dominated.

But it is not only regarding social or political organizations that Jerry and Rena part their ways. When Rena goes out at night, for example, much of the time she goes alone. Neither Jerry nor Rena inquire too closely into the whereabouts of the other so long as the absence is not prolonged. They are an amicable couple, never quarreling in public nor publicly humiliating each other as do some other couples in Hunter's Point.

Nevertheless, Jerry is absent most of the time. Only two days during the more than forty that I was in the house at some time or another did I ever see Jerry present for more than an hour or two after waking in the morning. Of course, starting in early evening he is gone all night, since that is when he works.

Although Jerry could be at home a great deal of the day because of his working hours, he does not choose to. He does not discipline the children, nor in fact does he, by and large, acknowledge their existence. He does not shoo them out of the house, does not dandle them on his knee; he does nothing.

Fanny Lou — Rena's eighteen-year-old cousin — is staying with them. Rena thinks it is about time she found Fanny Lou some boys, got her drunk and laid. She says this in fond, joking tones. Only a few minutes later, she will suggest lightly that "Jerry is finally getting to like Fanny. Ain't that nice?" Rena is basically quite cautious, however, since Fanny is a very pretty girl, and even though Jerry is not often home, she would really prefer for them not to be in each other's company too often. She shoos Fanny out, just as if Fanny were a child, and Fanny accepts this treatment with equanimity, deferring in general to Rena.

Rena's aunt lives in the next building, her mother two buildings away; both come to visit her often. While family relationships in extended families tend by definition to be close, in Hunter's Point they are especially so between women but not necessarily so between men. A particular scene is instructive of these as well as other values in Hunter's Point.

Geraldine, Rena's cousin, a striking, tall, sixteen-year-old girl, came into the apartment sniffling — an obvious paralinguistic signal, as she stopped immediately upon being questioned.

Rena: She beat you?

Geraldine: Yeah.

Rena: What about this time?

Geraldine: Yeah, she wanted me to do them old dishes. Oh, Rena, I'm just sort of upset. They took my little brother in for murder. He and some other kid for killing this kid. The other kid and my brother they both say the other kid pushed him off the roof.

That was two nights ago — you know, I just couldn't sleep last night. I tossed and turned. You know, every time something like that happens it's like something is wrong, you know? I never think that that's what the reason is. I just can't sleep. My aunty wouldn't tell me till yesterday, and then she beat me for not doing the dishes.

Rena: That's nothing — my mother, she still beat me and I'm twenty-six. Hell, they shouldn't have been on that building. You can get killed on them things. Them lousy roofs. Listen, I'll tell you, they just don't keep up the roofs on them old buildings.

Geraldine: You can't keep boys out of trouble. Lucky he ain't here or I'd beat his head in.

Jerry: I saw it on television. [*He makes no further comment.*]

The interaction is illuminating in several regards. First, there was, among the families involved, an absolute assumption of the accused's guilt, although no one at the scene had talked with him. No one even suggested getting a lawyer. The acceptance of violence (such as frequent child beatings) and even the almost casual acceptance of murder (though murder is by no means a common event here) are evident in this conversation, just as they are in the casual attitudes toward physical violence which are common throughout Hunter's Point.

Perhaps even more striking is Jerry's apparent lack of need to inform Rena of her cousin's misfortune even though he was aware that she knew nothing about it.

Even clearer, however, is the power of the matriarch in Geraldine's immediate family. Not only must her beatings be accepted with equanimity, but she has the power to make a completely arbitrary decision about when to inform the rest of the family of the boy's arrest. The old woman, as later conversations showed, was merely exercising her right to maintain control over the family. On the other hand, we suggest that Jerry's actions, though similar superficially, resulted primarily from his lack of interest and general lack of involvement.

Rena, joking in another conversation about Geraldine's "debut" on Third Street, suggests that she and Jerry should teach her (Geraldine) to smoke and drink in the house, under the assumption that, since she will learn anyway, she should learn under more congenial circumstances. Though Rena herself does not drink, she is tolerant of others who do. Even so, her concern about Geraldine's involvement with the crowd on Third Street is somewhat tardy. Geraldine at sixteen, and as beautiful as she is, has already had a rapid and thorough education in the social graces and techniques of Hunter's Point. Geraldine has already had one abortion that Rena does not know about. Geraldine's own mother, having run off some years ago, is little help in these matters.

But Geraldine is not Rena's major problem. Rena is most seriously concerned about Johnny, her eight-year-old son, who has recently taken to carrying a switchblade knife. Rena complains that she never knows where her kids are, but she is already starting to lock out little George, who is only two. Only the baby, Ann, who was six months old in the summer of 1967, is in the house continuously.

RENA LEA

Life History

"I was born, I came . . . I been here since I was born, in San Francisco. We, uh, lived over in the Fillmore on _____ Street, till I . . . we left I was fifteen.

"There ain't no . . . when I was little we stayed there . . . is where I had my baby."

_____

Q. What do you mean?

A. I was pregnant and I was seventeen so me and my first husband we got married. He, uh, was from Oakland. I, uh, went there to church. My aunty had a church there and, uh . . . we went over there for church. He was a good dancer, I liked that . . . but he left and now he sends money for the kids.

Well, I went to school in San Francisco, but I never liked school. I just never liked it at all. We used to go down the Peninsula and, uh . . . we, all them houses is like my daddy was gonna get us, but he didn't.

When I married Jerry, we got a better thing than Joe [*her first husband*] and I. We uh, came here 'cause Jerry's out of work, and by then I got three kids and I can't work at all.

That's like it was . . . my mother's thing . . . she was married too young . . . [*laughs*] . . . she never really got married . . . she just say she's married. See, she and my aunty is from the old country.

Q. The old country?

A. Man, that's Mississippi . . . you ain't never heard it? The old country? I was back there once only when I was twelve. My mother warned me about it and she was right. That's where they make sure you're a nigger and you know it . . . sheeit, man. These niggers here now come around thinkin' it's bad here.

Anyhow . . . I liked it here so much better when I got back, I ain't never had no complaint. Well, no, that ain't true. Thing is this bastard cop . . . see, after the riot they had down to the community center . . . I was about . . . it was a week later goin' home from the store and I was I guess staring at this cop on Palou . . . He told me, what I lookin' at, nigger? and if I don't want to get a slap alongside the head to [move] on.

Q. What happened?

A. I moved on – I was scared.

Q. What, I mean, what was it about?

A. Man, what you mean? . . . I mean, I don't know . . . you think there's always some reason for things? Sheeit, that's just the way it is. My little baby girl knows better than that.

Q. Yes . . . [*Pause.*]

A. There ain't no more to talk about me. I didn't like it here, I don't like it here and I'm gonna leave.

Rena Lea's life history as she relates it is sparse: she says virtually nothing about her childhood, beginning her life for us at seventeen. She became pregnant prior to marriage, as many in Hunter's Point do. For her, as for many, church is a focal area of social interaction for the young. Moreover, she indicates her essentially spontaneous and sensual orientation; her attraction to her husband is overtly and unselfconsciously physical.

By indirection she indicates as well the power of the older women in her society. Her aunty "ran" the church. Both her mother and her mother's sister came to California at about the same time. Both are dominant in their own families (from my observation) over weak males, and Rena Lea tells us how her mother uses the title "Mrs." as a status symbol, while abjuring any permanent conjugal tie.

A general undercurrent of dissatisfaction pervades her account, and though she is apparently quite fond of Jerry he plays a very small role in her life's history.

Her description of the social reality of Mississippi is instructive. She juxtaposes Mississippi and San Francisco, describing white and black relations in Mississippi as similar to the kind of treatment police tender blacks in San Francisco. Yet, because she needs to feel that she has advanced from so bad a situation, she seems to deny that what she says is really true. In both cases, the import of the denigrating term *nigger* (when used by a white) is inescapable. Rena Lea evidences some impatience with my "naïve" question, "What was it about?" The world is relatively inexplicable; explanations are merely chimeras. In any event, she evinces no satisfaction with the past or the present and a definite desire for future change.

TAT Responses

Card 1

A. What am I supposed to do? I supposed to make up somethin' up about this? Well . . . uh . . . this girl was lookin' at this violin, see . . . and, uh . . . you know . . . she gonna really try to play it.

Q. And?

A. Well, she gonna study to do it . . . if somethin' else don't catch her mind . . . like . . . uh . . . like getting married.

Card 2

A. This one's about a lady leanin' up against a tree . . . uh . . . I think, uh . . . anyhow, she's gonna have a baby and she's got the world by the tail. You know, see . . . she's got this house and farm and her man and he is keepin' her good. And she's tryin' not to show off too much . . . 'cause there's this young thing there who's goin' to school and she is wishin' she could have that, too.

Q. What do you mean?

A. You know this kid, no . . . she's probably her daughter and doesn't really want to go to school . . . would like to stay at home.

Card 3BM

A. This is like my sister — she's always gloomy and depressed, moping around.

Q. And?

A. And nothin'.

Card 4

A. [*Long pause.*] . . . This guy . . . he's goin' away . . . and this broad's tryin' to keep him and it ain't goin' to work. Once they git that thing in their heads, you might just as well forget it. Don't waste your time. He's thinkin' about some other woman and he's long gone while he's there.

Card 6BM

A. Um . . . [*Starts to laugh.*] . . . that old woman givin' him hell and what for. He's tellin' her somethin' she don't like and she's about to whop him up alongside the head.

Q. What happened?

A. He just thinks he's grown up . . . she gonna show him it ain't true.

Card 7GF

A. Um . . . this like my little girl, she's tellin' her how she should do when she grows up but she just ain't listening. She ain't payin' no mind.

Q. Why?

A. Oh . . . kids don't listen to none of that kind of stuff.

Card 8BM

A. This one's easy. This boy he's dreamin' he's goin' to be a great surgeon someday. He's goin' to do great operation when the situation is hopeless. He's dreamin' about bein' in an operating room and it's during a war and he's savin' the life of the guy he's operating on.

Card 13MF

A. [*Pause.*] . . . She and he and . . . they . . . he's feelin' bad 'cause he just found out she's gonna leave him and she just did it for him this one last time. He screwed her and then she tells him she's leavin'. [*Laughs.*] . . . That's pretty good . . . she really got him goin'.

Q. Why is she leaving?

A. She don't need him no more. She could do better . . . She ain't, he ain't — that is, he ain't . . . he ain't workin' steady . . . they ain't got much money.

Card 16

A. [*Laughs.*] . . .

TAT Analysis

A quantitative content analysis of Rena Lea's TAT responses indicates that her expressed modal concerns are in the areas of violence and aggression, aspiration toward achievement, and concerns with authority, with lesser modes concerning loss of love objects (especially through rejection) and nonmarital sex leading to eventual separation. Rena Lea is also concerned with economic aspects of life, reflecting a desire for the acquisition of material things and seeing monetary relationships between individuals as a focus for concern. Additionally, she indicates some unspecified anxiety, nurturant attitudes, a feeling of discord over autonomy in marriage, and a belief in the negative results of parental education.

Apart from quantitative measures, however, a qualitative evaluation of Rena Lea's TAT suggests a continual conflict over expressive versus manipulative urges. In Card 1, Rena Lea suggests the dominance of expressive over achievement themes. In Card 2, achievement and expressive themes in a positive sense are vaguely threatened by the possibility of jealousy. In Card 3BM, there is almost a total card rejection with an emphasis on the depressing aspect of the sibling relationship.

In Card 4, Rena Lea expresses her anxiety about the possibility of desertion, and in Card 6BM she defends against this feeling by showing female dominance over males.

The theme of the rejection of parental advice, and by extension perhaps the rejection of the achievement theme, comes up again in Card 7GF. Card 8BM, however, continues the idea of achievement, though on a somewhat unrealistic basis. This unrealistic assumption of the possibility of achievement simply through aspiration runs through many of the TAT results from the people in Hunter's Point. In Card 13MF, Rena Lea suggests that expressive behavior can have its manipulative aspects as well. Here, she reverses the aspect of male desertion by claiming that the male has been used and exploited sexually and is now being rejected. He is being rejected on the basis of inadequacy which is described as economic. However, in the context of Rena Lea's life, her descriptions of male inadequacies would tend to include the entire gamut of activity which is considered to be the prerogative of males, even though economic considerations loom large.

In Rena Lea's responses, there is a noticeable lack of routine work considerations or of excessive card blocking, whereas both of these kinds of responses were in evidence in large numbers in Jerry's cards.

JERRY

Life History

"I was born in Alabama, Mobile. I'm thirty-three now. My folks was farmers, moved to town for work after my old . . . my . . . father, my father, he lost his farm. Like . . . then we moved, I guess it was the war, he came, came to San Francisco. Like, uh, like, uh . . . he wanted to work at the shipyards. He died and my mama and I . . ."

Q. When did he die?
A. Nineteen fifty. Like, uh, my mama and I lived here, then I met Rena Lea and we got married. We was moved to the Fillmore . . . but I got out of a job and I had to look, like it was summer and I lost a job and we moved here August 15, 1963, and we been here . . . we gotta move down the Peninsula. That's all.

Jerry's life history is the sparsest of the individuals collected in Hunter's Point. He lists a history of moves and disappointments. Male actions are seen in terms of their inadequacy — specifically, loss of work. To Jerry, women are what one remains with for emotional support, and he lived with his mother until he married Rena.

Jerry's suggestions about the need to move are less specific than his remembrance of the day he moved to Hunter's Point. From this and other evidence, it is reasonable to infer that Jerry feels at home here or at least in a permanent situation. The decision to move to the Peninsula is Rena's idea; he merely acquiesces in this as he would in anything else. Surprisingly, for so sparse a life history, his TAT results give a much clearer picture of the underlying dynamics of his life.

TAT Responses

Card 1

A. It's this kid . . . he's leavin' his head down . . . he's thinkin' about this violin . . . uh, he, uh . . . he knows it's gonna be too hard ever to play it.

Q. Why?

A. It's just too hard. He ain't never got the schooling.

Card 2

A. There's these two men plowing that field and they wives is there.

Q. And?

A. They . . . one is goin' to school and, uh, uh, the other, uh, see she is . . . havin' a baby and men . . . that one is thinkin' . . . he is sure that it don't matter anyhow . . . it's okay she go to school, then that baby be smarter man than him.

Card 3BM

A. This man, he tired and he's resting.

Q. Why?

A. He worked hard today . . . he's resting 'cause it's so hard.

Card 4

A. [Long pause.] He's either gonna do what she wants . . . and get him somethin', or he's gonna go.

Q. Yes?

A. It ain't no fight . . . it's just she wants somethin' and he ain't feelin' like givin' it . . . he's tired . . . now he might, but he might not. It all depends.

Q. On what?

A. Just depends.

Card 6BM

A. The police is comin' and he stoled somethin' . . . it's he's with his — she's his mama. They is . . . he's tryin' to explain — he says to her he's sorry.

Q. What happened?

A. He stoled somethin' from the store he worked and this woman . . . and they caught him. He run away, but now he's gonna give up.

Card 7GF

A. This just a kid talkin' to her mother.
Q. What about?
A. I don't know.

Card 8BM

A. This man, he's afraid. He's dreamin' they're gonna cut him.
Q. What do you mean?
A. Well, he didn't mean nothin' but he just hit this guy and the other guys is gonna get him for it. But, uh . . . uh . . . or maybe he could be dreamin' about . . . uh . . . he's just standin' in front of a store window and that's a sign in the window.

Card 13MF

A. [*Long pause.*] . . . I don't know. It seems like . . . I guess he killed her.
Q. What happened?
A. He was with her on that bed. He just started puttin' his hands on her throat and couldn't stop.
Q. Now what?
A. Now he don't know what to do.
Q. What will he do?
A. I guess he's wait for . . . I guess . . . I guess . . . he'll wait for them to come and get him.

Card 16

A. There ain't nothin' here.

TAT Analysis

The modal areas of concern which Jerry expresses are those of physiology, control, authority and autonomy, superego responses, unusual blocking (which is highest modal response), general aggression and delinquent behavior, and routine everyday work. Jerry's responses concerned with physiology include two comments on physical exhaustion and one on sleep. He also has a response indicating an injury through accident, harm from outside forces, and inadequacy fears as well as concern about separation in a marriage due to discord. Jerry also includes a response indicating resignation, one about dreaming, and some aspiration for others. He sees, as did Rena Lea, dominance in heterosexual relationships as essentially the prerogative of the female. Jerry is very concerned over his self-control, and his superego responses include apologies and a wish to surrender to punishment, a fear for revenge by peers over an undeliberated murder, and the need to call in the police which seems indicative of a fear of the inadequacy of his own internal controls. It seems clear that Jerry's own aggressive urges have been very thoroughly repressed, and he feels that these aggressive urges can bring him nothing but danger. This repressed aggression comes out in the form of physiological concern as well as concerns of the superego and control areas. Another sign of this repression of aggression appears to be the unusual amount of bizarre card uses or blocking responses.

Resignation and defeat appear as the dominant qualities when we look at the qualitative aspects of Jerry's TAT responses to Cards 1, 2, and 3BM. In Card 4BF, even his potential for rebellion is presented in terms of fatigue, and that rebellion is not at all certain of success. But to respond even to so normal a rebellion as this in Card 6BM, it is necessary for him to call the police and to give himself up.

Card 7GF is a continuation of this fear of a very mild aggression expressed in Card 4, and is a totally blocked card. Card 8BM shows the theme of aggression rising again, however, and again the aggression is denied by claiming that in fact it is probably just a dream. Card 13MF shows the return of the repressed aggression now culminating in murder. Jerry feels unable to control his responses, and eventually must simply sit in passive resignation for the punishment which is due him.

4

BABALONA'S FAMILY

BABALONA is a heavy-set woman of twenty-nine with five children. She was married when she was sixteen, and four of her children are the result of this early liaison; the other was born since the separation of Babalona and her husband. Babalona is presently between consorts, and, as she points out continuously, since she is not promiscuous there is no child on the way. (Her neighbors tend to support her claims about leading a sedate life.)

Babalona is a pleasant woman with a tendency to try (at least in my presence) to use a level of standard English with which she is neither truly familiar nor comfortable. Her conversations thus have a stilted and artificial sound to them at times. She is, however, warm toward everyone and an easygoing person who is less interested in housekeeping than in entertaining visitors cordially.

Not working and at home most of the time, she trades off baby-sitting chores with other women in her situation to enable her to shop and occasionally "get out." Unlike Rena, however, she rarely gets out socially and is dependent for amusement upon visitors and "the television."

Babalona has an infant child of eight months (born December 1966), and although she handles him a great deal she has weaned him already from the breast. "It ain't good for 'em to stay on it too long." She permits him pacifiers whenever he seems discontent. She somewhat harshly and impersonally disciplines children — specifically, without ever showing overt anger, she may repeatedly and severely strike a child until he is screaming and crying on the floor. Almost any technique of discipline is permitted in her mind so long as it gets the children out of her hair. Thus, she may cajole, threaten, or physically attack a child to render him tractable.

Unlike Rena, Babalona is not compulsive about keeping children out of the house. However, she usually demands that the oldest ones stay outside during the day. On the other hand, the door is seldom locked — or at least a great deal less frequently than Rena's — and the house is usually full of children. This both tires and bores Babalona, as the apartment is not very large (four rooms).

In her household (as in many others in Hunter's Point), children are continually concerned with food. They are always asking for food, and she, like many other Hunter's Point mothers, gives out food as a reward for obedience. Commonly, she refuses food to a child at mealtime if he has not been "good," only to give him food later when he comes up to her begging.

Babalona, like Rena, does not drink, and she also does not smoke. "I don't keep none of that high stuff around, anyhow."

Babalona is less involved in the community, and her interests are more centered on her family than are Rena's. Once she thought of joining a block club when it was formed in her building, but one meeting convinced her not to be bothered with that "nigger stuff." She interprets such organizations as being simply the means for some people in the community to make themselves "feel big." Nothing, she is sure, comes of it.

"Them niggers aren't goin' nowhere, and they doin' it at top speed just like always. Hell, they can't even get some bus service here. You know that at night, they just run busses here till one-twenty? I seen them clubs come and go, baby, and it ain't no big thing."

Babalona professes no particular inclination to marry again.

"No, not much in that, I like babies, but I been married . . . what I want to do that for again? Course, I'm just soft, that's why that man

68

don't have to pay me nothin' for these kids, but I still ain't no bargain about bein' married."

_____

As she sees it, Babalona's own family life may have had something to do with her attitude. "I came from Louisiana years ago. My father left my mother when I was just a baby. Hell, I ran my own husband off. He was always comin' in liquored up and couldn't hold no job when he did come in which weren't often. I got no use for men like that. I can take care of my kids on 'the welfare.'"

BABALONA

Life History

Q. Well, where were you born? That's one way to start.

A. Well, I was born in Louisiana.

Q. Where at?

A. In Shreveport, and I left Shreveport when I was two years old, so I don't remember anything about it. From Shreveport, we came to San Francisco.

Q. Who is "we"?

A. My parents — my mother and father — and myself.

Q. That's all?

A. That's all. Well, we came to San Francisco . . . I can't remember much about when we first got here. I can remember about as far back as when I was approximately four years old, and we lived in a three-room apartment over in the Fillmore district.

Q. Can you remember any incident from there, from that time?

A. There's only one thing that I can really remember, and that was that there was a vacant lot across the street, and that my cousin and I use to play together. I really don't even remember too many of my friends there, and from there we moved to_____ Street which was also over in the Fillmore district. It's a little alley street. And I started Pacific Heights Elementary School. And, uh, at Pacific Heights . . .

I can remember going to this school, uh, it wasn't a school I don't know what you call it. Anyway, I can remember going to this thing the Salvation Army gave where the children go and sing, and they would put on stage shows and what have you. And this is the only thing — from there, we stayed there six months, approximately, and then we moved into a big house of our own my father bought. My father . . . and I had a sister and brother then . . . younger than I. I can remember a lot of things . . . it was on _____ Street. We had a big house that was three stories high. There was a lot of people living in there with us that my mother rented out rooms to — small apartments to . . . [breaks off].

And I can remember staying out late and never coming home, and my mother coming to get me from not coming home after school, my mother would get me. And, uh, we stayed there about four years . . . and from there was two flats upstairs and downstairs. And, uh, we stayed there about a year and a half and my mother and father separated.

By that time there were five kids in the family. There was myself and I had three brothers . . . no . . . two brothers . . . three brothers, my sister, and myself. And my mother and father separated . . . and my mother, uh, uh, got on I guess on welfare of ANC [Aid to Needy Children, her own term] and we, we'd still stayed in the house, but my cousin took over the — moved in with us and they took over the mortgage, I guess, and started paying for the house and we could pay them and then we would pay them more or less, rent.

And we would, my father, he would come over from time to time, and uh, I went to school that was there in the neighborhood and there were, that was when the, uh, _____Street projects were open, and as far as my friends, they were mostly friends that were either living around us, or from the projects, and I can remember there was a great big lot down the street from us, and we used to go down there and catch these tadpoles and pick blackberries and get in trouble. [Giggles.] Like going down there when we shouldn't have been going in the first place.

And, uh, I graduated from elementary school right around that district, and I went to_____Junior High and going to school I got average grades, nothing outstanding, but nothing really bad, although I was the type of person that mother had always told me if somebody hit me to hit them back, but to, um, not ever pick any fights. So, in school I got this attitude where I just didn't care about anything. If the teacher would say — tell me to do something if I were in a bad mood, I'd say, I'd — if I didn't want to do it, they'd tell me I get bad grades, I'd say I didn't care and, uh, they'd say I'll tell your maw . . . your parents, and I'd say I didn't care, 'cause my mother was hard of hearing so I could always tell her that I didn't do it, or it was the teacher's fault or something like that. So I got by with a lot that I really shouldn't of got away with. Although I don't *think* I was any worse than the average child. I didn't steal . . . I cant't remember ever stealing, really stealing anything, or picking up anything that didn't belong to me, but I kind of fell into, I guess, the wrong gang, and uh, we would have street fights with either another club or another gang, or what have you. And, uh, I, I, uh, from _____ Street while I was still in junior high school, we moved to_____. It was when the Potrero projects were first built, and we were . . .

Q. When? Do you remember?

A. I don't remember what year it was, but it was when the newer addition — a newer addition was first built. We moved into the projects when they were — we were the first people to move into those projects, because there weren't too many people, even as neighbors.

And, uh, when more kids did move into the area, like I said about this gang . . . we had a little club with the recreation center, and we would go down, uh, on _____ Street or Avenue or whatever, and, uh, we'd — and the name of our club anyway was the War Eagles — were the boys and War Eaglettes were the girls, and, uh, there was this gang called the White Shoe gang and, uh, they would get together and at night when we'd go down to Good Samaritan, that was the name of the center in _____, and they would fight or else they would run around and look for fights. It was more fighting than anything else. More arguing than fighting really.

And I was interested in playing . . . up at the center we would play basketball, baseball when we weren't fighting . . . [*laughs*] . . . Um, and from _____ , I graduated when I was still living on _____ and we moved again and when we did move we went, we moved over in the back to the Fillmore district and there was, by then I had, let's see, how many brothers, I had four brothers and one sister — two sisters because I had a sister — my baby sister was born on _____ which — she had, her father is not my father. She has a different father from the rest of us.

And, uh, I was going to, I had started, I graduated when we were living on _____ , and by the time we moved, I was going to college. So within that time I was going to college, nothing outstanding ever happened in college. Just go to school and come home, babysit every now and then.

And, uh, we moved from the Fillmore district back over to the _____ district. We didn't live in the projects, but we lived on _____ Street and on _____ Street. What happened . . . nothing happened. I, anyway . . . eventually I met my husband and I was fifteen at the time and, uh, before I was sixteen he convinced me to marry him. So, one of the reasons for me getting married was because my mother had a whole bunch of kids and I wanted to get out of the house and have a place of my own and they own everything because . . . [*At this point, Babalona interrupts her discourse to say,* "Go back in the back and be quiet," *to one of her children, whose cries are making it difficult to continue. The little boy had been hit by his older sister, who is eight. Babalona supports the older girl's right to punish the boy, who is one-and-a-half.*]

Anyway, where was I, anyway, I'd gotten worried when I was sixteen, I'd turned sixteen in March and, uh, in November, well, I was pregnant, a month before I got married I was pregnant, and so in November, I had my first child and still nothing exciting ever happened. I kept looking for this excitement, this big thing that's gonna happen. But it never happens. [*Laughs – but more self-consciously.*] Anyway, at the time, I was living with my sister-in-law and brother-in-law and we moved out and then we moved to Hunter's Point.

Q. What brought you here?

A. Because we lived in a place without a bedroom just a kitchen and . . . just two rooms and so I had applied for a project, being my husband was working part time and it was during the rain season and he was working at the car wash and part of the time he wasn't working and what have you . . . so . . . we figured that we couldn't afford . . . you know . . . to get you know . . . a larger place . . . because in the projects you wouldn't have your utility bills to pay and what have you, all you would have to pay was your rent.

And at the time in the old projects, in the old War projects the rent was at a standard. Your rent didn't go up and down with your salary. It was a certain amount for so many bedrooms. And with this it was cheaper so when I came home from the hospital, my mother, my husband, and my sister had gotten a place while I was still in the hospital.

Living there, and I, lot of people in the neighborhood where I'm pretty friendly anyway, I think I would meet people that are around me and, uh, my husband, he was a member of, he had a motorcycle, they formed a motorcycle club, and didn't see too much of him though. He'd go to work and come back and go out and ride motorcycles, come in and go to sleep. *But* during that time I got pregnant again. [*Laughs.*]

Q. He was home enough for that, huh? [*Laughs.*]

A. And, uh, I had my second child, and we moved to a larger project because I only had one bedroom so we moved to a bigger project up on _____. And there I got pregnant again [*laughs*] and during this time I think with me marrying so young, I didn't know anything about contraceptives and not getting pregnant and I guess I wasn't really, I don't think I was really old enough to. I was afraid to ask somebody I think and I wasn't old enough and maybe to understand, you know.

Q. It makes you look dumb if you've got to ask something like that? . . .

A. That — you should ask about these things and I guess it really comes with maturity or having somebody to sit down to talk to you in private. And not, you know, a public thing like Planned Parenthood. My husband has been working pretty good so we left and went on vacation, and went down to Los Angeles for a week. And while we down there 'cause it was nice and warm down there, and everybody, at least they're not living in projects. Most of them are at least renting houses, or renting nicer apartments at really reasonable rates, so we moved to Los Angeles.

Well, I — I come back to San Francisco and my husband got a house down there, a rent house and the rent was like seventy-five dollars for a four-room house was seventy-five dollars plus your utilities which didn't run too much. But a big back yard and a big front yard and a garage. And down there, we, my husband had gotten a job within that week, anyway we came back and we moved down there.

And, uh, so anyway while we were living there, my husband took his motorcycle down there and he joined another motorcycle club and, uh, he was gone so much of the time and I didn't know too many people down there and so I would come up to San Francisco like every two or three months and I'd stay a week or sometimes two weeks whatever it took from being lonesome and then I'd go back down. So, within that I think that we kind of started drifting apart and then I had four kids. [*Laughs.*]

And, uh, so when I got back we had incidents of him stayin' out and not comin' back home for a couple days or so. And we had incidents of him staying out two and three days and not comin' back home, and so eventually I just came back up to San Francisco and I stayed for a couple of months or so. But somethin' that really kind of shook me up was that, I was used to living in San Francisco where white and colored people all lived together. When I went to Los Angeles the section that we lived in, it was nothin' but Negroes and for two whole days I didn't see anything but Negroes and I couldn't believe this. You go in the grocery store, and the Negroes worked in the groceries and all the grocery stores and the only grocery store I went in was a great big grocery store called Shop Rite. And, uh, even walking around the streets . . .

Q. Where was this?

A. In the Watts area or right across Watts on the other side of Central. And there were, it was really, I was amazed, because as I was brought up, I was never brought up to really, my parents never talked about, well, that's a white now that's a colored man there's any difference. So I guess figured, well, what is this? And we stayed down there over the weekend. This was when we had went to stay over the weekend and, uh, on the way back we went to other districts where there was nothing but fights and, uh, I don't know, this kind of got next to me because I was feeling like I may have been like down South where they say, you know, the places are really segregated. Where the Negroes all have their own little section and what have you and I just couldn't get used to this. You know, with living down there, on our block there were only three white families on the whole block and one lived across the street and they were older people.

But, as far as younger people living next door to you and what have you, right around there it just didn't happen. There were a store which was owned by a Chinese person, but, I don't know, I just couldn't get used to it, even with living down there. And there was something about Los Angeles that I . . . I lived down there three years almost and I went downtown only once. And that was because there's shopping centers in every area, like, Compton has their own Crane Plaza.

Like here you'd have to go all the way downtown to buy things, but Los Angeles, I don't know, it seems, that every area you go in has their own shopping center with this big stores, great big stores and what have you and everything is, you know, you would need — and you would really have to go downtown.

Anyway, from this house the person who had the house sold it, they were living in Los Angeles and we moved down there to these apartments which was right in Watts, right in it, was on 103rd Place and Compton which was right in the center where the Watts area really was. And, uh, we stayed there for several months — almost a year, and during that time, well, what happened then, well, what happened then, my brother-in-law left his wife [*laughs nervously*] and he starts staying with us and, uh, he was the type of person that you really didn't want living with you. But, well, I don't know, I just did it because he was a friend of mine, and, uh, and of my husband's and with him living there, my husband was working at night and, uh, he started this big argument more or less between my husband and I, where ... where ... us, if anybody, I'm — I've always been the type of person where I always invite people in my house are — if somebody I know, I always been the type of person to have either parties of people around the house always playing cards. And if a guy, uh, would come there with his friend, would be a girl friend of mine, or three of them would come in together, it would always be that he was my boy friend and he was coming in my house and what have you.

And, uh, with this agitatin' my husband and I started driftin' more or less apart. So when he finally — my brother-in-law finally did move out of my house. He moved into a place of his own and, uh, he had tell my husband little things that really never went on but with him working at night he wasn't quite sure if it was happening or not. So we, we moved right after Christmas. We stayed there about nine or ten months and so right after Christmas we moved to this place over on _____ Highway which is really more or less the borderline. And we moved there in a nice little house that had two bedrooms and a big garage and another big front yard and so forth.

My husband and I, he was always making accusations I couldn't leave that house and what have you without somebody seeing, said they saw me with this guy or if I was in the car with a girl and her boyfriend or somethin', or her husband — it was always my boy-friend or what have you.

So, at that time I didn't know it but evidently I was pregnant, with my fifth child [*laughs nervously*] so we stayed there a couple of months till I finally moved back to San Francisco. Myself and my children, my husband stayed there. And, uh, I moved back up to San Francisco was stayin' with my mother, and she was staying at Hunter's Point. At Hunter's Point in the projects and I stayed there, and . . . well I got a job working for the place that I worked for before I'd left San Francisco, working for a presser. And, uh, I worked there for a while, but I really couldn't make too much money, then I went down and applied for aid to help me with the family and children and when I went there they, uh, asked me was I pregnant so I told them no and I had to go to a doctor.

So when I went to the doctor I found out that I was pregnant so they told me that I shouldn't work anymore. And I was just within a certain of time, which I think was a ninety-day waiting period that I would start receiving full aid, but they did give me a food order and they gave me one rent order so that I could move out of the house with my mother and into a place of my own where I moved over in the Western Addition and the place it had two bedrooms.

And from there — over there I had my fifth and so far my *last* child. And, uh, I . . . I stayed there and after I had my child I had started to work at this pressing place because I have always been the type of person that I never liked to depend on anyone else and I preferred working for myself and making my own way as long as my children were taken care of. And . . . when I was working, I was workin' at . . . anyway, this garment industry, and I was a presser and I wasn't satisfied, for one thing I wasn't makin' enough money to completely to get completely off the welfare but then I was at least makin' enough money to feel that I could breathe and I could get a paycheck every week or every two weeks, and I felt like that I was makin' it for myself. And, uh, about after I worked there for about six months I found out that I had this female disorder and I had to go in the hospital and have an operation so the day before I was, I was supposed to report to the hospital on Monday morning and on Saturday I decided I was going to go down and take the post office test. So, uh, I'd taken the civil service examination, I passed but when I passed I was in the hospital and when I got a hearing from them I was still in the hospital and I'd found out I'd passed and I was supposed to come down to get a job . . . you know, to apply for a job.

And when I was released from the hospital I went down to apply but the doctor had recommended that I wait until I was completely released from the hospital I had minor surgery to, um, wait. Until I was released, anyway, to start . . . to start working. And . . . when I did get released I started working at the post office and that was in October I started working and I've been working up till this time. And right before I started working at the post office I moved – I can't keep track of myself.

Q. That was when you moved . . .

A. Up on _____ . Livin' up on _____ , my mother was living upstairs when I first moved over there. And while I was living there, um, there was, there was a lady coming around making a survey or something of the people that were living in this Hunter's Point area. And in her comin' around I got associated with this block club that they had started. And, uh, the block club was supposed to be . . . the purpose of the block club was supposed to be so the residents could get together and, uh, do or at least try to do what their opinion of the things that was going on in this area and to try if there was any way possible, to improve the living standards and the recreation and just everything that, you know, that they thought was going on wrong or that should be improved in this area.

Um, during this time we had, we had meetings and talked about things like trying to improve the boys' club and makin' the place we lived in just a little better place to live in so, uh, those things we did got going is to get these projects repainted because what had happened were the Housing Authority would only paint them only five or six years or something like this. So we did get it where they would paint more often or at least you could call up and make an appointment if your house hadn't been painted or it was in pretty bad condition. That they would come in and paint instead of putting a normal one coat of paint on them it would be two coats. Where some people might not think this is important but it does last a longer time and it is a lot better. Another thing we did was that there was only one laundromat and there were, either it was closed early in the evening before you could get home from work or it wouldn't be open early enough in the morning for you to go in if you were a person that worked you had to try to do it on Saturdays when it was overran with people. And it was dirty and it was never cleaned up and the machines were out of fix most of the time.

And, uh, what they did was they came in and they lowered the price of washing but they took out the number of machines that was there and, uh, they painted the place, cleaned it up, and had someone come in at least once a day to keep the place clean and make sure the kids aren't tearing up the place. So, and, the people who did this were the people that were working for the Housing Authority so evidently it did go through them. And, uh, what else happened while I was in that there building — my house burned down. During the time I was living there I was working at night, in the daytime I was trying to sleep on Saturday morning waiting for my sister to come over and pick up the kids and my son set the house on fire.

So from there I had, I moved I moved from _____ to well I had to from _____ to _____ and I will say one thing about the Housing Authority that I really did like, they did come in and help me out as far as getting me moved, settled and, uh, a few days later everything that I could get from out of the place I did go up there and they moved it down for me and they didn't charge me anything. There is other problems you always have with the Housing Authority like they're never gettin' around to fixing little things but this would happen if you had a landlord.

And, uh, so anyway right now I'm living on _____ , I'm not perfectly happy, but who ever is? I think that's about it.

Babalona describes a childhood rich with pleasant experiences and, even at an early age, some tendency to avoid parental restrictions. Her family she describes as extended, but female-dominated, and with a sporadically employed father.

She attributes an aggressive and immediate gratification orientation to her mother, and recounts a childhood and young adulthood fairly typical of residents in Hunter's Point (and, we may suspect, the projects in which she lived as a child).

Very early in her life, her mother — the main socializing agent —

was replaced by her peer group, and she learned to exploit her mother's deafness to her own advantage. Also, Babalona's mother had a new husband by the time Babalona was a teenager.

The relative unimportance to her of her own husband is clear from her statement that "nothing happened": she got married, that's all. She also makes it clear that this marriage was no love match, but had the instrumental purpose of getting her out of her home. The man she married proved to be a poor provider (as her father had been) who found her company less interesting perhaps (or more unpleasant) than that of his motorcycle cronies.

Her eventual separation from her husband was the inevitable outcome of their continued physical separations and his suspicion of her fidelity. She finds fault, however, with his leaving, although she finds none with her own absences. Babalona tries to make it as clear as possible that she was blameless of any accusations of infidelity, but regardless of the truth of the matter her story is illustrative of the kinds of male-female tensions in urban black families. By and large, her account reveals her growing experience with what she sees as inadequate, unfair males, and a growing independence from and denigration of them. That is, as men prove less and less reliable she comes more and more to rely upon herself and her female friends and to make light of any need she might have for permanent male companionship.

Her account of her life after leaving her husband shows this movement toward a complete financial independence from men (based on welfare, AFDC, and sporadic work) and closer ties with her mother and sister. During this period she learned, in conjunction with others, how to deal with authorities, especially the Housing Authority. Babalona has established a pattern of life and generally accepts that pattern.

TAT Responses

Card 1

A. Well, it looks like a little boy that . . . he's looking at his violin and trying to make up his . . . well, he looks to me like he's kind of sad because maybe he can't play it and he wish he could, or somethin'.

Q. Well, what do you think will happen to him?

A. Well, just possibly . . . well, maybe he's more or less dreamin' that one day he'll . . . a symphony or somethin' . . . anyway, with an orchestra or somethin'. He's sittin' up, dreamin' about it.

79

Q. Think he'll do it?
A. Probably. If he practices.

Card 2
A. [*Laughs a great deal.*] Uh, it seems like . . . uh . . . that this is maybe
a little while ago where . . . uh . . . to me it looks like two Negroes,
a man that's out in the field that's plowing and the Negro lady, it
seems that she's leanin' up against a tree and she's expecting, to me.
[*Laughs.*] And, uh . . . this, uh . . . this white girl has been to school,
comin' from school, maybe with her books, she's been studyin' or
goin' to school, or somethin'.
Q. What's happening in there? Anything happening? What are they
thinking?
A. I don't know. She's not smilin' or anything . . . looks like she's
kind of sad. [*Laughs a great deal.*] . . . Looks like maybe the lady
with the baby leaning against the tree which I don't know, to me
seems to be a Negro, is maybe dreamin' about the times that later
maybe that her child will grow up and that she won't have to do
the same thing. If it's a boy that he might not have to do what his
father's doin' out plowing, what have you, looks like she's thinkin'
about that. Looks like she's dreamin about somethin' that might
happen later.

Card 3BM
A. Hmm. [*One-half minute pause.*] I can't tell what it is. [*Laughs.*] To
me it seems like that, well, this lady's sitting on the floor and looks
like she has a gun beside her [*laughs nervously*] and that maybe
she shot somebody or something, and she's crying 'cause she's sad.
Q. Why?
A. 'Cause she shot somebody, I suppose. Well, I don't know.
Q. Who'd she shoot?
A. Well, I don't know. Maybe somebody that she liked . . . or . . . may-
be she shot her husband [*laughs very nervously*] . . . or her boy-
friend, or something.
Q. Well, why would she do that?
A. 'Cause she was mad maybe? That's all I see.

Card 4
A. Uh . . . in this picture I see there's this lady and man . . . seems like
that, uh . . . he's sayin' somethin' like, I'm leaving you. And she's

beggin' him and pleadin' with him for him to stay and she's not gettin' too much across because he's gonna leave anyway, and she might be tryin' to convince him to stay, and I hope she makes it.

Card 6BM

A. Well, to me this seems like my foreman, Mr. Rice. [*Laughs mildly.*] He's tied to his mother's apron strings. [*Laughs a great deal.*] And, uh, he may of said something, like he's getting married. And, uh, she doesn't want him to go, so, she's pullin' this routine like, you need me, and what could you do without me, and he's tryin' to make up his mind whether he's gonna get married, or stay with mama.

Q. Do you think he will?

A. If she's convincin' enough, he will. [*Laughs a lot.*] If he's Mr. Rice, he will.

Card 7GF

A. [*A minute-and-a-half hesitation.*] . . . Well, in this card, uh, it seems like in this picture, there's this mother and daughter . . . maybe about twelve, eleven or twelve, and that, uh, that I think she has a doll or somethin' and that she is trying to explain or somethin' that she's growin' up and she's getting older and she would, she should put [away her] dolls, and that she explain the facts of life to her so that she can grow up and become [*long pause – thirty seconds*] a nice young lady, instead of bein' more or less a little baby.

Q. How is it going to work out?

A. She seems, as far as lookin' at her, seems like she really doesn't care to listen. And she might grow, would grow up, bein' the type of person that would not listen, and in the adult world, and they might, she might . . .

Card 8BM

A. [*Pause of nearly a minute-and-a-half.*] . . . Um, this here was an accident or somethin' here in this picture where I can't . . . I don't know . . . where, uh, these two men are . . . the lady's takin' a bullet out of this man. The reason I say a bullet is because of the gun sittin' on the side of the man. It seems like they're tryin' to operate on him. What's this thing here? [*Laughs.*]

Q. Well, what do you think can happen there after this is done? – this operation?

A. [*Very long pause – forty seconds.*] . . . I don't know what might happen. I hope that . . . I hope that the operations's successful as it is . . . maybe . . . I don't know . . . on this one, I'm more or less blank.

Card 13MF

A. [*Laughs.*] I think them kids ought to get out of the room. [*Laughs a great deal – for twenty or thirty seconds.*] Oh, this picture. Well, I don't want to say.

Q. Say it. Come on, it doesn't matter.

A. There's this man in be– . . . bed . . . no . . . it's this woman in bed and this man, he just couldn't do anything. [*Laughs a great deal.*]

Q. What do you think he'll do?

A. He looks pretty bad. I don't know if he'll try again, that's for sure. Well, anyway, that's what it looks like to me.

Card 16

A. I see only a blank card.

Q. What kind of story would you make up for it?

A. Well, I'd say a person'd have to be an idiot to make up a story on a blank card.

TAT Analysis

A quantitative analysis shows Babalona's modal responses to be in the areas of physical and physiological concerns, achievement, nurturance and dependency, separation, quarrel, unusual effects, authority control, and adequacy; she also showed some neutral and nonrealistic outcomes and one blocking response. Babalona also made responses in the areas of pregnancy, unspecified accident, negative parental training, undeliberated murder, nonmarital sexual activity and eventual separation, routine work, and general negative outcome of card.

The areas of achievement and physiology and physical responses were the most important modes, though at least two of the three responses in the physiology area were connected to a discussion of race, and two of the achievement responses were directed toward aspiration rather than specific achievement.

Qualitatively, Babalona's response to Card 1 was only vaguely realistic. There is a dreamy quality of aspiration to her achievement motivation, connected to a moralistic statement of the kind we have come to expect from Babalona since we know that she is, at least in part, identifying upward with what she deems to be the proper middle-class responses. On the other hand, Card 2 seems to be at least in part denying this response. In Card 2, we see two things. First, there is a kind of contentment with expressive behavior in the status quo and the suspicion that achievement as represented by the white schoolgirl is not really the most desirable aspect of life. On the other hand, there is a return to the achievement theme with the hope that the child will not have to work as hard as his parents.

Babalona's response to Card 3BM showed a great deal of nervousness about the possibilities of aggression. She was not very willing to see this as a possible aggressive card. When she did finally admit to her own agression, she was able to say that this aggression might very well be directed against either a husband or a boyfriend — or in any event against some male personality for whom she developed a very negative affect.

In Card 4 we perhaps get some idea of why this negative affect exists. The theme of male desertion is raised here along with the inadequacy of female pleading to alter the situation. But Card 6BM denies that this male desertion is really a form of independence. Men are seen in this card as being essentially tied to their mother's apron strings, not having the independence to make up their own minds.

These beliefs seem to be expressed in the responses to Card 7GF as well. In this card, she indicates the child's inability to accept parental strictures and advice. Here, perhaps, the achievement and duty themes are seen as less powerful than the expressive and autonomous ones. Still, she indicates some fear of what the result of these expressive autonomous urges might be in the absence of intelligent adult direction.

In Card 8BM, Babalona shows again her great concern and fear about aggression. The response time was very long on this card. In any event, we do know that there is a male who has been injured by a bullet and that a female is acting in a nurturant role toward him. Card 13MF may give us some hint as to how this injury came about. In Card 13MF, we have an extremely transparent and undefended statement about male impotence accompanied by an aggressive and even sadistic humorous response toward the situation. Whether concerns about adequacy of a more general nature and perhaps fears of penetration disguised by, first of all, seeing a male penetrated and, secondly, seeing a male made impotent are significant aspects of this response is not immediately clear. However, we might expect them to be so in terms of the general fear of aggressive impulses expressed in the earlier cards.

MARGARET (BABALONA'S DAUGHTER, AGE TEN)

TAT Responses

Card 1

A. He lookin' down at his violin. And, uh, he got a violin, a piece of paper setting on the table — whatever that is. And he's lookin' down at his hand with his one hand, on the one hand like that.

Q. And what's he going to do?

A. And he's sad, and he, and he might get mad and tear up this violin. Or else . . . or else play it.

Q. Why would he do it?

A. Because . . . he might do it because, because he is mad and he might not get to go outside and play like all the rest of the kids like we do.

Card 2

A. It's a man and a horsey and a lady and another girl and . . . [*Long pause.*]

Q. What are they doing?

A. The man is, look like he planting something. And the lady sittin' on a tree thinkin' and she's thinkin' about if she get married will she gonna have children and then she'll live happy and he, he might get on his horsey and ride away. The lady might go in that barn.

Card 3BM

A. Look like this here man has a gun and he's gonna shoot. It looks like he's dead.

Q. Well, what happened?

A. He's layin' on this . . . some kind . . . look like . . . looks somethin' like a couch. Somethin' like that 'cause we used to have this when we went swimming, you know . . . so nobody look at us while we change our clothes . . . [*Giggles.*]

Q. Hmm.

A. And, uh, he look like he on that.

Card 4

A. Look like she . . . she . . . she don't want her husband to go and somethin' . . . a lady way back where there, I can see her face, and that's her sister . . . 'cause they look alike.

Q. And?

A. And the man gonna leave 'cause he got this strange funny looks on his eye.

Card 6BM

A. We . . . he, the mother turned his back on him 'cause he promised somethin' like he gonna go away from home and stay away and find somebody to marry to.

Card 7GF

A. Looks like her mother had a little girl sitting on the couch, looks like I'm making this up.

Q. That's okay.

A. The little girl lookin' at somethin' but I don't know what she's lookin' at and she's holdin' this dolly like this.

Q. Why?

A. 'Cause she want to grow up and get married.

Card 8BM

A. Well, ugh . . . [*with great distaste*] . . . oh, it's this man looks like a man and two more men, one of the mans going to cut one of the mans that's layin' in the back of the other. Rifle alongside looks like he gonna kill, but look like, yeah . . . he's asleep. He's supposed to be asleep.

Q. Asleep?

A. Yeah, and he, I think he's the boss of those two tryin' to cut him up.

Card 13MF

A. There's a lady and a man and a table with a lamp on it and books. And the lady's sleeping in the bed and the man's going like that.

Q. Why?

A. 'Cause he don't want to see the lady.

Q. Oh? Why?

A. 'Cause he's 'shamed.

Card 16

A. Nothin' on there but a clean piece of paper.

TAT Analysis

Quantitative analysis of Margaret's responses shows her primary modal response to be one of unusual card handling — total blocking or bizarre responses in the form of indeterminant alternative plots. There were twelve such responses; this was by far the largest number of responses in a single category made by any of the subjects of Hunter's Point. In addition, she had two responses in which there was no outcome and one of a routine everyday work-type situation. Aside from these, the modal responses were in the area of physiology, autonomy and control, violence, and separation, with lesser modal responses in the areas of quarrels, marriage, and unusual affect. In addition, Margaret mentioned an unspecified death and shame.

A qualitative analysis of these responses shows, for example in Card 1, a conflict between achievement and/or duty and expressive desires. This conflict is only resolvable through violence. Card 2 rejects this violent response for a more dreamy pastoral scene: kind of a fairy-tale quality prevades the response, a happily-ever-after marriage is in store. But this situation is amended at the end of the story by noting the possibility and indeed the probability of separation through male desertion. After the male gets on his "horsey" and rides away, the lady then might go into the barn. We might suggest that the barn here is a security symbol necessary to overcome the anxiety resultant from father desertion.

The theme of father desertion and female retreat raised in Card 2 is not immediately apparent in Card 3BM. But in Card 3BM there is a great deal of blocking, taking the form of indeterminant alternative plots and unresolved outcomes.

The connection between the aggression and death of some man and the exhibitionistic tendencies indicated later on in the story is not clear, but is probably important to understanding this response. One possibility that suggests itself because of other evidence is a fear that her own competition with her mother for her father may very well have sent her father away. Card 4, in fact, suggests the theme of competitive struggle between two sisters over the same man. Parenthetically, Babalona's sister lives next door to her, and according to Babalona's sister and some of the other neighbors, there may well indeed have been some competition between Babalona and her daughter for Babalona's husband. Babalona's sister is also presently unmarried, and has four children. This situation may have provided something on which Margaret could project her own unwanted impulses and use to rid herself of the feeling that she was the cause of her father's abandonment.

The theme of separation — specifically, males leaving females — comes up again in Card 6BM. The argument between mother and son over a potential marriage is one which Babalona also suggested, and there is probably some overdetermination here in that the male figure may very well stand for both her father and herself. This interpretation seems more plausible in light of responses to Card 7GF, which suggests a simple theme on the part of the girl of growing up and getting married. Parenthetically, the early response to the card — "looks like I'm makin' this up" — was later explained to me as meaning, "You're going to think that this is just what I do at home." Card 8BM indicates a death, which is denied and then turned into sleep. The blocking here also indicates that Margaret is experiencing considerable difficulty handling her impulses. That the man who is killed is seen as the boss probably means that he is a parental figure — and her aggressive impulses against parental figures have to be disguised. Card 13MF was answered in almost a card response. That is, she merely described what was shown on the card without any attempt to discuss movement, motivation, or emotions. Card responses suggest significant blocking of affect. The indication of shame as the effective state in the male figure may indicate an incest perception or it may not.

In sum, Margaret's responses are quite difficult to deal with qualitatively. There is so much effective blocking that about the only thing we can say for sure is that in her present environment and stage of psychosexual development she finds it extremely difficult to deal with almost any of her impulses. Impulses toward autonomy, impulses toward her growing sexuality, impulses toward aggressiveness are all felt to be dangerous.

5

MARY ELLEN'S
FAMILY

MARY ELLEN is a different case from the others. She has five children and, she claims:

"I don't know who they father is. I ain't never kept track. They is always another one. You know, I can catch me a guy any time I want."

We may be justified in rejecting Mary Ellen's avowal of absolute promiscuity, as I saw no evidence of truly indiscriminate dating on her part, but it is highly probable that any such avowal indicates a special sort of attitude toward men and toward sexuality itself. It might also be important to note in passing that, as we have indicated, since sex mores tend to be somewhat different in Hunter's Point than in the rest of American society, such a profession may possibly not contain the same degree of either pathological or socially deviant content that might be assumed if it came from a middle-class woman of the same age (twenty-nine).

A profession of such promiscuity, however — even in Hunter's Point with its greater openness about sex — is seen by other members of that subculture as an essentially unhealthy preoccupation. While Mary Ellen and many of her attitudes and behavioral activities would be seen as deviant in American society at large and to some extent in Hunter's Point as well, her deviance in Hunter's Point is of degree, not kind. We estimate that Mary Ellen is representative of approximately a fifth to a quarter of the women in Hunter's Point in terms of exhibited life styles and attitudes (not, however, in terms of expressed promiscuity).

Rena with her Jerry is a competent shopper, aware of bargains, and determined to make it to the middle class and leave all that "nigger shit" behind. And Babalona is reasonably comfortable in Hunter's Point — although she considers the possibility of what life would be like outside Hunter's Point if there were no such thing as segregation and racial prejudice — and tends to exhibit a mild distrust of and unfriendliness toward whites. On the other hand, Mary Ellen has none of these overt characteristics. Professing no concern with any social issues, she is only vaguely aware of the existence of a food stamp program whereby low-income families can supplement their incomes by using low-cost stamps issued by the federal government. She is totally unaware of the kinds of available services and consumer aids for stretching a household budget. She implicitly believes that the more you pay for an item, the better it is. Thus, she chronically overpays, especially for consumer credit.

She claims that she has not yet reported the arrival of her last baby to welfare authorities, and thus has not yet been granted an increase in her Aid to Dependent Children allowance — although the baby is three months old. Mary Ellen, in fact, professes not really to understand how "the welfare" works or to have even the sketchiest knowledge of her obligations and rights. (This is somewhat typical in Hunter's Point. Most residents have varying degrees of sophistication about these matters.) Here too, however, she is representative of a certain minority. Rent payments seem to be made for her at various intervals by a variety of men, and she herself pays her own rent on those odd months when there is no man present or willing to pay it.

A somewhat flirtatious, attractive girl, she is very popular at the Long Island Club, a bar on Third Street where she spends much of her time. By her own admission and by the general consensus of her neighbors, however, she is totally lost when it comes to making things work. Having almost always lived in some form of public housing and spending ten of her twenty-nine years in Hunter's Point (although not consecutively), she has had many contacts with the welfare agency and the Housing Authority.

She complains that these agencies are always "bugging" her about men or pregnancies, and constantly asking to see if she has a man living in her apartment. All but two of her children have been put up for adoption through a city agency because she "forget about them and someone would find out and tell people they was down the street."

Light-skinned, as are her children, she was forced by her landlord to leave her last, first, and only private housing some three years ago. (She only lived there six months because the landlord thought she was Hawaiian and didn't like her. She didn't know what Hawaiian was, she claimed.) She has recurrent problems with the Housing Authority and claims to have had to pay several bills more than once. She has not remembered to keep receipts, and seems not completely to understand their function; and, of course, she has no checking account. How much she receives from the ADC program, she doesn't know, but she "has the paper and can show you."

Mary Ellen "gives the keeds some beer at night to put them to sleep so that they won't wake up." On such occasions, she doesn't bother to get a babysitter. She does, however, share a typical Hunter's Point predisposition to inflict severe corporal punishment when children "sass" her. She beats her children with two clotheshangers wired together. To demonstrate the effect of this punishment, she picked up the clotheshangers from the wall where they were hanging and immediately the elder of the two children present (three years and six months) began to whimper. Having made her point, she put the clotheshangers down. Discipline is not always imposed through such threatening gestures, but Mary Ellen prefers not to "spoil" her children.

Mary Ellen has few friends and acquaintances in Hunter's Point, and gets along well with almost no one. She is not especially hostile to others, just uninterested. "I making it, and I don't want nobody to bug me."[1]

MARY ELLEN

Life History

"I was born, uh . . . you know . . . in St. Louis, Missouri, and I *think* my papa . . . father's . . . now my mother's married to a storeman . . . he owns this little store on Third . . . but she says *my* papa, uh, you know, was a railroad man.

"It was shit. We used to remember, uh, you know, pick them fuckin' coal pieces up off the tracks . . . uh . . . you know, uh . . . the tracks, the trains had — this coal would get on them from the trains, would get it 'cause it was free . . . that's when I was three, we left. I, uh . . . we . . . uh . . . you know, we came here to San Francisco . . . and . . . uh . . . we lived . . . uh . . . in that place over there."

Q. Potrero Hill?

A. Yeah . . . you see, there's we moved then to Oakland and then to here again. When I got bigger, though, my mama and I would fight, you'd, uh . . . think we'd kill each other. There was this . . . she, then we . . . we, the place, she was always sayin' I was goin' with her man. She caught him feelin' me once while she was out . . . she thought somethin' else. Anyhow, I got married in 1953 and had a baby. But I left him . . . in a year or so. He was always runnin' around and then'd say I was. Any friend I'd have over . . . uh . . . you know . . . he'd think here is some stuff happenin' again.

When I was eighteen, I had three kids and we go to Menlo Park. This man . . . George . . . was with me then and I liked him . . . better than anything . . . he's, he . . . I still . . . he still comes over to see me . . . we was . . . he left . . . 'cause we . . . what happened we was in this bar and this guy was just cuttin' up he didn't mean nothin' and neither did I . . . they was just some foolin' around and he pours out his beer pitcher on George's head and he hits him with a chair and they's some cuttin' and the guy was killed so George went to prison for six years.

He's nice, though . . . George is good to me and he always brings somethin' over . . . that lamp is from him.

Well, uh . . . you know . . . I had to move then from the place we was to another . . . see, we wasn't married and they . . . you know . . . uh . . . it's that they always fuckin' with you . . . "You got a man?" "You . . . what you kids think?" Sheeit.

The kids, though, I got um . . . uh . . . well we come up here and go back there and now we stayin' here. My boy, he comes over all the time here. We goin' to move soon as I find some other place, I guess.

Mary Ellen's rather short description of her life indicates some concern with her parentage. Her doubts about her father's identity suggest more concern with his identity than she would admit openly, and suggest a veiled hostility toward her mother. This vague hostility becomes clearer in her discussion of fights with her mother. The theme of mother-daughter competition for the same man is overtly stated, but in the form of a denial of her own (Mary Ellen's) responsibility in the situation.

There is an interesting parallel between her description of husbandly accusations about her own infidelity and Babalona's. We might be justified in assuming that the accusations toward Mary Ellen, however, were more substantive.

Mary Ellen's seductive behavior, her promiscuity, and her concomitant lack of responsibility (which has as one aspect a hatred of men) is apparent in her description of initiating a fight between two men over her. Her reminiscence strongly supports our initial observations about her tendencies toward destructive acts.

TAT Responses

Card 1

A. This, a boy. [*Muses and laughs.*] . . . He thinking how he going to go to jail if he steal that ole violin. He see this violin in this store window, and he's gonna take it, but he don't 'cause it . . . he's . . . 'cause he's afraid he's gonna get caught on this old violin.

Q. What's he want it for?

A. It's . . . I don't know, I don't, what's this thing here laying next to it? Look like a sword . . . must be a pawnshop window.

Card 2

A. These is old folks. There, this man he's workin' in the field, and his wife and this other girl is watchin' him.

Q. What's going on?

A. They, well, uh, this okay guy . . . he's really got a good build . . . they's just livin' here, but that, if she want to go to town? You can see she got these old books. [*Pause.*] . . . She probably part white too . . . she don't look Negro like them other two. She ain't really like them . . . she's . . . they . . . want her to stay . . . but she don't go for all that old Baptist shit . . . so she's goin' to be long gone.

Q. How will it come out?

A. She gone to the old city and what she's goin' to do. Get herself some guy.

Card 3BM

A. [*Long pause – approximately forty seconds.*] . . . This here . . . [*pause*] . . . she . . . she . . . she, her mother, she is worn out . . . it's too much, or maybe she . . . she, I don't know . . . looks like something had happened. I don't know.

Q. What?

A. I don't . . . maybe . . . I don't know.

Card 4

A. [*Laughs.*] Hey, she got this old boy good. [*Laughs.*] I don't know . . . maybe I shouldn't say at all . . . you might think . . . 'cause he, he, he look like you without your beard. Hey, where you get these from?

Q. These are pictures from magazines . . . I didn't . . . that . . . I didn't cut them out, these are just pictures. What were you going to say?

A. [*Laughs.*] I don't . . . well, this gal, she's kinda . . . convince him that he's, he should stay there that night with her and not go home to his wife. [*Laughs – more self-consciously.*] Well [*laughs – easily*], I think she'll make it . . . looks she's sure of herself and he isn't.

Q. What will . . . what'll happen?

A. She'll get him. [*Laughs.*]

Card 6BM

A. [*Laughs long and loudly.*] Hey, this one's . . . uh . . . this same ole guy he's talkin' to his maw . . . she's sayin' "you gonna marry a nigger?". . . [*Laughs uproariously.*]

Q. [*Laughs.*] What's going to happen?

A. She . . . she gonna talk him out of that old shit. He's safe.

Q. How so?

A. You sure you want me to say?

Q. Yes . . . of course.

A. He done sleep with that girl, but they ain't no reason he got to marry her. That's just the way it is.

Card 7GF

A. Ain't nothin' happenin' here.

Q. What do you mean?

A. I don't know . . . this just a girl and her baby and she's listenin' to her mother. Same old shit . . . her old lady's givin' her what for 'cause she's got this kid. But it's same thing happened to her.

Card 8BM

A. It . . . this, this looks . . . this a police station?

Q. You tell me.

A. Yeah, this a police station. They's some kind of operation . . . I guess this kid . . . that someone . . . he shot someone, but he ain't scared. He just cool about it.

Q. What happened?

A. I don't know . . . he just shot this man . . . this storekeeper, I guess . . . I don't know.

Card 13MF

A. Yeah, well. [*Laughs.*] . . . This looks like this guy . . . they just done makin' it, and looks like he . . . he dressed and goin'.

Q. And? . . .

A. Well, he can't see 'cause it's dark . . . and he's tryin' to get out so she won't hear him.

Q. Why?

A. Well, he leavin', I guess . . . I guess he ain't comin' back.

Q. Why?

A. I don't know.

Card 16

A. [*Laughs.*] Now *you* tell *me*!

TAT Analysis

A quantitative analysis of Mary Ellen's TAT responses shows modes in the area of blocking and of physiological concern as well as areas of authority and sex, and lesser modes in delinquent behavior, physical aggression, and separation. Mary Ellen also has responses in the area of expedient behavior and self-initiated achievement, and has one of the few responses concerning self-esteem of any of the Hunter's Point people who took the TAT. She also used no unrealistic endings. Specifically, Mary Ellen's physiological responses had to do with race (two entries), musculature, pregnancy, and clothing, so that there was a range of the meaning of responses. Those responses concerned with authority had to do either with dominance in heterosexual relationships or outside imposition of authority. There were no noticeable superego responses. The delinquent behavior noted was illicit sexual behavior and nonmarital sex leading to separation. Nonmarital triangles as well as extramarital relationships all played roles in her responses.

Qualitatively, Card 1 shows nothing of a normal achievement theme, but the purely expressive theme of theft is suppressed because of the possibility of punishment. The continued domination of expressive themes is clear in Card 2, where the manifest duty and obligation themes connected with Baptist religious attitudes are rejected. The Baptist theme of repression is raised after a covert sexual remark directed toward a male and is in turn rejected by a retreat from the conflict situation. But the retreat itself is in the direction of expressive themes. Card 3BM is completely rejected. The physiological concern in terms of exhaustion, the recognition of a maternal figure, and the anxiety-ridden "looks like something had happened" response all indicate that the card is extremely threatening.

In Card 4, Mary Ellen identifies the male with the ethnographer (i.e., me) and the female in the card with herself. Mary Ellen is suggesting that it would be easy for her to seduce me, and she indicates a great deal of self-confidence in the manipulative use of her expressive sexual urges. This fantasy is carried on into Card 6BM, where Mary Ellen feels that such sexual liaison would inevitably lead to a rejection on the part of the male, but suggests that this is primarily the result of the inadequacy of the male. Mary Ellen raises a theme of safety (sex is dangerous) in suggesting that the male will be talked out of any sexual contact with the female by his mother. Sexual contact is seen as leading to the abandonment of the female by the male.

In Card 7GF, the response "ain't nothin' happenin' here" is followed by the recognition that the girl has given birth to an illegitimate baby. Conflict is implied because of parental anger. It is probable, too, that the "nothin' happenin'" response is a denial of sexual interest in males and of the ability of male sexual activity to produce anything. On the other hand, Mary Ellen did become pregnant many times in real life. Female parental strictures, however, are rejected on the grounds that the female parent is essentially no different from the daughter. It will be remembered that Mary Ellen expressed some concern and interest in exactly who her male parent was.

The need for outside authorities in the absence of internal controls becomes clear in Card 8BM as well. Aggression, a child or young man shooting someone, is followed by a denial of affect: "cool" here is used, as we have indicated earlier in the text, as a denial of meaningful emotional expression. The genesis of expressive feelings is denied or claimed to be unknowable. Expressive feelings, especially aggressive ones, simply arise and resolve themselves in an explosive manner; only outside authorities can do anything about it. The denial of affect is also a denial of responsibility, and we have suggested that Mary Ellen has difficulties in the area of responsibility.

Card 13MF continues a theme of expressive behavior, personal autonomy, and male abandonment of females. Such behavior is inexplicable: it simply exists. The male here is avoiding responsibility, we suggest, since he is attempting to leave without wakening the woman. There appears to be at least a covert assumption that this is not proper behavior, indicating at least some conflict over such behavior.

FRED (MARY ELLEN'S TEENAGE SON)

Life History

"I was born May 27, 1953, in Letterman Army Hospital at the Presidio. When I was small, to keep me in the house at nighttime my mother, she used to send my friend out in a sheet, to scare me like he was a ghost or something. Well, anything else . . . and I used to have everything I wanted except, well, my sister she's, well, my little sister was born. That's when I used to have a lot of fun 'cause she used to hit me in the head with bottles and everything to make me learn that you just can't pick on people for nothin'.

"And when I grew up I started playin' basketball for gyms and everything and last year I won the trophy that I was supposed to get this year for the boys' club 'cause we took first place in the House League. And this year I won the scholarship to Bishop O'Dowd."

Q. You always lived in Hunter's Point?
A. No. I lived, when I was born I was living in San Francisco. We moved to Palo Alto, we moved to San Francisco, we moved to Menlo Park, we moved back to San Francisco, moved to Menlo Park, we moved back to San Francisco, then we moved to Los Angeles . . . then we moved back.

Q. How come all these moves?

A. I dunno. See, I know she moved to L.A. 'cause she wanted some hot weather once in a while. And I was glad to get back 'cause I was missing all my grandparents and everything.

Q. When did your mother and father separate?

A. I dunno. It was back in about 1955 or something like that. I was still small.

Q. What are you planning? What are your plans for the future?

A. To be a biologist. See, I sent over to, uh, Woodrow Wilson High School those after-school science programs, and I took geology, biology, and chemistry. I finished biology 'cause I liked that the best and I had two certificates in it . . . over at my grandfather's house — and the school safety award certificate 'cause I was the captain when I graduated from elementary school.

Q. What do you like most?

A. Basketball. I play basketball and eat. Those the best things.

The account given by Fred suggests very little about his early life (he is fourteen) except to indicate with positive affect both being frightened by one of his mother's pranks and being struck by his sister. It appears that he has had to repress aggression against siblings more than he wanted and has turned this negative feeling positive as a defense.

His achievement desires are high, by his own admission, and he clearly believes he will be able to qualify academically, just as he has athletically, for a high level of performance. He has little to say about his mother. He merely categorizes her bewildering moves and indicates his need for the kind of stability his grandparents offer. The expression of a great love of eating is difficult to evaluate, but in light of Mary Ellen's rather abrupt feeding techniques with her infants, it may indicate a deep hunger for an as-yet-unsatisfied emotional life.

Of great interest is his complete refusal to discuss his separation from his mother, initiated by the welfare authorities. He is not presently living with his mother, but visits her nearly every day.

TAT Responses

Card 1

A. Make up any story?

Q. Yeah, what do you see there?

A. Johnny went to school one day and he wanted to know how to play a violin and he was studyin' the strings out and everything. I don't know if he ever learned to play it, but he should the way he lookin' at it . . . he's lookin' at it.

Q. Okay.

Card 2

A. What's happening here, what is that? Um, a man in the background plowing the field and this girl she's goin' to schoo— . . . looks like goin' to read a book or go to school. It looks like a Bible and another book. And another lady's watchin' the man plow the field.

Q. What's the story?

A. Uh, I don't think I can make one up on that one.

Card 3BM

A. This man looks like . . . this is the story about a murderer 'cause I see part of a gun on the floor. And looks like after he killed his wife or somethin'. 'Cause he shot his wife and probably didn't mean to do it and he's so sorrowful.

Q. Why did he do it?

A. He probably did it to get rid of her 'cause he had another lady . . . that he wanted to go with.

Card 4

A. This is the story about a man who looks like he's doesn't like this lady and she loves him real bad. Looks like he's lookin' at another lady, and he's mad at the lady and he just turns his head from her.

Q. What's gonna happen?

A. I think he's gonna go with the other lady, the way it looks in the picture looks like he is. Looks like he doesn't love this lady.

Q. Why?

A. She don't feed him . . . never give him nothin' to eat.

Card 6BM

A. This is about a boy and his mother. The boy is a man but his mother is kind of old. And she's lookin' out the window like she's mad at him 'cause he did somethin' to one of her best friends or somethin'. Doesn't look like she wants to talk to him neither.

Q. What did he do?

A. He did, he was fightin' one of her best friends and she told him not to.

Q. What's gonna happen?

A. I guess she'll just put him out of his, her, her house.

Card 7GF

A. This is about a mother and a little girl. She was playin' with her doll one day and her mother — she wanted to read her somethin' out of a book. She was reading, ah, about the adventures of Tom Sawyer, and the girl was just lookin' away like she don't want to listen.

Q. What will happen?

A. She won't learn nothin' . . . much . . . unless she learn how to read.

Card 8BM

A. This is about a boy saying somebody killed a man. I think the man was his father. And he's going away. And he went to the police station and tell on the men, and there was two of them. And one has a moust— . . . one has a moustache and one has a moustache and a beard. [*This is what I am wearing.*] It looked like his father was layin' down to sleep.

Q. Why did they kill him?

A. I guess they killed him for money. 'Cause the son is dressed up good. [*The subject is neatly and well dressed.*]

Card 13MF

A. This about a man came into his room and saw his wife dead, and turned his head like he didn't want to see her 'cause he had always loved him [*sic*] and everything.

Q. How come she's dead?

A. Looks like she was killed, stabbed or something. And this man right here, he turned his head.

Q. What will happen to him?

A. He'll probably go crazy for a while and then probably have, he'll probably have psychiatric treatment. He doesn't know who killed his wife.

Q. Does he care?

A. Yes, 'cause he turned his head around and didn't want to see her. You could tell by the expression he had.

Card 16

A. This is make up anything?

Q. Do what you want.

A. This is a story about a baseball player, and after he hit his home run the next man came up who just came on the farm club. He couldn't hit a home run, he struck out. And he was mad 'cause the people was booin' him. And then a famous baseball player walked up and struck out on purpose to show the people that anybody could strike out. And the purpose of this story is to show that just because you're new, and strike out a while, that doesn't mean that you won't be any good.

TAT Analysis

Quantitative analysis of the descriptive categories used in Fred's responses indicates modal interest in the areas of physiology, violence, and blocking, and lesser modes in the areas of separation, unrealistic outcomes, quarrels, unusual states, authority and autonomy, achievement, economic concerns, and sex.

Additionally, his responses include reference to a dead person, nurturance, unspecified delinquency, and a rather peculiar Card 16 response in the form of a fairy tale.

All of the violence is connected with either planned murder or unspecified murder, and, interestingly, the physiological response to food is similar to the response given in the life history. The response concerning nurturance and the responses on separation due to rejection — and especially separation from the mother as punishment — may well suggest that Fred sees nurturance needs as manipulated by nurturant figures.

Card 1 qualitatively seems to indicate a belief that expressive attitudes and simple aspirations are adequate for fulfilling an achievement need. Card 2 is a simple card response indicating some blocking. In Card 3BM, male aggression against wife is apparently viewed as a rather threatening situation, as Fred denies that it is planned and suggests sorrow as a result of this accidental killing. The motivation for this accidental killing, however, becomes clearer in the next part of the response, where the murder is indicated as being deliberate because of the desire to leave the wife and take up with another woman.

Card 4 further clarifies this theme of desertion: he notices the second female figure in the card, which is rarely perceived (although it was perceived by Babalona's daughter as well). This second female figure is seen as the attraction to the male, who is in the process of leaving the first female figure. The reason for the desertion is the lack of nurturance of the first figure. Thus, we suspect that the nonnurturant qualities of Mary Ellen's mothering which resulted in the removal of her son for adoption has been transformed in this story: Fred's apparent defenses against the feeling of abandonment and nonnurturance are to indicate that he will be the abandoner in the case of nonnurturance.

Card 6BM continues this theme, but shows the difficulty of leaving the mother. In this card, it is not the son who abandons the mother, but the mother who forces the child out of the home. Mary Ellen's son is not precisely sure why he was forced out of the home at such an early age, but has taken the responsibility upon himself, believing it to have been his fault as a result of some fight he had with his mother's friend. We surmise here that Fred has interpreted the results of his jealousy and antagonism toward his father and/or Mary Ellen's early suitors as the cause of her rejection of him. This card is also notable for the confusion of sex identities which occurs at the end. Mary Ellen has come to take on many of the aspects of both father and mother to her son. His confusion in this regard is evident in his inability to decide on the proper pronominal adjective to apply to the house.

The theme of autonomous concerns and of expressive versus duty concerns is shown in Card 7GF. Here the expressive affective life of the child is interrupted by the mother's wishes. The defense against this intrusion into the autonomous life is to take a noncooperative stance. But while this serves autonomous needs, it interferes with internalized moral strictures. Thus, a penalty for autonomy is found in the ignorance that will result from not paying attention to parental strictures. In Card 8BM the father is killed off, and the aggressor is identified as the ethnographer (i.e., me). The identification of the father is overdetermined with reference to the son. This card is relatively unclear, but it does indicate some concern for external controls over aggressive tendencies. And, in fact, these aggressive tendencies are very inadequately denied by claiming that the father was lying down to sleep instead of dead. Unfortunately, it is not clear what perception Fred had of me.

The aggressive tendencies against women are more carefully defended in the next card, Card 13MF. In this card, a man sees his wife as dead, but Fred denies that the man had any aggressive intent against her — despite the murderous impulses suggested in an earlier card — claiming that she is deeply loved and that as a result of her death the man will go crazy and will have to undergo psychiatric treatment. Thus, not only is the death denied but the punishment for the aggression implied in the story is built-in.

There was a response to Card 16. This response was initiated by the subject. In this card, what appears to have happened is a very common type of fantasy, that of a nurturant adult figure lending support to a child (or at least a younger person) by means of his own deliberate inadequacy. Nonetheless, despite the introduction of this supportive defensive theme, in the story neither protagonist is depicted as a failure. The theme of achievement raised in this story is only in terms of aspiration. No meaningful instrumental activity or techniques for achievement are suggested. Achievement here is magical, the result of totally incomprehensible forces. These forces are organized in terms of some kind of fate which is just as possibly good as bad. Such a perception of fate offers defenses against feelings of inadequacy.

NOTE

[1]Parenthetically, Mary Ellen was relieved of her remaining two children in June 1967. It seems that, with the help of two eight-year-olds who were "babysitting," they were tearing up the apartment and throwing small furniture (such as the radio) out the window and breaking all the windows.

6

MANGO AND ADELAIDE'S FAMILY

IF Mary Ellen's family represents one extreme in Hunter's Point, that of Mango and his wife Adelaide represents the other. Mango is in many ways atypical of the black males at Hunter's Point. Mango has a permanent, moderately well-paying civil service job and is active in the community: he is, in fact, a community leader. Reputed not to chase after other women, he is the head of his family: clearly dominant over his wife and four children without being domineering, he commands their respect and has gained their apparent admiration and love. Mango has convinced his wife to wear her hair Afro style, which is now (1967) beginning to become fashionable among a few women in Hunter's Point. (Afro-style clothing is characterized by looseness of fit, bold, colorful African prints, and flowing lines emphasizing grace rather than kittenish sexiness.)

A friend of Mango's who had not seen him for five years came to visit him once while I was there and was astonished to the point of disbelief to see the way Mango's wife dressed and wore her hair. He could not hide his admiration and deep envy of Mango's marital situation. He left musing that he would never be able to convince his wife to do that.

Mango has little doubt as to the main problem in Hunter's Point, and his opinions on the matter are firm: "The problem here is that all men is pussy-whipped."

Mango himself initially had a very difficult time getting the older women who ran the local organizations to accept him as an equal and as a natural leader. By and large, however, there has been relatively complete capitulation on this point. He has by now the grudging respect even of some of the oldest and most entrenched matriarchs in Hunter's Point.

What makes Mango a rare phenomenon in Hunter's Point — and by extension, I suggest, in urban black communities in general — is that he has succeeded in becoming a dominant member of political and social community organizations by means other than through association with his wife or other women (some men have achieved prominence in this way, albeit prominence of an essentially powerless nature). Moreover, he has done so without benefit of a governmental appointment or a professional administrative occupation. That he has developed a base of followers for the most part by his own personal efforts while holding a full-time job would make him unusual by any standards in any community.

Within his family, he controls expenditures without parsimony, and his decisions are central in family activities. Mango disciplines his children, but tends to do so in terms of verbal castigation if reasoning does not work; he will spank his children but apparently rarely feels the need to.

In some ways, of course, Mango is a person of unusual ego strength and, one suspects, would be so regardless of the culture in which he lived. On the other hand, he is not very much unlike large numbers of middle-class Americans in terms of his position in the family and his relationship to social forces in the community. That he is unique in Hunter's Point is perhaps the greatest testament to the strength of the matrifocal family there and its essential differences from the family structure most commonly found in the rest of American society.

Yet it is instructive to note that Mango's level of integration has not been achieved without anxiety. Both in his life history and in his surprisingly sparse TAT responses (with his verbal facility and overt competence, I expected a great deal more out of his TATs than actually showed up, although they were not actually impoverished), Mango clearly indicates the degree of strain he is under.

MANGO

Life History

"I was born in Arkansas, a town called _____ . Oh, I was born 1935 — I was conceived in Illinois but my mother had to go to Arkansas for family reasons to birth me, and I stayed in Arkansas till I was two years old and I was brought back to Illinois to be raised. I was the only son my father had, and, uh . . . "

Q. Did you have any sisters?

A. Not by my father. My father died, ah, before I knew him, he died I think I was about three years old and I was raised by my grand-mother, great-grandmother, and my great aunt. My mother had little to do with me, ah, she didn't have much to say so over what I did because she was quite young when I was born and the, uh, older people kinda took me on.

Q. You lived more with the older people in your family than with her, huh?

A. Yeah, right, and at that time I was the only male in my family, my immediate family, and I carried on a pretty normal childhood, I guess.

Q. Well, what did that mean? Was it your grandmother, your aunt, and your mother living in the same house?

A. Yeah.

Q. And you?

A. And me, and I was more or less dominated by women from the sense that, uh, my family life consisted of nothing but women, but my outside activities here with boys, you know my age and older. I always dealt with, uh, played with kids older than me. And I guess I grew up a little faster than, uh, normally I would. And, uh, I, as my childhood was spent in Illinois, in Southern Illinois, I ran with kids as I say older than I was, and I gotta lot of male image I guess from them, was the only place I could get it in fact, until my cousin moved with us and he was a year older than I was, but it, uh, didn't make any difference, to me, I had my circle of friends and he had his. So I started running with guys four and five years older than I was and around my eleventh or twelfth, well, one thing that stands out in my life, I think pretty strongly was the first time I went to jail, it was the year when I was twelve years old, uh, for curfew.

In my home town there was all-Negro town and it was a very strict curfew.

Q. This was in what town?

A. Illinois, in a little town called _____ , Illinois, and curfew there was for kids under sixteen years old. Was nine o'clock, I mean you couldn't be on the street after nine and I was caught coming from the movie one night about eleven o'clock and I was put in jail and I stayed in jail till about three o'clock that morning. And all, it was quite a scare for me. And, uh, after that, ah, I got into trouble, ah, with some more kids older than I was for, uh, petty theft, uh, stuff like that. One summer I went to jail three times for petty theft, and, ah, each time it was, ah, I felt it was all fairness because you know in my town you couldn't cry discrimination, you couldn't cry you know people were prejudiced against you and putting you in jail because you — they thought you did something. There was always a case where I had did something and, uh, I knew people wasn't takin' it out on me because of the color of my skin or something like this.

I was wrong, and, uh, so I had one more time to jail before I would be sent to reformatory till I was twenty-one. In Illinois they have a law where so many offenses you go, you stay in reform school till you're twenty-one years old.

It so happened that year I, my mother moved to California in 1942 or '43 and I was still with my aunt and grandmother. So 1950 my grandmother died — my great-grandmother — and so my aunt moved here and I came with her — and at that time I had, my mother had had three more kids, two brothers and a sister, but I was, oh, about seven years older than the oldest one so that meant that I was thrown into a situation where I was almost twice their age, well, you know, now you really young and my father, he my stepfather, had his problems, uh, because my mother was raised as a Christian — huh! [*expressively and somewhat bitterly*] if you can use the word, she was a very strong church woman. She worked in the church, she lived in the church. In my early life, uh — between as far back as I can remember up until I was fourteen or fifteen years of age I was brought up in the church, and, uh, I had to go to church not because I wanted to, but because my family made me go to church. And when I came to California and my mother carried on this practice of steady churchin'. But, my father, my stepfather, didn't believe in it too much, he did his drinkin', and he had his problems, he had problems then as a child you don't understand, but now as a grownup I do.

Q. What do you mean?

A. Well, they were domestic problems, you know, between my mother's life and his life. He wanted to — uh — ah, do the normal — have the fun that men have and drink. My mother didn't like it and so as a consequence of it their marriage broke up. And I was about seventeen, sixteen or seventeen years old when their family, when he broke up with my mother, and that left me in the position of being still the only, the oldest son, and, ah, responsible to some degree for my younger brothers and sister. And that mean discipline, uh, set an example for 'em, uh, uh, keeping my nose clean and, uh, and raising them, you know.

Q. Well, were you raising them yourself, how did it —

A. Yeah.

Q. You mean you were taking care of the kids?

A. I was, yes.

Q. Were you working then?

A. No, I was still in school, but, uh, I felt strong, I guess one thing that always bothered me is that, you know, I never knew my father, and, uh, I never wanted my kids to be put in that situation, and I didn't want my brothers to — to, uh, come up without any male guidance because, ah, I was lucky in a sense that like I said before I was raised around kids that was much older than I was and they kinda lent some type of a male image to me where my brothers and sisters were in a city dwelling where all the kids around our neighborhood was younger or they wouldn't have anything to do with them, uh, because of my mother's beliefs in religion or the kids that they should have been playing with or associating with wouldn't play with them or associate with them because, you know, we were, the family was too religious. So, that left 'em to me, ah, I had to exert that male image and, ah, to pick up the responsibility where my father, ah, stepfather, left off.

And there were, ah, times when, you know, we were thrown into situations where, ah, before he died, I was, before I learned how to drive a car really, ah, we would go someplace for a family ride, and

107

he would get drunk and couldn't drive home and I would have to bring the car home and the kids home and, ah, you know, be really responsible for 'em at a young age and so finally I couldn't put up with my mother anymore, uh . . . *huh!* [*special grunt of a deeper, more emotional tone*] . . . in a sense I, ah, did, I, I, she didn't understand me and I didn't understand her because she had never had anything to do with me because, ah, she didn't raise me, she just birthed me.

Until, ah, so we were, ah, poles apart, uh . . . *huh!* . . . I, uh, when I finished school, I quit school, high school in my, I, ah, one month from graduating out of high school, and my family was on welfare, and it bothered me because when I was in Illinois my aunt was on what they called relief and that meant, ah, she used to get twenty-six dollars a month on relief and she had to take care of me, send me through school, keep me in clothes.

Q. On twenty-six dollars?

A. On twenty-six dollars. And keep a house up. Ah, so that meant when I was younger I —

Q. Well, you can't do that. I mean, where did she, she must have had some other money coming in.

A. Well, the house was paid for for one thing, so all she had to pay was gas and light, and she used to get twenty-six dollars in money and about once a month, I forget whether it was once a month or once every two weeks, she'd buy commodities, you know, ah, cheese and potatoes and stuff like sugar and, and stuff like that.

So, when I was about, going back to when I was younger I can remember, I, I realized the situation my family was in, uh, I knew they were very poor — *huh!* — so I would, uh, I had a wagon, and in my home town you could sell scrap iron a penny a pound, copper a nickel a pound, bottles, milkbottles a penny apiece and rags, you know, so I used to run around selling iron and bottles and rags, but I was fortunate, I didn't, my aunt never asked for any money from me, uh, I used to mostly keep the money for myself and show fare and my little expenses I had, and, uh, I would, I would even go fishing on the river and catch fish and sell 'em for show fare and my recreation. Didn't make nothin' — dollar, you know, two dollars — but this kinda built a sense of responsibility in me, you know. I had, I would shame, I would be embarrassed to ask my aunt for, you know, money, because I knew what the situation was, I knew she didn't have it. So I got a job in a grocery store when I was about twelve, delivering groceries when I first started out and then I started clerking because I could always count pretty good even when I was little, then I used to make about six dollars a week, I think it was about six dollars a week and sometimes I'd bring meat home, some food from the store and I would offer to help 'em, and, ah, but one thing I respected, ah, with my aunt was that she never asked or made it mandatory, you know, that I contribute to the family, ah, she didn't make it a duty on me. And it kinda embarrassed me, I guess, into a situation, where, you know, you feel you gotta do something if you're a man at all, or I wasn't a man, but I was the only male, and, uh, I, uh, would every once in a while bring some groceries home, and I'd feel real big then, you know, and, ah, so when I came to California, the situation was reversed in a sense, I had a stepfather that was working shipyard, but to me he was still a stranger, ah, my mother was a stranger and he was a stranger. I didn't know 'em, because as soon as they got married they left and came here and left me in Illinois, and, uh, I wasn't afraid, I wasn't ashamed to ask them for anything. And, since I had never asked anybody for anything and I got into the position where I didn't want to start begging, so I would earn some money from him, from like I'd wash his car every Saturday, and, ah, or, either I would just, uh, do without.

And then after he broke up with my mother, ah, I was just about finishing high school and I quit, I quit high school. I was in the twelfth grade and not lacking one month from graduating in May. And the pressure on me got so great that I felt like I was, uh, a burden to my family, because, uh, my relationship, my aunt was there and I was there and we were both, I felt, uh, burdens to my mother, and her situation after my stepfather left.

Until it came down to the situation where I was supposed to get a graduation suit and my father was there then, my stepfather, and he made this remark about, he wasn't gonna spend any money on me for a graduation suit. So I quit school and I went to work for _____ – *huh!* – downtown. And I worked for him for a week.

Q. What's _____?

A. It's a mail delivery, uh, delivery service.

Q. Oh, ah, yeah.

A. Ride a bicycle. And I worked for him for a week. And finally my aunt talked me into going back to school, into going to school. She, ah, say that she would get the graduation suit for me. So I went back to school and graduated, and after I graduated, I went to work for Comptons, and I worked for them.

Q. What's that?

A. It's a mailing house, a mailing firm. They get those mailing – and I worked for him from the time school was out all the way up until May the following year, and I was trying to contribute as much as I possibly could to the family and yet still maintain a certain amount of individuality, and, uh, it got to the point where I just couldn't make it anymore, you know, I had to leave – I had to get out on my own, I had to get away from the domineering-type mother, uh, that was still pushing me into religious – *huh!* – field when I didn't really feel it at all, I didn't care about it, so I went in, I volunteered and went in the service. I put my age up three months, so that I would, so that she wouldn't have to sign for me, and, ah, I went into the service. In the service, I, I –

Q. This was what year?

A. This was in 1954. I graduated in 1953, went into the service in 1954. I, um, learned quite a bit, I learned how to be independent, more independent than I already was. I was quite independent when I went in there, but learned a lot. I learned people, I learned how to get along with people and learned who to avoid and who to associate with. And, uh, I, I did my, I did whatever I wanted to do, if I wanted to do it and I felt I wanted to do it bad enough, I would do it.

I, like I, I wanted to be on the pistol team, and being a Negro was one strike against me because that was special duty and it meant gravy, you know, it was a good life to be on special duty. So I went out for the pistol team. Never shot a pistol in my life – *huh!* In fact, I didn't even qualify with it when I took the test in, ah, boot camp. But I went out for the team anyway and I made it. I stayed on the pistol team thirty months, as, ah, one of the only Negroes on the pistol team. There was one more and he was the alternate, but he, ah, never made it. Ah, he just kinda, his rank kept him there. He was sergeant and I was private, so – huh! – but anyway it was a good experience. I got to travel a lot, and see a lot of places. I went to the South for the first time in my life that I can really remember. I went when I was younger, but I went there in the service as an adult and my experiences there were about what I

110

expected them to be, ah, a little shocking in a sense, but otherwise I knew where to go and where not to go. And so, I had no difficulty getting along, and I think one of the biggest problems or one of the biggest letdowns I had the whole time I was in the service was when I went to Germany, and I found out in Germany where I was, in Augsburg, that it was segregated, ah, by race, ah, they had a Negro section of town in Augsburg and a Caucasian section.

And we had just left Tennessee where the same situation had existed and to get in Germany [*sighs*] you know, five thousand miles away from the South, and run into that same situation is a little too much, so during the course I was there we got in a, into a few fights. And I remember, let's see, our company was about, as I told you before, about thirty-five percent Negro. And —

Q. This was an airborne company?

A. Yeah, and when we got to Germany it was just too much to take, you know, another segregated city — [*wryly*] huh! So, we got in a few fistfights around there. They put everything off limits for a whole weekend. Finally, everything opened up to anybody, you know. Still wasn't welcome, but we went anyway.

Q. In other words, you really unsegregated the town.

A. Yeah, while we were there we did — [*wryly*] huh! We, ah, you know, the riots that's happening here now, was nothing compared with the ones we had over there. This, these was real race riots, uh, uh, wasn't disturbances. These was guys that knew how to kill each other and —

Q. But you won?

A. I don't know whether we "won" or not, uh, whether we won the fight, but we won the issue. You see, uh, it's kinda bad publicity for the military, the U.S. Army, when they get over there and be fightin' each other — so — the commander over there put the whole town off limits to everybody, until an order was passed that all places be open up to anybody, any soldier — no matter who they were. If they didn't open up, they would put 'em off limits to everybody. So, then the whole town opened up.

Uh, so I got out of the service. I come back home, and I was a little more wiser and a little more experienced in, uh, the worldly ways, I guess, and I came back. My mother was alone and she had two brothers. I had another brother then and one sister, two brothers and a sister. And I tried to stay at home again, but she was still on this

111

religious kick, and, ah, it still wasn't my cup of tea, couldn't fight it.

So, I stayed there and I got a job and I tried to help her as much as I possibly could, and it just, we just didn't get along. So — I stayed home about almost a year, got a job working construction work with a construction company, and, ah, I worked for him for nine months. And I was packing up to leave, I didn't know where I was going, I was, I think going to try to hitchhike to the east coast, uh, Midwest or something. And I — my wife, now my wife, uh, talked me into takin' [a civil service] exam. And I didn't want to do it because I didn't want to stay here. So I went down with her and my mother to take the exam and about a week later or two weeks later, I passed it. And they called me to work in about three weeks.

So — they talked me into going on takin' the job [at] _____ . And I started workin' at _____ in 1958, and I'd been workin' at _____ two months? — one month — [here Adelaide corrects him: "May to July"] — May to July and I got married, and, uh, but I was fittin' to move away from home anyway, so marriage was just, was gonna help me out a bit, when I left home, you know.

So, ah, we got married, we eloped. Because I didn't want no big wedding and I didn't know whether her mother would approve of me or not.

Q. Whether whose mother would approve?

A. My wife's mother. And, uh, in fact we didn't even tell 'em we were married till about when? August? September? [Adelaide: "July."] ... [Disbelieving.] We got married July fourteenth. [Adelaide: "The end of July, I guess."] ... [Turns to me.] I thought it was longer than that.

But, anyway, we, uh, got married and I moved out and, uh, been married eight years, but, uh, I think, you know, you just exist, you go to work every day and you come home in the evening and that's it, you know, your life ends. Uh, we, I never have been what they call, care for a lot of parties, and, uh, I never been an alcoholic to an extent where I just had to have a drink, or I never messed with any drugs, uh, very little, uh, and more or less then it was to prove to a guy, you know, you done it.

Uh, but something always has been in my mind since I been married, is that I've been tryin' to make it, I been tryin' to be the man in my house, in the sense that I, I've been around lots of friends of mine and a lot of people, and I've noticed how women dominate men for one reason or another, but to me this has not been a prob-

lem . . . [*meaningfully*] yet I — I will say this right now — and I
strongly believe it and I think my wife do, too. [*Looks at her.*] If
that day ever come then she's minus one husband. [*I nervously
laugh very lowly.*] That's right, I, I can't, uh, I, you see because to me
I'm responsible for what happens in my family, uh, directly responsible, or indirectly. Uh, if my kids do something, uh, break a window,
or hit another kid on the head with a rock, uh, you know, they
won't go to the mama, you know, if you got an old man at the
house, you are responsible, you know.

You come, you pay, or you go to jail, most especially if the kid's
young. So — all these things to me, you know, a man has a certain
role in life, in family life, uh, either you do it or you don't do it,
you give in to the pressures of society, which let women dominate
it, or you don't. You stand up and say no — no, ain't gonna be that
way. And I think, I think something else that bothers, I don't know
whether it bothers the old lady or not, but it bothers me, is if
there's a conflict in my family, which I can truthfully say very seldom there is, but sometimes, you know, everybody gets depressed
and you want to sit down and talk about something and —

But to me, you know, things happen, say, for instance, that there
is a conflict between my wife and I, something I did and she wants
to sit down and discuss it. All right, now, I may take it the wrong
way and I may jump on the defense, you know, and you draw back
on a whole lot of old problems that you haven't brought out before,
you know, and then it compounds the situation. And the next thing
you know you got a real argument going. And then a fight, and then
boom, it's all over.

Now, every human being on the face of the earth suffers at some-
time, you know, you are born, you accept it. You should know how
to throw it off and say, that's life. You know you can't let every
little issue bring you to the conference table, you know, uh, because
life is not gonna be easy. There gonna be difficult moments and conflicts between man and woman, most 'specially when you been livin'
under the same roof and puttin' up with each other, you know,
little problems and faults, if you can say that. Nobody's perfect, uh,
I do things, I know, that probably annoy my old lady and she do
things that annoy me.

But, every time you do something that annoys me, I don't have
to jump on you for it, you know, I can accept it as being part of

113

you. But we haven't had any major conflicts in nine years, uh, because I guess, because this attitude, uh, or if there's a decision to be made, uh, major, there's no such thing as a conference. I make it and I'll suffer the consequences if it's wrong, but I won't pat myself on the back if it's right.

Q. When did you first come to Hunter's Point?

A. When I first came to California I came to Hunter's Point and I came to — lived on _____ — that's when _____ was in existence, uh, it was an all-Negro neighborhood. The Hill was integrated in a sense; they had, uh, Negroes on this side of the Hill, whites on top of the Hill, Negroes on the other side of the Hill. Then they had _____ , was all Negro and _____ was all Negro.

No Negroes in homes around here, very seldom, very, very few.

Q. The _____ was all white then?

A. All white, all.

Q. Other side of Third Street, that was? . . .

A. All white. And, uh, I, I remember the first day I went to school here, it, being raised in a city where, a little town, where everybody was, that was everybody was a Negro, the mayor was a Negro, the superintendent of schools, the teachers, uh, in that school there was very, very strict discipline. Uh, you didn't get in trouble in school — there was no such thing as suspension, you didn't get suspended. There was no such thing as kids cuttin' [laughs], ah, because we had a very effective truant officer. He could run everybody down in one day, you know. Here I guess the problem is bigger. You couldn't get lost, uh, every child was an individual, you know, uh, to the teacher. The teacher knew you personally, he knew your parents personally, my aunt knew the teachers personally. They — in fact, it was such a close relationship it scared me. I mean, you know, I couldn't do anything, you know, sometimes boys have a tendency to want to do things to get away with, little mischievous things. I couldn't do that. Very few kids could. We could do it after school, you know. We'd get into our fights and everything after school, but this was a normal boyhood life . . . uh, the, the, uh, complications that I ran into here was one I could go to school and I could get lost in a crowd. See, like I went to_____ when I first came here. They had about twenty-five hundred kids, and in twenty-five hundred kids, you know, you can get lost. And if you just be quiet and don't say nothin' the teacher don't ever know you're there.

Plus, I had to travel a long ways to school which I never had to do. The only time I ever rode a bus in my life was when I was going what they call into town, which was about three or four miles.

But, here I had to ride on the bus miles or more to school every morning and it was quite different, uh, to have to get on a bus to go to school, eat lunch at school, then come back home in the evening.

And to me Hunter's Point was the most beautiful place I'd ever seen, uh, because most of the cities in the East are smoky and, you know, we lived right around the railroad tracks and the old smoke engines from the railroad, uh —

Q. Well, you lived between _____ and _____, didn't you?

A. Yeah.

Q. Bound to be smoky.

A. Oh, it was quite, quite. I mean it looked real different, uh, and the projects at that time were kept in better condition than they are now. The grass was cut, the grass was green, and I think that a lot of the wild oats here now wasn't here then. There was green grass on the hillsides, and, uh, the people, well, I don't think at that time they had any — I never really thought about it much, white people were here and did they leave? Or what? I just accepted it the way it was. In fact, I was kinda glad to be in a new city; I was getting tired of my home town.

But, the first, my first day in school here was quite an experience, you know, to sit in, say, for instance, you go all the way through school, through the ninth grade in a segregated school. No white nowhere. And then you be thrown into an all-integrated school, ah, in the tenth grade, uh, I guess it took me a little while to overcome it. You know, where you could, you know, stand up and be counted. But I was, I don't know, I met a few kids around here, but they didn't go to the same school I did, and I had to make all new friends, and, uh, well, one thing I learned about this area is so different from most cities in the East and most especially where I lived is that in San Francisco people are hard to make friendships with. You know, you don't make friends easy here. It takes years and years and years of, of, uh, of really going at it to make friends. Which is something in the Midwest or in the East, I found you're accepted easier, people will accept you easier. They're friendly, they speak to you on the street. And here it's so seldom you can see somebody you don't know and they speak to you or even talk to you, or your neighbors

115

here, they, they're, I don't know what this is contributing to this, but
this is one difficult time I think most people have when they come
to a city like San Francisco, is the unfriendliness, and, uh, even up to
today, it's, it's still not easy for a newcomer in this area to make
friends, even if, even somebody's been livin' here five, six, seven,
eight, nine, ten years that, uh, only know three or four families good,
you know.

But, I, I like, you know, to get off into this deal where, uh, I became really aware of this situation, ah, to me, San Francisco has
always been a place where, you know, California to a person that has
never been here is an ideal place, it's a dream come true like, you
know. You come to California and you gonna get rich and all, man,
the Golden Gate and all the myths you hear.

Q. I remember that same thing when —

A. So I come here, I knew I had it made, you know. And, ah, I found
out that, you know, real quick just how different things was. So I
went to work, went to work at _____. I was married then. I,
uh, my mother was still going to church and, sort of, she had dropped
off a little bit. She had gotten involved in the community. And, but
these was all the people that she was working with, were all big
church members, uh, a big — the clan, you know, from church — the
women that ran the church and they were now turning their energies
toward running the community and, uh, I never had any feeling for
community organizations or community activities because it was too
closely related to the church for me.

It wasn't broad enough — where a lay person, uh, not a lay person,
but uh, an individual person that didn't have Christian ideals could
come and express himself. And I think, it's a lot of young people
here feel that way, but anyway — they were very involved in community activities. They were, uh, I think, they were workin' on a
freeway problem or somethin' when I first started noticin' what they
were doin'.

And me having my own family to worry about, it didn't bother
me too much, that. All I was trying to do was keep bread on the
table and keep a roof over my head and enjoy some of the luxuries
of living, like, you know, I like to fish, and I'd go every weekend.

So, finally, it come to a point where I moved to the address I'm
at right now — right here. And — I was still not too swift on community organizations and community activities and so forth and so on.

116

Then, one day I came home and a Caucasian family had moved into [the neighborhood]. And this guy was very active in community organization, you know. And, ah, I didn't know him at the time. All I knew he's a Caucasian and uh, he had moved into my neighborhood, and gonna clean up the problem for me. And I think this was too much for my ego. [*Laughs.*]

I, I think when I first got involved, uh, to me now this happened down inside me. I told him about it since, was that, you know, it kinda riled me up, to why you come here and here I am, I'm livin' here and I've accepted this, or at least I haven't said anything about it. Well, I guess I had accepted it, and an outsider come in and tell me, that, you know, look it's this way, it's that way, it's the other way. And, ah, he was going to the meetings and so forth and so on. And it seems ridiculous, you know, to me, to – for me to say that I'm a father, a responsible person, ah, at least responsible to my family, to have somebody else do my work for me, you know.

And, uh, so I got involved, I got involved with, ah, block club, and at that time I think I was the only Negro male – huh! – people involved in, I mean indigenous person involved in, ah, community work. Uh, I knew I was one of the only ones around my age. And, uh, but it, the more, you know, it was, it was sort of like competition. You know, where you competin' against a man, you know. I had a lot to learn.

Q. Even no matter how nice a guy he was, you could, in some way, see him as a representative of "the man."

A. I don't know whether that was entirely what I looked at him as, a representative of "the man." I looked at him as a threat to my manhood, you know. Uh, you know, uh, you know, in other words, he was being more of a man about the situation than I was. Here I am sitting in here living in it and not saying anything and this guy comes in and don't even know what's happening and is more involved and cares more about what's happening than I do.

So I had to find out why, you know. What was I, why was I so complacent with the whole situation? And, ah, then when I got to know him, I, uh, found out, you know, a lot about him and got to be very good friends. But, still yet the competition, not competition but the, well, you can call it competition between us from my standpoint of view, it may have been competition, from his it was somethin' else since, uh, he wanted to do this. But, uh, that meant I had a lot to learn. I had – huh! – a lot of readin' to do, and uh, lot of hard work to do. I think I talked it over with, with my wife about it before I really got too involved. It meant stayin' away from the kids, and, uh, bein' gone at night.

But it, by that time I had been established, you know, I had established myself, I think with the family, so it wasn't too much of a problem. [*Addressing Adelaide.*] Was it? [*She shakes her head quietly.*] No.

Ah, ah, so that I had begun to be aware of things that I hadn't even thought of before, like, uh, like a lot of the prejudices that exist in San Francisco and a lot of the underhanded dealings that go on in a community like this, and the neglect that the Establishment affords this community, and, and then you start getting mad about it. You start gettin' very angry and it starts makin' you work harder and then you wonder why other people aren't interested.

But, I guess they haven't been touched like I was. They, the competition, or the threat, hasn't been placed before the, where they would, uh, get up and wanna do something about it. Now, maybe in some situations, it's a, people have political ideas and want to go some place like that and they get up in community work and start working, but this has never been a factor in my life. In fact, I, I, I don't think I would take a political office if it was offered to me on a silver platter. It's just that I feel that my kids, all that I can do for them in the way of making San Francisco and wherever else we go a better place for them to live, and not have to put up with the things that I had to put up with, uh, not that it was all bad, but, uh, uh, that's what fathers are for, to make a better world for your kids.

Mango describes his early life in an absent-father, female-dominated family. He is very sensitive about this pattern, and continually refers to it. His childhood, however, with its emphasis on peer group importance and mildly illegal activity, resembles those of other Hunter's Point residents.

Mango expressed his fear of jail and the impact that that fear had upon him in quasi-ethical, moralistic terms. But his moralistic tone is modified by ambivalent attitudes toward "Christian" beliefs, which he remembers as being essentially repressive and the cause of his step-father's abandonment.

He developed a strong sense of responsibility toward his siblings because of his stepfather's abandonment (quite possibly as an ego defense) and, in the absence of any intense emotional relationships with his mother, was apparently able to avoid some of the more overwhelming aspects of a poorly defended cross-sex identity. What seems important, however, is the effect on him of the continued theme of male irresponsibility in paternal abandonment on him. The conflict over dependence-independence eventually leads him to join the army, where he is able to develop more personal security.

It appears, however, that he has bought this security at a price of some emotional and social sex-role rigidity. Mango's descriptions of the proper male role include both nurturant and abandoning elements (he will abandon his wife if she does not act as he expects). Thus, he is able effectively to integrate what appear to be a set of usually unproductive personal feelings.

Mango has had to be provoked into independence both as a young man — by his stepfather's abandonment and his mother's religiosity — and as an adult, when the impetus for his becoming active in local social and political issues was provided by a white neighbor's concern for their virtually all-black community.

TAT Responses

Card 1

A. Now, I'm supposed to say what this picture reminds me of?

Q. Well, what — well, make up some, see what's the story in there that you see.

A. Well, uh, it seems to me like this child is, uh, thinking of the history of this violin, or if he'll ever master it, uh, if, uh, or, uh, who before, you know, used such an instrument, uh, and, uh, what's it for and what's it all about.

Q. What do you think he comes up with?

A. You mean his solution, his —

Q. Yeah, his, to — what is the outcome of the situation?

A. Well, I think he really thinks that it's a puzzling instrument, that he can't make anything out of it.

Card 2

A. Well, this to me looks like a man, his wife, and probably could be his daughter. And, uh, he's toiling to give his child an education, uh, seems to me that, uh, the woman in the picture she look like she's pregnant. Is she? [*Laughs.*] And that, uh, she seems to be looking, you know, for a brighter day, uh, and the child, the girl in the picture seems to have a sort of respectful look in her eyes for her parents, uh, she's not exactly looking at them, but it seem to me there's a, she seems to say that she wish her parents didn't have to go through the problems that they have, uh, toiling with the soil, uh, uh, living in this, uh, condition, and, and probably hope that, uh, they were educated like she is, or, or in the process of being —

Q. What do you think the outcome of it is?

A. Well, probably, uh, when this girl does finish, uh, her education, uh, seems she's headed that way, uh, she'll find out in the end that her parents were doing what they knew how to do and liked to do and, and they wasn't such a bad life after all.

Card 3BM

A. Uh . . . huh! — well, this one is a little difficult to really say what he's doin', ah — man, woman, person, uh, could be meditating, could be sleeping. I don't know, you know, it's hard to say what his whole — he may be, uh, just suffered a trauma and this is the position it led him to. Almost to the bed and not quite there — he kind of fell down in that position.

Q. Okay.

Card 4

A. Uh, this man and this woman seems to be in conflict, uh, she has a look of understanding in her eyes, and, and he seems to be rejecting that, that feeling she's trying to communicate to him. Ah, he seems to be determined to go another direction, uh, than, she's trying to restrain him from going, or either she's offering him love and he's turning away from it.

Q. What do you think will happen?

A. Well, I think that from the look that he has now, that he will complete his mission, whatever it is he determines to do that, uh, that her pleading and her, the look in her eyes, and the, the kind of hold back she has on him will not, uh, not stop him from doing what he wants to do.

Card 6BM

A. Well, this seems to be a mother and her son and he has just told her that he has made up his mind to do a certain thing. And she seems

120

to have some doubt as to whether this is the right choice and he has some look of doubt in his face about whether he has told his mother the whole truth or has hurt her in some way. Or he seems reluctant to, to the ways he's, uh, his position is that it was a pretty hard thing to tell her that he was doing, and, uh, seems to me she was looking out and wondering, you know, "Where did I go wrong?" [*Laughs.*]

Q. So, how's he gonna resolve this situation?

A. Well, again I think, uh, she will have, uh, mothers usually do, have understanding of their children, sooner or later. And I think that, uh, she'll, if she's turnin' her back on him now, that, uh, later on he will, she will embrace him, and, uh, all will be forgiven.

Card 7GF

A. Uh, this is, uh, seems to me like it's, uh, a mother or, uh, trying to teach her child, or read to her child something from, uh, some book. And the child is far away from the thoughts of what her mother's tryin' to relate to her and she seems to be thinking of something unrelated to what, uh, the woman is trying to read, uh.

Q. Why do you think that is?

A. Well, I believe it's because, uh, the gap between the youth and the adult of the old type of learning process that, ah, the adult is probably trying to teach her is so out of date it doesn't attract her attention, it, uh, it, it, it's not interesting for her, and, uh, she's, she's just wandering in another world.

Card 8BM

A. Well, to me this is a child that, a young man that's daydreaming, uh, I believe he sees himself in older life as being a very successful person, possibly of being a surgeon, uh, of performing, uh, operation on a wounded person or sick person and he has a lot of optimism in his eyes of doing just that, a lot of, uh, ambitions looks about him. That, uh, he looks very determined to do the things he sees.

Card 13MF

A. Well, this seems to me like it — uh, would be a man that, ah, probably tired of, he seems to me as though he might have had a, a sexual relationship with this woman and, uh, now he's, uh, a little tired and she seems to be knocked out and, uh, and he feels that, ah, well, he may be, uh, getting up to go to work now, or, uh, or, uh, probably to, I see books here, it might be hers or his but could probably be that he's, has to go to school or somethin' like this.

Card 16

A. [No response.]

TAT Analysis

Quantitative analysis of Mango's TAT responses indicates a significantly different pattern, at least in terms of the quantities of responses in certain categories, from the rest of the TATs collected in Hunter's Point. Mango's modal concerns are in the area of achievement. Very much lower modes are shown in the area of physiology, discord, and self-expression. Autonomy, affiliation, succorance, and positive outcomes also show minor modes.

Most interesting is the small number of loss-of-love-object responses; the fact that Mango gave the only affiliation responses (those indicating a positive need for the companionship of other humans) in Hunter's Point; and that his numerous self-expression-satisfaction responses represent higher self-image than do anyone else's responses (only one other subject had any). In the achievement responses, in addition to simple aspiration, the idealization of the parent, the recognition of certain character traits necessary for achievement, and aspiration for others all play important roles. Only one specifically sexual response is given, and we may suspect that the suppression of sexual urges is in favor of affiliative, family-oriented, self-expressive concerns and achievement concerns. The number and quality of physiological responses, though, indicate, as we have suggested, that Mango pays a somewhat heavy price for this deviant (for Hunter's Point) orientation. References to sleep and exhaustion, unspecified anxiety, and family discord suggest that positive concerns are not achieved without struggle.

Qualitatively, Mango's Card 1 response is an expressive, investigatory one rather than an achievement one. Whatever implied achievement orientation there is in Card 1 results in an essentially negative response. Mango is not really sure of his ability to master that violin. We suspect he is also not really sure of his ability to shoulder the large responsibilities that he has taken upon himself.

The theme of heavy responsibilities and striving toward a better future is raised in Card 2. We might suspect that the nurturance needs which Mango does not permit adult females to satisfy for him are at least in part satisfied in fantasy through the belief that his children will respect and eventually reward him for his sacrifice. The hope that the achievement striving will not be useless is implicit in the last part of the response.

The theme of covertly and overtly stated difficulties continues in Card 3BM, where the difficulties are great enough to drive the individual, whose sex is left undeterminant, to a prostrate position. There is a possibility, however, that in the first two cards there is a significant blocking — in Card 1 of sexuality as implied by the child's not looking at something which is quite difficult for her parents (perhaps for her father) — which may be part of the trauma which the nonspecified individual in Card 3BM suffers. We may suggest now that the major concern probably exists in the area of the ambivalent attitudes toward sex, and a rejection of the male sex role in specific in favor of a more generalized androgenous role stressing male nurturance. (We might term this: socially positive cross-sex identification through sublimation.)

In Card 4, the repressed sexuality seems to come a little bit closer to the surface. The specific mention in Card 4 of the rejection of the love of a woman and of the close contact of a woman is defended by making reference to an unspecified mission. The sexual hold — perhaps a nurturant hold — that his wife has on him, he suggests, will not so much elicit his dependency and fulfill his nurturant and expressive needs as prevent him from a certain type of achievement.

This need is alluded to again in Card 6BM. Conflict between the mother and the son over a specific choice that the son has made is the theme of the card. It is not clear in what way he has hurt his mother or what it is that he has not told her. If we remember, however, that Mango and his wife eloped and that he has always been concerned with the dominant role that women played in his early life, we may surmise that his decision to adopt the role of an adult male was very difficult and painful for him. This interpretation is more easily supported in light of Mango's apparent desire for his mother's embrace once more in the future. This desire is disguised in terms of forgiveness and understanding, and appears in this context to be an understanding of his need for autonomy which he permits himself magically to have at the same time that he enjoys his mother's embraces.

In Card 7GF the lack of communication between the child and the mother indicates something slightly different from the conflict between duty and expressive behavior. On the manifest level, there is no specific affect involved; there is a denial of any affect by suggesting that the child is in a dazed, dreamlike state. In light of the other things that

Mango has suggested to us in his other responses and in his life history, there is an alternative explanation to the manifest contract: the thing that he fantasizes the mother is suggesting to the child and which is "out of date" is an incestuous relationship, which the child must reject in order to attain adulthood. The lack of affect expressed in this story is probably a blocking of the affect that would be associated with the conflict resulting from such a perception.

The dreamlike state at the end of the response to Card 7GF is reintroduced in Card 8BM. Here there is a continual determination expressed to achieve adult status which will permit the adult male a nurturant role in keeping with his partial feminine-sex identification while offering a secure haven in life through a social sex role as a male. Here, as in many of the responses from Hunter's Point, achievement, while closely related to aspiration and hope and determination, seems a little weaker in its instrumental aspects. There is a fantasy, wish-fulfillment aspect to this response that implies a refusal (or inability) to acknowledge the difficulties in attaining the perceived goal.

In Card 13MF, the theme of sexual fulfillment as fatiguing and physically debilitating and as a distraction from achievement and duty appears again: sexual activity can best be defended against by seeing it as interference with greater, more important plans.

ADELAIDE

Life History

"I was born in the South, and I spent the first three years of my life in [the South], uh, I don't know anything that went on or what happened, and, uh, my family moved, my mother and my stepfather and I moved to Oakland, California."

Q. When was that?

A. That was in 1941. I was three. And we spent four or five months in Los Angeles and then we moved to Oakland. And my grandmother at the time had come out very early when the war first started and bought a house. And she fixed us up a basement apartment. What was two families lived in the basement, my aunt and her children. We stayed there up until '44, '45, '46 we bought a home in Berkeley. We moved to Berkeley, California, and, uh, I attended school in

Berkeley and I did, when, uh, I was five years old, no, I was seven years old, and I returned to Houston to visit my father's people, my aunt took me.

And, uh, he at the time, my father, was still in _____ and his wife and my grandmother. And, uh, I had rheumatic fever and I was out of school for two years and I had a home teacher. When I returned to school I was more advanced than the class, so, they suggested to my mother that they skip me and she said no, that I could take a trip to_____ . So we left about September and stayed until January. And, uh, I knew, I didn't notice anything different when I went to _____ , but here in the last couple of years I found out that I did notice things that were different that I'm just realizing now. Little things that happened there.

Q. And you just forgot them at the time, huh?

A. Didn't seem like, well, one thing that I remember was, some, I had, you know, I was going to visit my father's people and I took school pictures and a little girl asked me did I go to school with white children and I said yes. But, it didn't bother me, and we got on the bus to go downtown one day and I sat down on the first seat I found and my aunt caught me up and took me on to the back and I didn't pay any attention to that.

And then I was telling Mango here, oh, I guess about three or four weeks ago, that on my train trip, I asked him something about taking a train trip across the country, "Did they put you in separate cars?" And he said, "Yes." When you get ready to go into the South, they put all the Negroes in one car. And then I was telling him about our trip and I remember we had a layover in New Mexico, and, uh, we got off the train. And I remember we getting back on a different coach. But I didn't and I just now really realize what that was for.

And, uh, I came back, went through school, and, uh, attended all schools in Berkeley, and I went on to, uh, one junior high school. Well, they have, at that time they had three junior highs in Berkeley. One was Negro, one was white, and one was mixed. And I happened to be in the Negro school, but, uh, that didn't bother me, and I attended Berkeley High. Then, after I finished school I came over here to go to school.

Q. What do you mean? To go to school where?

A. I went to San Francisco City College. And, uh, I stayed over here while I was going to school, and I attended City for a year, then I got married and I didn't go back. And, uh, well, let's see, I've been married almost nine years. I worked a little since we been married and then I've just been a housewife. That's all. [*Laughs.*]

Q. Well, what did you think about it when Mango started being active in community organization here?

A. Oh, I was very glad. Um, but he wasn't very active up until we, uh, he got involved with, uh, this family and they were very active, uh, little by little he's become involved. Sometimes I think he takes on too much, and, uh, I've asked him to cut down. And he'd cut down one then here comes along two other things. [*Laughs.*] But, uh, I have my, I'm very glad. He, he enjoys it and I enjoy it for him because he enjoys it. Doesn't take him away that much. [*Muses.*] Sometimes it's too much, but sometimes I think the problems get on him and he looks like he's very depressed, sometimes. Community problems.

Q. Do your kids go, do any of your kids attend the schools?

A. No, my oldest little girl will start in September.

Q. Where she gonna go?

A. She'll go to Jedediah Smith or either Hunter's Point, either of them. Depends on where we move, I think. And then we'll get involved in the school situation. Because from what I understand they're pretty off.

Q. How so?

A. Well, Mango's little sister, I followed her very closely in school, and she went to Jedediah Smith, then to Pelton, then to Mission. And she finished from Mission and she just had a diploma, so far as she just, just graduated from High School. She didn't know anything and it bothered me. And, then, uh, I have a few friends whose, uh, kids are in school, and their, I have a little niece, I have four little nieces, and they all attend school in Berkeley and the schools are so different, uh, Berkeley schools and this. I don't know about any other schools in the city except these around here, and just comparing the kids in the two different school situations, they're just, there's so much work that needs to be done over here. Because there's a lot of things that they're missing — or either they're getting them too late.

Um, like in Berkeley the schools, uh, start Spanish and French classes in the second and third grade, and, uh, over here, the earliest you can get them I believe is in the sixth. And six, seven, and eight and ninth grades — they're too old.

126

Adelaide, like Mango, also experienced an early parental split. In her case, however, her mother not only remarried quickly, providing the child with a father substitute, but Adelaide actually knows who her father is and is in contact with him. We see here, as with Mango, that when the family moved to California the entire set of female relatives came along. The extended matrilineal family has been as important in her life as it has in Mango's.

Immediately after discussing her earliest experiences with racial prejudice, which she encountered on a trip back to the Old South, she relates that she experienced what she might very well have felt as discrimination in the Bay Area in terms of a segregated high school. Her professions that this did not bother her may well be defensive.

Unlike most Hunter's Pointers, she actually attended college, at least for a while. She expresses contentment with her life as a housewife, but I wonder if it is her own feelings of mobility that have subtly assisted Mango in his determined drive to better things for himself and others. Or it may be that he picked her for a wife because they complemented each others' drives and intelligence.

Her faith in education, perhaps based upon her own experiences, is reflected in her analytic concern over the inadequacy, which she can detail specifically, of the local schools as compared to those available across the Bay in Berkeley.

Not tied to the past as much as her husband appears to be, she has both strong present and future orientations in her life history. Overall, in my observations of the family I found that she is pleased with Mango's work and is essentially comfortable in her life, perhaps more so than is Mango.

TAT Responses

Card 1

A. Okay, little boy sitting there, uh, he's been told to practice his violin and he's just debating if he's going to pick up and practice or if he's not.

Q. Do you think he will?

A. Eventually, if his mother is around, he will.

Card 2

A. Let me see, there's, ah, reminds me of a picture — movie picture. Anyway, uh, there's a mother standing by watching her, um, son, I'd say, fixing to plow a field, the young daughter's getting ready to go to school. That's about all I can see in it.

Q. Do you think, what do you think is going on in the minds of the people? Is there anything else that they're, is there anything they're thinking about?

A. The mother seems to be just daydreaming, and, um, very weary look on the girl which is, uh, I-don't-want-to-go-to-school bit.

Q. Why do you think?

A. I don't know.

Card 3BM

A. Uh, suicide victim.

Q. This is a suicide victim? What do you think happened?

A. She shot herself.

Q. Why?

A. There's a gun.

Q. You can see a gun. Why?

A. Why? Love, distress, I don't know.

Card 4

A. Um, for some reason he's fixin' to leave here, a typical family fight. Or a lovers' fight. And he's fixin' to walk out on her, and, uh, she's tryin' to give him one of them good old hugs and kisses to tell him to stay.

Q. Do you think he won't?

A. Yeah.

Card 6BM

A. Somebody looks like they come in, to me it reminds me of a, um, son who's come in to see his father or grandfather who's just died or something like that.

Q. What do you think is happening?

A. And, uh, well, I can't. The reason why I say grandfather, she looks like a grandmother, and, uh, she's just staring into space, and, uh, he's just looking at the dead body or such.

Card 7GF

A. Well, it's a young girl, holding a baby, I think.

Q. What do you think is happening?

A. The mother is reading to her. And, uh, she looks like she's in another world. That's about it.

Card 8BM

A. Reminds me of a, um, um, well, anyway, they're operating someplace, but it's not an operating room, it's um, um, like when the tents, where they do it when they're out to war.

Q. Yeah?

A. On a ship or something. This reminds me of a makeup light. There's a shotgun so you think of war. Window so it would remind you of a place. Makeshift place like during wartime or something like that.

Q. Why are they operating?

A. Appendicitis? [*Laughs.*]

Card 13MF

A. Well, okay. It's somebody's a student there. Don't know which it is. And I can't tell if he's just murdered her, or just come into a murder room or a rape room, and, uh, he's kind of 'shamed, or he doesn't want to see it.

Q. Uh-hum.

A. That's it.

Card 16

A. [No response.]

TAT Analysis

A quantitative analysis of Adelaide's responses shows them to be rather sparse. In fact, her responses were the fewest in number of any of the respondents. Modal areas of concern are those of blocking, separation, violence, unusual affect, autonomy and control, and physical exhaustion. There are additional single responses of nonspecified accidents, shame, unspecified quarrel, and parent-initiated achievement.

Qualitatively, Adelaide expresses a recognition of female dominance within the nuclear family in Card 1. She indicates no belief in the existence of autonomous achievement motivation, suggesting instead that achievement motivation is initiated through parental concern. Maternal dominance is continued through in Card 2 in a less obvious form. That is, the mother is standing by watching her son work — or better, preparing to work. The rebellion is suggested by the daughter's reluctance to go to school. Adelaide, however, chooses to refrain from suggesting what the outcome of this conflict will be. The response is essentially a card response, and indicates a certain amount of affect blocking.

That the repressed emotions are unable to remain repressed becomes clear in Card 3BM, which she identifies as a suicide story. She chooses, however, not to attempt any explanation for this suicide other than to indicate that it was probably over love and distress. Card 4 does indicate a theme with which we have become very familiar in Hunter's Point — male abandonment of female and the female's inability to prevent this abandonment. Possibly this choice of theme was made more likely by the depressive content of the preceding card.

The continued theme of a refusal to inject affect into the responses continues in Card 6BM. In this card, the death of a father or grandfather is recognized, but emotional affect is attributed to neither the son nor the grandmother. We might suggest that the death of the male figure in this card is the punishment for the abandonment theme first stated consciously in Card 4.

In Card 7GF, a girl is seen holding a baby. The remainder of the response is essentially a blocking one or card response. In Card 8BM the problem of the aggressive theme is continually denied and defended against by removing the affect from the situation. The card responses are in terms of the place, the situation, and the conditions, and Adelaide refuses to involve herself in any kind of story. When asked the reason for the operation that she had identified, she answered "appendicitis" in a laughing manner that suggested she didn't really believe this to be the case. In this card also, then, there is a kind of absolute refusal to get involved with the possibility of the results of aggressive feelings, as well as a repression of their cause.

Card 13MF does indicate some of the possibilities that Adelaide sees in such relationships. There is a discussion of the possibility of committing a murder or, alternatively, of stumbling onto a murder or rape scene. I believe that this response indicates some shame, perhaps over the kind of aggressive feelings felt. By and large, Adelaide has given us very little affect to deal with, but has indicated that she has great concerns in the area of autonomy, female dominance, and aggressive feelings toward males. These are, however, normal responses in Hunter's Point.

GENERAL COMMENTS ON TATs

In analyzing responses of TATs from Hunter's Point, I have been guided by the belief, which seems borne out in my analysis, that later card responses are influenced by emotions aroused in response to earlier cards. In many cases, such an analysis gives the impression that cards are being analyzed in the reverse order of their presentation. This is not so. In any event, sufficiently convincing internal evidence exists that responses to the cards include responses to the entire situation of presenting the cards, rather than just responses to each specific card.

The responses from the Hunter's Point residents show a relatively uniform pattern of concerns. In looking at such responses in terms of broad overall themes such as expressive behavior, instrumental behavior, and realistic perceptions, it becomes immediately clear that the Hunter's Point respondents are more interested in expressive behavior than in instrumental behavior, at least when judged in terms of realistic perspectives.

Additionally, there are a significant number of responses indicating that sexual activity itself is seen as an instrumental act as well as expressive behavior. This tends to force on us the conclusion that sexual activity in Hunter's Point is far from the joyous, spontaneous, and carefree behavior which popular public opinion suggests it to be in black urban communities. It also seems clear that the male respondents are uniformly concerned with their own adequacies and that they view sexual activity as essentially dangerous. While this is not so clearly the case for the female respondents, they quite obviously agree that this concern exists for males.

The theme of desiring achievement for children is a normal response for lower-class parents. Nevertheless, this theme, which crops up in several of the TAT respondents in Hunter's Point, is not simply based on the obvious desire to see one's child get ahead and avoid suffering the way the respondent has, but has other important dimensions as well. A theme stressing achievement for one's child may also defer the need to act out that achievement oneself. In fact, it may represent a passive defense against social inadequacy (though this is not to deny that the external obstacles to real personal achievement are immense).

Another general comment that can be made is that there were significant differences in the richness of responses: some individuals gave very sparse responses, others very rich ones. This was equally true for the life-history materials. Sparseness in the TAT responses is usually an indication of the blocking of very disturbing affect, and this seems to have been true in these cases. The sparsest responses, those of Jerry and Adelaide, are also those with the most seriously disturbed content as well.

Finally, the central significance of the matrifocal family, which I earlier identified as the dominant form of social organization in Hunter's Point seems to be borne out in detail by the responses on the TATs.

The responses also give some idea of the manner of psychological integration in individual cases. For example, though Jerry and Rena Lea show some serious antagonisms for each other, they have found a technique of integration which appears to be working for them. Rena distrusts and denigrates males. She has in this a more or less willing partner, her husband. She can be content with Jerry's economic support and companionship while denigrating it, with little expressed fear that he will abandon her. He seems to need her just as much as she needs someone to run down.

Jerry can thus permit himself his own passive tendencies and accept her denigration because at least he knows he supports the family to some extent. He keeps tensions from reaching too high a level simply by being absent much of the time. But his control is tenuous, and his aggressive tendencies can only be kept in check by lack of contact with Rena. In fact, he is apparently afraid of what would happen if such contact became too intense. He may some day abandon Rena, probably both she and he expect it.

In the case of Mango and Adelaide, the defense systems operate differently. Mango, too, has great concerns over his adequacy and an ambivalence toward and fear of his passive urges, indicated by his overt control of his family and demands that he be the boss. He handles his desire for passivity and the feminine role by finding a constructive nurturant male role to take. The genesis of this cross-sex anxiety is clear from Mango's description of the absent-father family in which he was raised.

Adelaide's integration is less clear. She blocks affect more, not having integrated as well as he. She can console herself with the fact that she has an active "male" husband, while actually fearing male abandonment. Her depressive tendencies probably help support the overt identification of her as passive vis-à-vis Mango. Or perhaps Mango's covert passiveness helps support her belief about male inadequacy. This covert level of role reversal may be what makes their marriage work.

For both Babalona and Mary Ellen, in a sense the game is over: each has achieved the pure matrifocal family. The pervasive influence of this institution is clear from the TATs of their children, which reveal lack-of-achievement themes in one case and totally unrealistic achievement themes in the other. Obvious concerns with father abandonment and an orientation toward expressive themes with the fear of the results of self-expression are present as well. They will quite probably reproduce the environment from which they came.

III

The Community

7

COMMUNITY
VALUES

THE term *values* in anthropology usually refers to the attitudes people openly express or covertly hold toward the world and the objects and people in it. The term has also been used more specifically to indicate the attitudes which people express toward their basic relationship with nature and each other. Values further act to constrain or broaden actions and in this sense are part of behavior. Kluckholn (1951) gives some examples of areas of basic human concern regarding which all men hold values — such as man's basic nature (one can view it as good or bad — or neither), man's relationship to nature (dominance over it, dominance by it, or harmony with it), his relationship to time (present, past, or future orientation), his relationship to life (one of being, becoming, or doing), and his relationship with other men (in terms of lineal, collateral, or individualistic ties).

While it is perfectly natural, and certainly relevant, to seek to determine where Hunter's Point residents stand on all these questions, I shall be more concerned here with specific aspects of some of these — especially where the values held by a majority of the Hunter's Pointers are at variance with what I perceive to be the dominant values of the community at large and thus tend to leave them at a disadvantage in dealing with it or render them the objects of ethnocentric contempt.

We have seen how the life cycle in Hunter's Point, and the conditions of life as it is lived there, tend to create a certain kind of person. For example, the structural situation of living in poverty and being relatively powerless to control significant aspects of one's daily life creates feelings of smoldering helplessness which, when combined with a destructive family situation, tend to produce a withdrawn, nonproductive, and affectively "dead" individual.

Within this process, and as a result of it, a series of values are generated — values that preceding chapters have only implicitly described. Here, however, I shall explicitly discuss some of these values, their ontogenesis, how they are maintained, and their implications for future behavior.

POVERTY

In the early 1960s some charitably motivated white middle-class people in the Bay Area (San Francisco, Oakland, and environs), in conjunction with some Hunter's Point residents, attempted to start a consumers' food cooperative in Hunter's Point with federal funds allocated by the Neighborhood Development Act.[1] A co-op affiliated with the highly successful Berkeley Co-op, which has several branches, it was felt, would bring badly needed consumer awareness in Hunter's Point. It failed miserably.

The reasons for its failure are rooted in the differences in values held by those who wished to establish the co-op and by the majority of Hunter's Pointers. A cooperative supermarket is financed somewhat like a corporation, each customer being permitted to buy shares up to a limited number for a minimal fee well within the reach of even the Hunter's Point poor. The staff of the co-op then tries to save money for its customers by using no advertising and buying selectively while carefully training consumers how to judge "quality" in merchandise. It then redistributes "profits" at the end of the year to customers in proportion to their shareholdings.

Basic to the successful operation of a co-op is the self-conscious desire of its customers, particularly its shareholding members, to save money. This essentially means avoiding the trap of highly advertised brand names which may be of poor quality or overpriced and the economic pitfalls of credit, to which end an effective consumer co-op teaches members how to approach installment buying and appraise the relative quality of merchandise, as well as how to deal with associated problems. Ideally these efforts are aided by a generalized feeling of "community" serving to defend the individual against the contemporary corporate economy with its attendant frills and traps. Thus, a certain "ethos" is a part of a successful co-op – or at least has been so in Berkeley.

Taken point by point, these aims and attitudes are self-defeating in Hunter's Point; taken together they pose a presently insuperable barrier to the successful organization of a consumer cooperative on the Berkeley model.

First of all, pinching pennies may be an enjoyable (though perhaps mildly necessary) task for middle-class, college-educated housewives. It is something they can do for enjoyment in the same way that they spend hours looking for "bargains" which they might not really need. Deprecating one's own economic position is a style of life among many middle-class, college-educated Americans as a reaction to what they conceive of as the crassness of economic boasting which they may feel is prevalent in the United States. Families in this class whose bread-winners are professionals or semiprofessionals have little economic insecurity in the grossest sense. The game of "let's see how cleverly we can manipulate the economic system" is not so much a financial necessity as part of this style of life.

Hand in hand with this is the common emphasis on off-brands of goods and a conscious refusal in many cases to buy the most popular brands – sometimes precisely because they are the most popular. A common feeling among the middle-class Berkeley Co-op group is that their refusal to buy the heavily advertised items constitutes a blow to the "crass Madison Avenue hucksterism" which promotes them, and sounds the call for a return to simple Spartan virtues and intelligent understatement. Such people find no difficulty in rejecting a part of what they have (access to many consumer goods) without feeling deprivation, since the decision not to buy certain things is their own.

In Hunter's Point, most residents do not understand the basis upon which quality differentials, price differentials, and credit and install-ment-buying gouging exist – or, more importantly, that there is any-thing that can be done about it. And that many are unwilling to admit that they are so ignorant as to need "consumer education" further complicates the matter.[2] Poverty and stupidity are equated by Hunter's

139

Pointers, who do not choose to admit to the stupidity and personal inadequacy that they feel are associated with admissions of poverty. Moves aimed at increasing the "political awareness" of the inhabitants of Hunter's Point flounder on this same rock. Political "education" movements imply somebody needs education, an attitude which irritates Hunter's Pointers.

Furthermore, many inhabitants of Hunter's Point have assimilated what they *assume* to be American middle-class mores — i.e., as they are presented on television. They believe implicitly that brand name goods are inherently better and that the more you pay for the merchandise the better it is — even if the higher price is due to installment or interest. To be told to buy unadvertised and thus obviously inferior products on the pretense that they are actually better is simply not believable.

Hunter's Pointers tend to be completely unaware that much of the college-educated middle class in America (to whose material possessions they overtly aspire) has, at least verbally, eschewed the ethic of the upwardly mobile huckster. In Hunter's Point the patterns of consumption presented in Doris Day movies are patterns of consumption worth striving for.

Hunter's Pointers do not want to be reminded of the poverty, and thus the implied stupidity and backwardness, reflected in the practice of penny pinching when penny pinching is their everyday concern. To have to admit to this practice, which they associate with poverty, and, even worse, to institutionalize it in the form of a co-op is totally unacceptable. The only way to live (even if it is an unattainable goal) is to get the best, whatever it costs. Never having this goal in reach, but believing it is worth striving for, many Hunter's Pointers find it difficult even to question the goal.

Finally, a feeling of community simply does not exist in Hunter's Point. By far the vast majority of the population feels no particular love for or allegiance to Hunter's Point; perhaps even more importantly, it feels no particular solidarity as a *black* community. Organic solidarity (in Durkheim's terms) or mere contiguity has bred no real meaningful feelings of interdependence and camaraderie. Even the "riots" (Chapter 10) failed to do this, and understandably so. There is a high turnover in occupancy in the housing area, and more importantly there is a general feeling of self-disparagement which, at times, almost reaches the level of negrophobia. In discussing the embryo co-op in Hunter's Point, Maggie B. could find no other way to discuss the problem than in terms of her own negative feelings about other blacks:

"Niggers, we don't deserve no civil rights. When I go shopping, I go where they ain't no crowds of niggers around. All them people hoodling up. I don't like no gum on the floors, it sticks to your shoes, and soap-boxes broken all over the floors."

Such comments are typical. Many Hunter's Point residents indicate either that they shop elsewhere (i.e., in white neighborhoods) or would if they could get transportation, usually citing local crowding as a reason. However, at no time during the eighteen months I observed Hunter's Point did I ever witness crowded conditions in local groceries comparable to those customary in stores in white middle-class neighborhoods. Stated secondary reasons such as the dirtiness of the area and the perceived "quality" of the crowd seemed to be the actual primary ones. Many Hunter's Pointers, then, fearing that being poor really does mean being backward and stupid, fight very hard against consciously acknowledging their poverty. A consumer's cooperative obviously has a difficult time operating in such a community.

Such attitudes even seem to be held by those in Hunter's Point who have some higher level of personal achievement motivation – by Pete, for example, an eighteen-year-old boy of serious demeanor who is the oldest of four children. Both Pete's parents reside in the home, and his father has a steady job. Pete is thus not from a typical home of the new housing area; indeed, he lives in the old housing area. Pete acts as a general office boy and switchboard operator in the local Youth Opportunity Center. His attitude toward the white community and questioning social scientists is direct, forthright, and revealing. In a general discussion, Pete suddenly and forcefully directed the following to me:

"We ain't poor. I could buy just as good a jacket as you got. You all think we're poor, we just ain't interested in what you guys got, or what you are. You just think we're poor, we ain't no more stupid than you are."

In this and other conversations Pete is telling us three different kinds of things at the same time. First, he is telling us that he resents social scientists looking at him as if he were some sort of bug to be dissected under a microscope, a strongly held feeling in Hunter's Point. Further, his concept of "poor," unlike that of most middle-class whites, is not merely an economic one. To him, being poor is equated with being "stupid," backward, and unable to "tell where it's at." These are the very qualities Pete is trying to deny in himself and hates most to have attributed to himself or his peers.

The third thing that he's telling us is that degrees of sharpness, education, and status are reflected in one's clothing styles and other aspects of overt and obvious consumption. A style of life which includes "sharp" clothes is clearly a superior one. If Pete can believe that such things as his clothing styles are at least as sharp as those of most whites, he can deny the status differences between whites and blacks. In fact, this attitude permits a charade of actual status hierarchies for blacks vis-à-vis whites by the manipulation of predetermined outward signs such as "cool threads" (fashionable clothes). In addition to being one of the expressive aspects of life in Hunter's Point, the continual concern with clothing permits a form of competition for "coolness" of dress (thus offering another nonviolent aggressive outlet) and the development of local "soul styles."

Black "soul styles" not only serve as expressive aspects of individual personality, but permit intragroup competition and comparisons; perhaps most importantly, they act as pseudo-status heighteners in their relationships with whites. Whites "ain't cool," they "can't even throw on good threads," they "dance like drunken dogs." Such obvious different food items as barbecued pork ribs, chitlins, and hominy grits, through their function as particular "black" styles, are made into differences of pride. There is a strong, persistent lack of communication of such information to whites, though some blacks in Hunter's Point are more willing to hint at the existence of these particular soul styles since certain whites now seem to covet them.[3]

Thus, Pete, in his revealing response, was not using the word *poor* in a completely idiosyncratic fashion. The denial of poverty and of status inferiority vis-à-vis whites is an important aspect of the behavior of black youths in Hunter's Point. (Denial, as I have suggested above and elsewhere, is a common form of psychic defense in this community.) Nonetheless, good clothes cost money, and no matter how much a person lies to himself about his financial condition, he must have money to buy clothes.

This is the genesis of the clothes lending which is so much a part of the young men's culture in Hunter's Point. Individuals continuously lend "sharp" clothing to one another. Since this tends to dilute ownership, problems inevitably arise. There is a general pretense, aided and abetted by all, that what a man is wearing is his own; yet any time a dispute breaks out between two persons who are part of such an informal arrangement, one of the strongest "putdowns" is to point out that a man really does not own what he is wearing. As might be expected, violence often erupts over either ownership or use of a particular article of clothing, the length of loan of clothing, or the condition of the returned clothing.

These values concerning clothing also affect black-white relationships in Hunter's Point — indirectly through the addition of one more covert culture item, but directly through the hope that whites will misperceive the situation and the fear that they will not. Without making any conscious effort to do so, the denial of reality is fostered by hiding this widespread pattern from whites under the assumption that it is a shameful aspect of poverty, backwardness, and general stupidity.

Interestingly, the denial of poverty and of the general cultural backwardness assumed to be associated with it is so strong here that the only person who lives in Hunter's Point that I ever heard mention poverty as a condition of her existence, aside from one woman who remarked that being poor makes you a victim of circumstances, was the white wife of a white minister who lives in Hunter's Point and serves a congregation there. Her reference to herself as one of the "poor," however, was primarily a political attitude, and related to her militant political attitude toward the "white power structure." Militant political expressions about the need for solidarity among the "poor" and "underprivileged" in Hunter's Point are rarely, if ever, made by residents with reference to themselves. Their life view is usually a hopeful if often unrealistic desire to escape from, not identify with, the poverty of Hunter's Point.

Even when expressing sentiments which are almost openly self-hating, most of the residents of the area still keep hidden their beliefs about the relationship of their own poverty to their (supposed) stupidity. Even such minor aspects of Hunter's Point life such as "CP time" ("colored people's time"), which is a common joking reference to the tendency of Hunter's Point residents to be late wherever they go, is carefully hidden from whites because of its implications of backwardness.

Lipset and Bendix (1959) contend that impoverished people tend to turn to otherworldly religions instead of effective political action as a solution to their problems. If the present is unchangeable and unpleasant, it is easier to postulate a future in which present roles will be reversed.

This, in effect, permits a denial of present reality — since it is transient — in favor of an eternity of bliss. In Hunter's Point, in addition to otherworldly religions, which in fact are not as extensive as they have been reported to be in the South, there are other forms of denial of reality. Such forms of denial act in terms of personal ego defenses against an unbearable present reality. In addition, denial can be a form of "hiding" the realities of their own life, i.e., their self-perceived backwardness, which they feel the dominant culture despises. These devices serve the same function as otherworldly religions in Hunter's Point in that they reverse the reality and express a belief in the dominance of the underdog.

For example, Hunter's Point residents will often state how "bad" some "niggers" are. This is not, as might be expected from what I have said before, an expression of self-hate. It is, rather, a denial of reality. "Bad" in this context may be taken to mean "dangerous," clearly a higher status position than "stupid." The assumption is that "bad niggers" are dangerous to "the man" (any white man). The facts, of course, belie this. Hunter's Pointers have very little in the way of a record of aggression against whites. "Bad" (and therefore dangerous) "niggers" are in fact seldom dangerous to whites. Aggression in Hunter's Point is almost always directed against other blacks and fantasized against whites, a phenomenon most obviously true in "the riot" (see Chapter 10). In fact, the high valuation of aggression is hardly ever borne out in interaction with whites, with whom a passive and acceptant stance is taken. This is so even in the face of the massive changes which have come about in the United States in white-black relations in the last few years.

However, the myth of black "dangerousness" is as carefully cultivated in Hunter's Point as it is among the most rabid white racists. Elaborate legends are created about individual Hunter's Pointers who are said to have "killed a dozen whites" or to have "shot three cops." All throughout the Bay Area, in fact, Hunter's Point youth have the reputation for being "badasses." This is a reputation assiduously sought, attributable, in part, to the kinds of personal needs I have described above. In addition to providing individual boys and young men with feelings of power which they cannot derive from other sources, such an image provides a kind of general communal black feeling of superiority vis-à-vis whites. Though such a feeling is based on very little in reality, it acts as a vitally important reality-substitute where the real stuff of equality with whites (let alone superiority over them) is totally lacking.

144

Hunter's Point youth especially hang onto the belief in their danger-ousness to the white community, not as a potential, but as an accom-plished fact. This permits them feelings of power over whites and allows for fantasized aggression against whites with none of the dangerous con-sequences of actual confrontation. Some young men in Hunter's Point have begun, in fact, to try to integrate this defensive (and imaginary) aggressiveness into a political context as well. This would seem to be the genesis of the signs which in the last few months of 1967 blossomed out all over Hunter's Point — painted on walls with spraypaint cans and splashed onto sidewalks and on fences — reading "Black Power."

"Black Power" as a slogan, however, serves the same function in Hun-ter's Point as most of the other fantasized aggressions of its inhabitants. It is a stirring slogan, it sounds militant, and it can make a black person appear dangerous to whites. In terms of the actions flowing from it, its content not only is nonexistent in Hunter's Point, but in fact may actu-ally be negative. Whereas "Black Power" is used here as a slogan that permits the sloganeer to sound meaningful, it has led to no kind of political, social, or economic organization, formal or informal, which might in any way implement the ascension of Hunter's Point residents to power.

On the other hand, "Black Power" may be a great deal more than a shibboleth. It may well be that in some still not fully articulated way it is a recognition of the basic realities and needs of Hunter's Point blacks (and by extension of other black Americans as well). If the structural factors of segregation and discrimination and the vicious circle these factors create in league with the family structure and socialization prac-tices in Hunter's Point mean that few individuals can hope to "leak" into the dominant culture, then perhaps it is necessary for the group as a whole to develop power. In other words, if individual upward mobility is nearly impossible for Hunter's Point blacks, then the cry "Black Power" and its implied separatism and group movement is perhaps becoming realistically perceived as the only possible human alternative commensurate with human dignity. It is thus not surprising that when consciously articulated by Hunter's Pointers, the content of "Black Power" is essentially separatist.

There are, therefore, very destructive aspects to the intertwining of the reality-denial mechanism and the value system of the Hunter's Pointer. Basic values are essentially those that use denial as their psychic component. Placed in a position of minimal power by the weight of the dominant community's prejudice, and victimized by both structural and familial attacks on his personal self-esteem, the Hunter's Pointer retreats to denial of this impossible situation. But that very defense which permits him to manipulate his environment in fantasy makes it almost impossible for him to manipulate it in reality. The net result is a continual decrease in self-esteem.

SELF-PERCEPTION

If the particular lack of self-assurance and self-esteem which characterizes the black male can be seen in his relationships to white authority and the white community at large, an even deeper and more pervasive self-hate and self-denigration is felt within the black community in the sensitive and all-pervasive area of skin color. Both the self and others are constantly subjected to unflattering comparisons on the basis of skin color and hair texture, as well as what are seen as other "nigger" habits of food, gestures, and styles of life. This is so even though there is at the same time some overt positive valuation of many of these traits. Such self-denigrative attitudes persist even in the face of increased "nationalism" on the part of militant Afro-American groups and "Muslims" (the Nation of Islam, usually referred to in the white press as Black Muslims). But such groups had at this time (1967) little influence in Hunter's Point. No Afro-American group had its headquarters there and the well-dressed and soft-spoken Muslims were never seen proselytizing in the neighborhood.

On the other hand, the internal glorification of "soul" and "soul styles" which proposes in its essentials that negroid physical characteristics — "kinky" hair, everted lips, broadened nose, darkened skin color, and so on — are inherently good is in continual clash with the covertly and often even overtly expressed belief that all of these and other negroid cultural and physical characteristics are inherently inferior.

Whites are seen as powerful, wealthy, and ubiquitous. They symbolize the hated oppressor, but because of the higher standard of living and power associated with white skin, and because of identification with the aggressor, they are also seen invariably as *the* standard of emulation.[4] Whites, therefore, serve as a status criteria for all good things. This hated and feared skin color is also the admired standard of personal beauty in Hunter's Point. Such an admiration is, of course, reinforced a thousand times a day by mass media, advertisements, art reproductions, popular amusements, and the glances of strangers and friends, as well as the very fact of the content of the English language: "black" applies to all things bad, evil, dirty, tainted, sick, and unlucky, and by extension to everything disgusting, lowly, lazy and unintelligent; whereas "white" applies to everything good, pure, wholesome, healthy, beautiful, and inherently positive. Brody (1963) notes this to be a common point of view in black communities; Hunter's Point is no exception.

No matter how much defensive derision is directed toward whites for their supposed lesser ability to dance, enjoy sex, or understand life, no one is ever really fooled. No matter how much effort is expended in saying that whites are useless, stupid, ugly, untrustworthy, and square (all of which are common, openly stated attitudes about whites in Hunter's Point), the reality of the behavior of the Hunter's Point black overwhelms the protest. Negroid features are continually modified by conscious effort in the direction of the "white" norm. The shelves of nearby drugstores are jammed with skin lighteners and hair straighteners. Most Hunter's Point males spend much time and effort and not a little of their limited financial resources to get a "conk" every month or two.

The "conk job" (as of 1966-1967) is one of the most familiar sights in Hunter's Point. A "conk" is a hair-straightening process involving the use of lye to remove the "body" from the hair, making it less stiff and curly and more pliable, more like the texture of whites' hair — i.e., "good hair." "Good hair" is that which has little or no curl to it, "bad" hair is that which has the more typical negroid curly or cornrow form.

This attitude is even more pronounced in women. Women almost universally "burn" their hair, a process usually involving some degree of physical discomfort because of the home use of the lye-containing "process compounds" — a pronounced burning sensation occurs if the lye is left on long enough to do a thorough job. Hunter's Point women also use skin lighteners. The fact that the young white woman is a desired sexual companion for Hunter's Point males (to have a white girl friend or to be a pimp for white girls is a mark of very high status) is deeply resented by Hunter's Point women. (See the section on education in this chapter.) Regardless of overt protestations to the contrary, ideas about the beauty of black as a color and associated negroid cultural phenomena have not taken much of a hold in the minds of the inhabitants of Hunter's Point.

That the concept of the sexual beauty of "whiteness," especially in

147

women, is a key item in understanding Hunter's Point attitudes is easily revealed by casual conversations that can be overheard anywhere at almost any time of day. From infancy through adulthood this attitude, reinforced by the mass media, is reiterated again and again. Having extremely dark ("black") skin often makes one somewhat of a pariah among other Hunter's Point blacks. Black mothers in Hunter's Point often humiliate a child by direct reference to his skin color, and this is especially pronounced if the child's skin color is one of the unacceptably dark shades. "Get your black ass out of here, you get on my nerves." Or: "Listen, black boy, you don't know shit. I'll whop you, you keep talkin' back to me."

Mothers often address such phrases more frequently to their darker children, not too subtly implying the wish that they were lighter. In most families it is obvious that maternal love is handed out in far greater quantity to, and that maternal appreciation is deeper for, the lighter-skinned offspring. Yet the denigration need not take the form of expressing overt dislike of black skin. Often mothers when punishing a child will say, "I'll whop that black off your ass, boy," or the children may indicate that the darker one's skin is, the "worse" it is for you. Further, sibling fights are often based on skin color. Children are quick to use skin color differential as a sore spot to hurt their siblings if they are darker.

Perhaps the most revealing aspect of interactions which have to do with one person denigrating another's skin color is that there are never any defenses offered that such darker skin is of equal value. Direct physical aggression, counterattacks in another direction, or some form of "you're not so light yourself" make up the bulk of responses to attacks on one's skin color. I have never seen, and doubt the commonness of, a response suggesting black is as good as any other skin color.

Marriage is seen by many as an opportunity to ally oneself with someone lighter. The ideal marital partner is very light-skinned. While some blacks suggest that they want to marry light-skinned blacks because "opposites attract," this does not seem to be the real reason. Often when talking with young boys or men I would point to a group of girls and ask which one was the most attractive. Invariably, the lightest-skinned girl was picked.

Finally, even the way in which references to physical beauty and skin color are combined in normal speech indicates this definite preference. Physically unprepossessing people are "black *and* ugly." Attractive

148

dark-skinned people are termed "dark *but* cute." Light-skinned individuals who are not attractive are called "light *but* ugly." It is almost impossible to be considered handsome *and* dark or light *and* ugly in the normal course of events.

Blacks in Hunter's Point, then, have accepted the definition of "black is bad," and the self-image of a dark-skinned black is not a very positive one. He has come to believe, to some degree, all the derogatory things said about him and his skin color. There is some reason to believe that most of the Hunter's Point residents accept negative racial stereotypes about blacks at least as easily and perhaps more so than some middle-class whites. It is one thing to suggest condescendingly from the security of white middle-class life that there is no evidence for the belief that black skin and intellectual inferiority are at all causally correlated. But it is another matter to have that black skin and to have to face what seems to be, to the unsophisticated viewer, the overwhelming evidence of one's own inferiority.

Naturally, the effect of this goes far beyond the immediate responses of the affected individuals. Local whites also recognize this preference for lighter-skinned sexual partners among Hunter's Point blacks and interpret it as overt sexual aggressiveness of black males against their women. (Interestingly, no white males ever expressed either fear of being seduced by black women or, indeed, objections to such possible sexual aggressions toward them.) White females, on the other hand, often expressed fears that their men visited "nigger" women "'cause they're all loose." The stereotype of the sexual prowess of blacks continually acts as an irritant in the white community. On the other hand, expressed belief in black sexual superiority itself makes up an important part of the defense system of Hunter's Point blacks.

There are, in Hunter's Point and the surrounding white communities, a series of stereotypes about black male hypersexuality and black female hyperattractiveness[5] (some of which I have discussed above). Hunter's Point residents simultaneously value the white norm of beauty as the highest possible and make overt statements about the greater sexual excitability of black females and their joyful participation in sex activities. These apparently inconsistent values coexist without the apparent cognitive dissonance which Festinger (1962) describes. One of the techniques used here to resolve such a dilemma is the compartmentalization of contradictory ideas. Still, the "compartments" apparently leak.

Black females seldom formally date whites. Some black women in

149

Hunter's Point have had sexual relations with whites, usually through some form of prostitution, but since certain information about women was not possible to get, no generalizations will be attempted here. Black males, on the other hand, claimed a much higher level of sexual contact with white females. Whether most of these claims — usually in the form of boasting — represent fantasy or fact is irrelevant to this study. What is important is that such claims reflect a pattern of desires indicating the high value placed on achieving sexual congress with white women.

In the light of the particular social-structural and family-structural facts of life of the black family in Hunter's Point, the sexual values concerning skin color and contact with whites may be described as having at least two dominant causes. First, the particular values of the entire society, which in part have been accepted by blacks as right and proper, stress the value of light hair and skin in female sexual partners. Simply because this is a dominant value everywhere in the United States society, it is also easily accepted in Hunter's Point. Additionally, sexual activity, which as I have indicated is viewed in Hunter's Point as involving aggression rather than love, is perhaps the one way in which black males can "avenge" themselves on white males for their deprivation and denigration. If one sees sex as aggression, then to "steal" white women is the height of revenge. This also obviously reinforces the myth of black hypersexuality.

Hypersexuality of blacks is a self-belief fostered in feelings of inadequacy and in the recognition that this is an area where white Americans are "hung up." Not sharing in the same degree the Puritan ethic which equates sexuality with sin, Hunter's Pointers are free to pursue this particular form of instinctual gratification more openly than middle-class whites have traditionally been able to do. This is especially true in comparison with the lower-middle-class white community surrounding Hunter's Point. Members of this community, continually aware of their own ambivalent attitudes toward sexuality, cannot help but be aware of this greater sexual freedom among Hunter's Point blacks.

"They're just like animals there."

"All they do is fuck."

"Man, I heard that them niggers got cocks a foot long."

"They say a woman gets fucked by one of them black bastards and she's ruined for white men from then on, she's got to have that black meat."

Fear of this alleged hypersexuality, combined with fears of sexual inadequacy on the part of white males and sexual curiosity on the part of white females which are vociferously denied but poorly disguised —

"Do them niggers really do it better than whites? — of course, I don't really care, I'm not interested, but I heard they do."

— lead to explosive attitudes toward blacks in general. In San Francisco, as elsewhere, the real question and fear behind all the excuses for dislike is still, "Would you want your sister to marry one?" Or: "How'd you like some big black buck to do it to your wife, huh?"

This total acceptance by a substantial part of the white community of the concept of black hypersexuality operates in feedback fashion to confirm blacks in their belief that it is true. Any area in which blacks display, or are thought to display, greater competence than whites is eagerly grasped as a support for otherwise poorly organized ego defenses against feelings of inadequacy. Since sexuality is so central an area in human activity, and since these misperceptions and explosive desires and denials continue to feed back and forth between the black and white communities, these shared perceptions (or misperceptions) and values operate to increase social distance and fear between the two groups.

Hunter's Point blacks, then, have an extremely difficult time developing a positive self-perception. The overwhelming power and dominance of the white community and its negative stereotyping of blacks takes an invariable toll. In spite of themselves, Hunter's Pointers have come to accept "white" values about skin color and have turned paranoid white fears about black sexual aggressiveness into a defensive positive value. The net result is a complex feedback in which both groups continue to view each other and themselves through the stereotypic vision that white racial prejudice has created.

EDUCATION AND ECONOMICS

The values and attitudes I have described for Hunter's Point are extremely important in determining how much formal education Hunter's Point youths attain and what are their life chances (not just in employment, but also in other crucial areas of life). In a subtler but definite way the quality of education and the kinds of work available to Hunter's

Pointers provide an almost perfect form of feedback into the value system.

I have suggested above that youth socialization follows in reasonable conformity with the basic matrifocal family pattern. Values of defensive aggression and violence give way in the late teens to an emotional distancing termed "coolness." Male attitudes toward women stress manipulation, minimal emotional involvement, and little or no responsibility. Women, we have noted, characteristically develop attitudes of manipulation toward and denigration of males. As we have seen, adult male attitudes of deference to women — acknowledging their power while harboring an aggressive dislike for them because of the threat they pose to their masculinity — are also reflected in the pattern of youth attitudes.

In addition to these attitudes regarding people, Hunter's Pointers have a general distrust of the value of hard work, based at least partly on real-life experiences and a present-time orientation which seems to mitigate against any strong "need to achieve." *Need achievement* is defined by McClelland (1953, 1961) as a set of attitudes which center around internalizing a work ethic, striving against internal norms, and working toward achievable but difficult tasks for the feeling of self-accomplishment that follows the achievement. People who have a high "need to achieve" tend to want continuous information on how they are doing.

Regardless of McClelland's concepts concerning the relationship between need achievement and economic development, it seems clear that some form of need achievement has characterized the American middle class in the past and that need achievement can very easily begin in school. Studying is best done by internalizing positive attitudes toward it; it is quite difficult to force someone effectively to study who is not or cannot become internally motivated. Good students tend to work best toward achieving difficult but feasible ends, and they generally use grades to tell them how well they are doing.

Such need for achievement is very limited in Hunter's Point for both structural and subcultural reasons. There is minimal involvement with intellectual pursuits since parents have not been socialized in that manner and therefore do not so socialize their children. Lip service is paid to education as an idea, though education is not phrased in terms of intellectual achievement as an end but as an instrumental activity which will lead to increased opportunities for wealth. What precise mechanisms will transmit education into income are only vaguely, if at all, considered. Thus, an inadequate comprehension of what is involved in education and an inability to achieve an education prevent the Hunter's

Pointer from attaining the normal middle-class fruits of material welfare available through education.

The reasons for this state of affairs seem clear enough. First of all, the educational system to which the Hunter's Point child is exposed is geared toward minimal achievement from the beginning. Besides being predisposed to see schooling as instrumental activity, Hunter's Pointers tend further to assume that merely "putting in time" is sufficient to "get an education." Studying as a technique toward mastery and comprehension is poorly understood.

Teachers in the local grammar schools typically see their charges as mentally inadequate at worst and inadequately motivated at best. Teachers expect a lower standard of achievement than they would be prepared to accept in white middle-class schools and rarely attempt to aim for a higher one. Candid reactions of grammar school teachers in Hunter's Point reveal that they see their job as primarily custodial. Until quite recently, it was considered "cruel" to attempt to inculcate aspirations for achievement in black youths who could not help but be frustrated by the facts of life of the discriminatory society into which they had to move. "Proper" behavior and neatness of penmanship were considered achievements as significant as a competent grasp of American history, mathematics, or reading with comprehension. It seems clear that such teachers' attitudes affect the performance of pupils (Rosenthal and Jacobson, 1968) even when those attitudes are subtle — and teacher derogation of Hunter's Point pupils is seldom subtle.

Complementarily, many parents, having little against which to gauge such schooling, raise few or no objections to an essentially custodial curriculum. The assumptions of black parents in Hunter's Point regarding the need simply to "put in time" and their limited concern over truancy tend to reinforce a minimal achievement motivation among their children.

Such inadequately trained children reach high school already far "behind" their white contemporaries. The practice of shunting black youths — and especially those from Hunter's Point (who are seen by high school teachers as the most backward of students) — into manual training and home economics courses in high school completes the cycle of inadequate precollege training. High school competition with whites almost always shows the Hunter's Point youth to intellectual disadvantage and thus discourages him or her from attempting future achievement.

153

Very little of the content of academic courses is actually understood by Hunter's Point youths, and much of what is, is misperceived. At least in part, this seems to reflect a very low level of literacy. It is very difficult for the Hunter's Point youth to see the relevance in his life of that which he cannot read with comprehension. Much of what he is taught simply does not touch him. The horizons of the Hunter's Point youth are not global (and realistically so). Very often, for example, mathematical operations – such as the extraction of square roots – may be mechanically performed while their meaning and application remain totally mysterious.

The attitudes responsible for such behavior do not, of course, exist in a vacuum. Typically much more experienced sexually than his or her white counterpart, the Hunter's Point youth finds that high school offers an unusual opportunity for finding new sexual conquests. For black males, this often involves a large degree of curiosity about and desire for white females.[6] Moreover, establishing dominance patterns within new social groupings through fighting and verbal dueling takes up much of their time. Black youths find little reward or virtue in strictly intellectual achievement, since they are already involved in all the means of achieving status which they can realistically perceive and the meaning of a status derived through academic achievement is not clear. Apparently because of the gross irrelevance of their education, there is also by this age a contempt for the educational process itself. Such contempt is extended to professional educators, and social scientists who are considered essentially ignorant of the "real facts of life," although they practice a profitable "hustle." For example, of thirty high-school-age Hunter's Point youths who were queried about the Moynihan report,[7] none had read it. All had heard of it, or claimed to have. All but five had negative opinions about it, based on a belief that it "put down" blacks. That sociologists, anthropologists, or psychologists might actually have tools which could explain part of the world in which they lived to them was not only disbelieved, it was not even understood.

High school teachers respond to black Hunter's Point youths' lack of interest in subject matter by giving them little personal attention. Such custodial-care situations breed antagonism between teachers and students, with the result that students have remarkably unanimous opinions regarding the meaning of high school education and its possible effects.

154

"Man, this ain't nothin' but a goddamn jail."

"They just keepin' us off the streets, man, that's all."

"You can tell by how they look they hate it when you talk to a white girl."

"You know what I'm gonna do when I get out of here? I'm gonna join the fuckin' army."

"Sheeit, man, I ain't learned nothin' gonna get me no job here. Man, we workin' on an old Chevy in the shop — ain't even got an automatic transmission. Sheeit, everything's got an automatic transmission."

"I like it, man. I like the dances. They are somethin' else."

Teachers' sentiments echo these:

"We're only keeping them here as long as we can. God knows it's not very long. They drop out like flies when they're sixteen. Nothing they learn here will do them any good anyway — they'll never go to college — they couldn't really get in *here* if you're honest about it. I pass kids here who literally cannot spell at the third-grade level."

"It's a social situation for them. To the degree that the social situation is pleasant, we have no trouble. When we get tough, they get tough. I've been beaten once. I'll never try to discipline seriously again."

"Possibilities for achievement — that's a cruel joke. They have nothing when they get here and they have nothing when they leave. I don't even really know how to tell which ones of them would truly benefit from intensive individual tutorials."

Thus, high schools, by shunting Hunter's Point blacks away from academic courses for which they are ill prepared in the first place, continue the vicious circle by educating day laborers whose saleable skills are obsolescent even before they graduate. While this pattern of education — or, more accurately, noneducation — is going on, black youths and their parents are being exposed to the current upsurge of public statements about the structural position of blacks in American society. Such information is interpreted in Hunter's Point as meaning: "Whites

155

have been and are keeping blacks down systematically by depriving them of the vote, money, jobs, political power, and status. This should stop. Blacks should be allowed to be the economic, social, and political equals of whites. This means whites, through the government, should give us good educations and jobs and political power."

Unfortunately, black Hunter's Point youths complicate their own self-denigration by adopting an attitude that suggests no type of achievement motivation is either needed or valuable. The community obviously owes them jobs and educations. They need only demand strongly enough. Often this acts to prevent just that kind of personal involvement in study which would make education meaningful.

Those few Hunter's Point blacks who go to college find the same problems there. Often they are poorly prepared. Moreover, an interview with three Hunter's Point college students (students at San Francisco City College) revealed that all felt there was nothing reprehensible in cheating, and all indicated they felt they received low grades because of racial discrimination.

The minimal amount of achievement orientation[8] is reflected, for example, in 1963 San Francisco Board of Education figures showing approximately a cumulative 40 percent dropout rate for all the grade levels in school from this area (including the Bayview district). The median educational level in the Hunter's Point area itself in 1960 was 9.4 years (U.S. census). This has not been improving. The dropout rate is increasing, according to local school officials, and though exact figures are hard to come by, private estimates from local officials indicate a total 25 percent dropout rate by the eighth grade.[9] Truancy is so rampant that enforcement of truancy laws in Hunter's Point tends to be completely arbitrary, according to local social workers and Youth Opportunity Center personnel. (Here, also, public school officials and teachers disagree as to the level of truancy.)

Girls are expected to stay in school longer than boys, perhaps because they are more amenable to the discipline. Those who do not get pregnant tend to finish high school, thus continuing their superior competitive position vis-à-vis black males for jobs. Boys are expected to play in the summer, girls to work. Thus, teenage socialization both inside and outside the school furthers the pattern of male irresponsibility and female responsibility.

The general pattern of attitudes about education is part of the broader world view which stresses a present-time orientation[10] (Michel,

1961; Smith and Abramson, 1962; and Radin and Kamii, 1965, all indicate this general pattern for black Americans), high consumption, low savings, and a propensity not to postpone pleasures. While in part a response to poverty, this world view is also a response in part to white values as expressed through mass media. "Distinction" and "class" are what you buy when you buy clothes to wear, a car to drive, and food to eat. Achievement orientations do not flourish in such surroundings.

However, a curious contradiction arises regarding the "unique" world view and value systems of Hunter's Point when they are contrasted with the white-dominated world. Although the "official" ethic of the dominant majority in the United States has long been considered to be the highly responsible, almost obsessive, and puritanical "hard work" ethos, Riesman et al. (1953) have noted a shift in this orientation. There is no reason to believe that this shift (which they suggest is in the direction of "other-directed" and consumer values) has been reversed in recent years, and there is at least impressionistic evidence that it has continued to increase. This new value orientation, as Riesman notes, stresses a present-time orientation, the futility of postponing pleasure, and the uselessness of hard work — if the work is not *inherently* enjoyable and rewarding in its own right. Clothing once considered undignifiedly colorful and styles once thought of as bizarre due to their unusual expressive content are increasingly more acceptable if the individual wearing them finds them personally satisfying. (We are not attempting, of course, any rigorous statement about these value shifts, but they seem self-evident enough merely to need remarking upon.)

This shift in values for whites is curiously similar in content, in large measure, to the world view and at least the overtly expressed values of the inhabitants of Hunter's Point. Add to this only an increasing openness about sex and a (possibly defensive) stress on honesty (similar to "telling it like it is," and in some cases with the same kind of hidden aggressiveness), and this all sounds more and more similar, at least superficially, to the ethos of the black Hunter's Point youth.

Why is it, then, that the black Hunter's Point youth cannot enter this economy and social order on any but the lowest levels? Clearly, there is no great discrepancy between his overt values about consumption and the consumption-oriented desires of a highly productive economy.[11] It seems possible that the most important levels of explanation lie in the differences in educational attainments between the Hunter's Point youth and the average white middle-class American. Clearly,

157

one of the surest and, except for the exceptional individual, perhaps the only way of getting onto the "economic escalator" is through higher education. But there are clear structural and personal reasons, some of which we have already discussed, why Hunter's Point blacks fail to gain much in the way of education.

Instead of coming from a family where literacy is taken for granted and where high levels of educational attainment are expected as a matter of course, the Hunter's Point youth often comes from a family where literacy is barely functional and clearly at inadequate levels for scholarly activity. Literacy is not merely a skill, but a group of habits relating to the use of words, a familiarity with all types of literature, and a continual exposure to books, magazines, etc. and the ideas contained in them. No such habits and expectations exist in Hunter's Point.

Further, instead of coming from a family where the concrete results of education are clear, where the mechanisms which act to create individual wealth out of knowledge — through professional training, for example — are abundantly evident, and where all the familial support and expectations channel the individual in the direction of higher education, the Hunter's Point youth comes from a family which contains in it no such motivations. Not only is it difficult for the Hunter's Point youth to see, through example, what practical ends can result from education, but his family doesn't understand, nor is it able to make clear to him, that this is a major road to economic viability.

Moreover, instead of coming from a family which assumes scholarly failure to be the fault of the child but believes that corrective discipline can overcome such faults, the Hunter's Point youth often comes from a family which, when it does not expect failure as a matter of course, is beginning to assume that such failures are primarily the result of racial prejudice.[12] Under such conditions, the family (more accurately, the mother) usually takes no personal corrective action aside from lending the failing child verbal and emotional support, usually in the form of statements about the innate prejudice of teachers and the impossibility of beating the system.

Finally, if such a family background were not enough to discourage educational achievement motivation, the overt and covert attitudes of his predominantly white teachers adds the final necessary dimension to failure. Expecting inadequacy from black Hunter's Point children, teachers foster that very inadequacy and help create self-fulfilling prophecies.

158

White middle-class American life sets a child on an "up" escalator at an early age, in that it supplies him with all the equipment and most of the motivation to do well in school, or at least to stay in school. The middle-class child can get off the escalator at any level he chooses, but rarely does he do so at a level which dooms him to involuntary poverty. Usually no one in the Hunter's Point family understands this escalator's ramifications (or, knowing of its existence, understands even how to get onto it). It is unnecessary to restate in detail what so many studies have already determined (such as DeVos and Hippler, 1968) — that there is no apparent difference in average innate intellectual ability among the races. There is little doubt, though — and this is an almost entirely different matter — that certain types of family structures and value orientations make academic achievement almost impossible.

The concomitant world view of the people in Hunter's Point tends to be mildly pessimistic and resigned. Outside factors are characteristically attributed as causes of the particular life situation they find themselves in. The unemployed and others on welfare feel themselves to be victims of situations over which they have no control. Poverty is seen as an endemic effect of poverty. That is, a common point of view in Hunter's Point is that entering the job market as a poor person ensures a lack of advancement and that such an entrance guarantees continued poverty.

It's not easy to characterize the general attitude toward welfare and unemployment insurance without having recourse to terms which have negative emotional connotations. It appears that most welfare recipients and unemployed persons in Hunter's Point have strong dependency needs which are exacerbated by a situation in which they must make a virtue of necessity. As we shall see in the account of the sit-in in the Youth Opportunity Center (Chapter 9), the complaint concluded with a demand for jobs. Yet the ability to hold a full-time job (eight hours a day, five days a week, fifty weeks a year) is completely out of the range of experience of most of those who demanded work. Little or nothing in the subculture of Hunter's Point fosters a point of view which values hard work for a productive lifetime to be followed by retirement. A combination of reality orientation and lack of achievement values does not permit the development of attitudes toward work common among middle-class Americans. Only too common is the pattern of the elderly black man who has worked hard all his life for very little only to be "dumped" after his productive years, usually on inadequate pensions (if any) or the dubious economic sufficiency of Social Security.

159

To be able to "make it" while avoiding the "work game" is a strong, pervasive, and consistent goal in Hunter's Point. The characteristically infantile attitudes which have been demanded of blacks by whites, and which become psychic defenses for oppressed groups (Bettleheim and Janowitz, 1964), also find their fruition in "welfare culture." Welfare culture develops in families who, for two generations or more, have been entirely supported by public assistance payments in the absence of a fruitfully employed male parent. One of its dominant aspects is a dependency on welfare payments as a way of life.[13] There is security in welfare (more security than many black males can ever attain through employment), and it creates a situation in which males believe they need not work if they so choose. Refusal to work permits males to live off females (as indeed they are accustomed to doing), and also permits this supposedly degrading situation to be seen as "taking advantage of white society."

Both the dependency needs and aggressive (but passive) attitudes of Hunter's Pointers toward the white community, in conjunction with a reality orientation toward the extreme difficulties for black males to get jobs which are good paying and not degrading, are thus satisfied through living off welfare. The general lack of education and lack of orientation toward education can be, and are, seen by Hunter's Point adults as due to circumstances of life over which they have no control. The general attitude is to "roll with the punches" and to take it as easy as possible.

As might be expected, this set of values fits well with the present-time orientation mentioned earlier. The present is seen as the only significant time of life, and the past is usually either too bleak to consider or remembered, if at all, in idealized, thoroughly unrealistic terms. The future, which is either too hazy or too potentially discouraging to consider realistically, is dismissed as irrelevant to the present or dreamed of in grandiose terms. Men discuss the great jobs they will have, the "big money" they will make, and the fine consumer goods they will acquire. However, it is my impression that they seldom believe it themselves.

The present-time orientation lends itself to a general disregard for the value of time as well. Attitudes meaningful to certain segments of middle-class life as expressed in such adages as "time is money" have little meaning in Hunter's Point. CP time is observed here — CP time ("colored peoples' time") being a way of describing a general tendency to be late for everything, as I have noted above.

"We'll start at two o'clock."
"Is that CP time?"

. . . implying the event could not possibly get started before three o'clock.

Easily associated with such an orientation, though it has other roots as well, is the high valuation placed on consumption as opposed to saving. Consumer goods are a prime value in Hunter's Point. This is especially true of furniture, clothing, and, to a much lesser extent, automobiles. Furniture is often of the very best, but just as often is second-rate (though purchased at a high price). A representative incident occurred when I was shown a living room couch which was proudly described as having cost $750. Subsequent checking showed that it had, indeed, cost $750, but $300 of that price represented interest on a time-payment plan and the couch usually sold for $250, not the $450 she paid for it.

Price tags are an important status consideration, and the price of a costly object is flaunted even though – or perhaps even because – it may be far out of proportion to the purchaser's income. As might be expected, Hunter's Point residents are often the victims of repossession. Unscrupulous local merchants quite often sell goods of inferior quality at exhorbitant prices and on time, then quickly repossess when the beguiled purchasers are unable to meet payments. A single piece of merchandise, if it is important enough (e.g., a color TV), may be sold, repossessed, and resold a half-dozen times by the avaricious seller.

Another aspect of the present-time orientation is the fact that few families buy groceries or similar consumer supplies in large amounts, but seem constantly to be buying small amounts of things from day to day. Inevitably, this leads to waste and inefficient spending. This pattern of immediate gratification and impulse spending furthers the inefficent allocation of already inadequate resources.

The particular patterns of consumption tend to indicate at least two ontogenetic factors. First of all, this is a pattern common to lower-class groups in the United States regardless of racial character. The feeling that the future is hopeless, that one has been used and abused by society and had best get what one can as quickly as possible, has at least some reality orientation to it. On the other hand, it might be noted that this is also a pattern easily predictable from the child-rearing patterns and family structure of the area. As McClelland (1961) and others have

161

pointed out, achievement motivation of the quasi-Protestant-ethic type demands a kind of maternal and paternal behavior and role models virtually nonexistent in Hunter's Point. According to McClelland, achievement motivation which might be expected to lead to certain patterns of postponement of gratification, hard work, capital investment (say, for personal education), and the like demands a father who provides a non-authoritarian, secure, male role model and, more importantly, a mother who encourages independence and rewards each sign of achievement with love, showing disapproval only when achievement is not accomplished. Such parental models do not exist in Hunter's Point, and if they did would be considered out of place.

Yet another factor is important here: once more, the all-pervasive influence of white middle-class culture and values. Such instant communication media as radio and television as well as the inherent communication value of the simple sight and sound of the vast consumer complex of San Francisco continually suggest to the resident of Hunter's Point that his personal worth is determined by his level of consumption. There is little reason to expect the resident of Hunter's Point to be any more immune to this message than the rest of the inhabitants of the United States. Further, the changed and changing value of white middle-class America itself is moving in the direction of present-time orientation and quickly toward consumption rather than productive values. This is no inherent disadvantage to the middle-class youth who already has or is getting the kind of education which will permit him to consume at a high level because of his income (which income, of course, is largely due to his higher education). It is not even terribly important that he have any achieving values at all. The social system has largely been programmed to send him through, as we have noted. The middle-class youth's parents, having an adequate income and certain expectations as a result of their structural position in society, simply assume their children will also receive an education. By and large, such an assumption is communicated to the child, who in many cases gets an education simply as his filial duty in the normal course of events.

Thus, while many generations of strivers and achievers have prepared the way for present-day white middle-class youth to enter the economy on a high income level through no particular effort, even if they do not really have strong achievement values, Hunter's Point youth face an entirely different problem. While values of the larger society may be moving toward theirs, blacks still have no way of "getting into" that larger society. Lacking the tradition of higher education, discriminated against in schools where they are shunted toward "shop" and away from "academic" courses, they are trained into obsolescence even before the end of adolescence. It would appear, then, that while it doesn't matter which set of values you have once you get into the economic system, if you don't have the right "ticket" (i.e., diplomas and degrees) there is no way of entering it at all.

NOTES

[1]Information on this attempt is available through the Berkeley, California, branch of the Co-operative Association.

[2]As Babalona pointed out, it is just as degrading to be asked for birth control information. As an adult, "You're already s'posed to know them things."

[3]This is a phenomenon common among both middle-class college liberals and lower-class whites. The epithet "bad motherfucker" as a description of an unusually dangerous and thus respected man, while current fifteen years ago in lower-class white circles in St. Louis, for example, was clearly derived from interaction with blacks in what whites called "spade bars."

[4]Both Kardiner and Ovesey (1951) and Elkins (1959, 1961) have noted this, quoting Bettleheim on the similarities of some aspects of the infantile regressions of Nazi concentration camp inmates and the identification with the aggressor which characterizes some aspects of black Americans' personality structure.

[5]Having grown up in St. Louis in a white semislum neighborhood, I remember the common belief that somehow boys from middle-class neighborhoods were not as "rugged" or as sexually interesting to girls as were boys from our neighborhood. Further, "our" girls were much more interesting and eager sexual partners. Boys from our neighborhood nevertheless seemed uniformly eager to "land" some middle-class girl in order to parade her as a trophy — and girls from our neighborhood accepted with amazing alacrity whatever dates they could get with middle-class boys.

It became apparent that much of the same thing was going on in Hunter's Point, though some of the action was symbolic and the intensity of feeling apparently greater.

[6]While such a statement runs the risks of being considered racist, it is the closest approximation of the discernible truth that I can make. That I perforce must anticipate the antagonism with which such a statement will be received in both the white and black communities is simply a reflection of the state of tension between the races in the United States.

[7]The Moynihan report (1965a), a strong demand for federal action to aid disadvantaged urban blacks, emphasized the destructive aspects of poverty and powerlessness on black urban families. Moynihan's making public what many social scientists already knew drew severe criticisms from many blacks who viewed the report (I believe erroneously) as racist.

[8]This is just as vociferously denied by other public school officials. Part of the confusion seems to stem from the definitions of dropout and the implications of truancy below age sixteen. However, girls who become pregnant, boys who go to

jail, and children who "disappear" from the rolls have to be assumed to be drop-outs. The Board of Education refuses to reveal dropout or truancy rates for given schools.

[9]The TAT results (see Chapters 3-6) also make abundantly evident, especially in Card 1 responses, that achievement is seen as difficult, if not impossible, and that internal motivation toward achievement is almost nonexistent.

[10]*Present-time orientation* as described by Kluckholn (1951) and Kluckholn and Strodtbeck (1961) is an attitude which stresses the meaning of the present (as opposed to the future or past) and is often accompanied by a hedonistic appreciation of the present moment as the most important aspect of life.

[11]See Galbraith (1958) on the necessity of this orientation for the survival of the U.S. economy.

[12]Such an assumption is basically correct. My entire argument is that the condition described here is finally attributable to the structural position which black Americans have been forced into for the last 350 years (including the phenomena of slavery, segregation, race hatred). A pattern of responses to these conditions are set up, however, which themselves are maladaptive.

[13]I might stress that I do *not* view this "welfare culture" as unhealthy simply because individuals in it are "feeding at the public trough." Certainly commercial farming operations which receive massive public payments through farm subsidies as a reward for their nonproductivity are an example of truly efficient "feeding at the public trough." Though there is current general concern over the results of farm subsidy programs, these concerns are not usually phrased in terms of fear about what such payments are doing to the "character" of the recipients. I am stressing here that the way in which both the dominant community and Hunter's Pointers view welfare continue to exacerbate interracial tensions and systematically prevent the development of feelings of personal worth in Hunter's Point.

164

8

SOCIAL ORGANIZATION

THERE are at least two kinds of formal social organization in Hunter's Point: those with an indigenous history and organizational structure and those which have come to be superimposed on the community. Though some organizations do not fit easily into one or another category, in cases where the difference is apparent it is significant.

Many of the same factors are involved in both kinds of organization, however, and thus the social structure of Hunter's Point is basically comprised of a series of overlapping personal fealties originating in the matriarchal structure of Hunter's Point itself. Informal social organization leaves its mark, advantageously or not, on formal organizations whether the latter develop from or are imposed on the community.

INFORMAL ORGANIZATION

First of all, Hunter's Point as a community, it must be remembered, owes its existence to vagaries of fate and the public housing efforts of the city of San Francisco. As I have noted, the San Francisco Housing Authority (SFHA) has had in the past absolute authority over much of

165

the personal life of the tenants in Hunter's Point. There indeed was a time when the Housing Authority, without being responsible to any other governmental official or body and immune to any legal action taken by the tenant, could simply evict any tenant it designated as undesirable. This helped create extremely antagonistic feelings toward the Housing Authority which have lasted until the present. Local lawyers have expressed considerable doubt that such actions could ever have survived appeal to higher courts. Technically, this absolute authority still exists, and the SFHA exerts a continual and daily influence on life in Hunter's Point through its offices there. Apart from this structure, however, the community is informally organized along kinship and fictive-kinship (relationships which reflect the closeness of personal ties) lines which extend through neighborhood and church fealties into more formal organizations.

Ties of real and fictive kinship are understandably important elements of social organization in Hunter's Point because of its family structure. As among the British Guianese discussed by Smith (1956), multigenerational matrifocal families are common in Hunter's Point. While it is only sometimes true that three generations of women share the same quarters in Hunter's Point, it is nearly the rule that two generations of adult women do. Additionally, women by preference tend to live near their mothers and grandmothers in Hunter's Point. Because Hunter's Point has only been a residential area for twenty-five years, this pattern of the matrilocality of these matrifocal families is not thoroughly established, but the process is developing. In totally absent-father families, it is more and more common for daughters to reproduce an absent-father family and to live geographically near their mothers. Only the continual influx of new residents prevents this pattern from reaching fruition.

The Housing Authority has slowed this process through its unstated policy of breaking up families which appear to be obstreperous. "Uncontrollable" children (not very well defined by the Authority) are often put under the guidance (custody) of the San Francisco Youth Authority which prevents, by nipping in the bud, the formation of matrifocal "sister groups."[1]

Such "sister groups" come about when several sisters and/or their mother and/or their oldest daughters live adjoining one another and tend to leave all their minor children under the care of one older child, or none at all, while pursuing their own ends. When such children get into too much trouble, the courts are called upon to intervene. Thus, many families through time become absent-father and matrifocal and are then dispersed and become nonexistent because the Housing Authority and Youth Authority deem certain families as undesirable influences on children.

On the other hand, there are many instances of sisters or mothers and daughters being located near one another because the women consistently want it that way. I suspect that by now this tendency is stronger than the effect of any actions by the Housing or Youth authorities. In any event, it appears that there is a gradual build-up of kin-tied geographical groups forming a series of small, tightly knit social groupings.

Fictive kinship operates as a social organizer as well. The importance of the "granny" and the "auntie" in socialization cannot be overemphasized. It is perhaps for this reason that those terms are the favorite fictive-kin terms. As might be expected, because of the matrifocality of the family, female relatives, especially "aunties" and "granny" (mother's sisters and mother's mother, respectively), take a large role in the socializing of the child. They are called upon as babysitters, and the frequency of intervisiting makes them a common sight in the house.

Thus, most female friends of mother are introduced to the children as "auntie" or "granny," depending upon whether they are of the mother's or mother's mother's generation. These fictive-kin terms appear to hold long-term significance and are even used among adults. Someone who has once stood in the relation of "auntie" to a child always remains in a revered position. Duties of a mild degree of filial piety exist between anyone and his fictive "auntie" or "granny."

The "auntie" or "granny," for her part, is expected to bring small gifts and birthday remembrances and on occasion to act as a buffer between the wrath of mother and the child. Such ties are a strong force in the social organization of Hunter's Point. The extension of fictive-kinship ties also tends to promote political and organizational power for some individuals, though this is never a stated objective.

Kinship (real or fictive), however, is not the only social force tying people together in Hunter's Point. It is complexly interrelated with church and church sodality membership. Often women are brought into church sodalities by their female kin. Involvement in the same church organizations by kin members strengthens the kinship bond and permits it to be extended fictively to even more women. Since formal organizations have been in the past and, though to a lesser extent, still are cen-

167

tered around churches and community action organization, the importance of church membership would be hard to overemphasize. No matter what its content, almost any organization of community importance in Hunter's Point has at least one "tame" minister (that is, one who is easily controlled by his female parishioners). Of course, some organizations also contain much more independent ministers.

Moreover, church membership as such is an important aspect of other social organizations, since the organizational structures and power elites formed in church sodalities and the resultant jockeying and competition for power are often transferred whole into social action organizations. That is, the same personnel and the same political struggles that exist within the church sodalities are reproduced, with little modification, in whatever social action groups the particular church members choose to ally themselves with. In fact, ministers are often induced to join or at least support social action organizations by their most vocal and powerful parishioners.

Ministers are felt to have an inordinate power over the women of the community by many non-churchgoing men. There is a great deal of jealousy based on fantasied and perhaps occasionally real acts of infidelity by parishioners with their ministers. On the other hand, it is just as likely that this antagonism toward ministers by other men is based on the fact that ministers are, by and large, supported and even controlled by women. But instead of having to deny this, or to produce a convoluted defense system against the reality by labeling it as manipulating women, ministers are culturally permitted to claim that they are doing a desired and desirable thing. Thus, the church as a social organization in Hunter's Point is a mirror of the familial situation in which female dominance is the rule.

The other important bases of social structure in Hunter's Point are the face-to-face neighborhood personal fealties, developed through time and involving widespread communication networks throughout the area. Individual women, having gained prominence or power through church-affiliated organizations, become local neighborhood leaders of other women. They function both as opinion molders and social action mobilizers. Thus, the two networks of social relationships among those people who count most socially, women, are inextricably intertwined.

It is best not to give the impression that these social ties are more far-reaching, deeper, and pervasive than they are. In reality, perhaps only 30 percent of the adult women in Hunter's Point are involved in such networks. Personal jealousies and bickerings over position common in any racial grouping reduce the strength of these ties. Moreover, the continual process of self-degradation which is endemic in Hunter's Point and the rapid movement out of Hunter's Point of the abler community members act as further entropic forces in community organization. Nonetheless, the personal force of the dominant matriarchy whose very presence creates so many problems for males is the most important anti-entropic force in the community. To the extent that any real sense of community exists in Hunter's Point, it is due to these dominant women and their organizational prowess.

Most of the matriarchs of Hunter's Point have been involved in social organizations connected with the community or local churches for about twenty years. Only a small percentage of this group is socially active. The rest are vaguely "wired in." All of the women have evolved styles of organizational competence and skill at organizational in-fighting of a very high level. While certain aspects of their formal education may be minimal, I cannot stress too strongly the organizational sophistica-tion, at least in terms of internal jockeying for position, shown by these women.

Reference to these group leaders as "matriarchs" is deliberate and advised. Only one of the major social, political, or church organizations in Hunter's Point is not both dominated and almost entirely led by middle-aged black women.[2] Youth gangs and ad hoc protest groups tend to be led by males, but the significance of these organizations, the former now all but defunct and the latter typically disbanded the day after their inception, is extremely limited. Interesting with regard to the male role in the community was the way local newspapers discussed the problems leading to the "riots" in Hunter's Point considered in Chapter 10. Of the supposed "community leaders" (all men) whom reporters quoted only one actually lived in Hunter's Point, and none controlled anything — except perhaps his own temper. This is not to say that the women could control riot situations — they most probably could not — but day-to-day organizational activities are undeniably in their hands.

Thus, in summary, one of the most important informal social group-ings in Hunter's Point is the matrifocal power group. As might be ex-pected from what has been said before, in the consequent interaction among adult females, female superiority is strengthened and male worth deprecated. Since most informal organizations involve face-to-face interaction and discussion in the home, children are exposed early and often to this pattern. Recognition of this pattern of female power is thus a significant aspect of the child's socialization experience and prepares the young girl to take her place in this grouping later in life.

Furthermore, this kin-church-based female power is important in more than church sodalities and connected informal groups. Until quite recently, all formal power positions in the community (in different types of political and community action organizations) have been filled by women who received their training in these informal associations of matriarchs. Thus, power struggles and fights in formal organizations not only reflect, but directly result from, the jockeying for power existing in more informal groupings.

FORMAL ORGANIZATION

That the presence of a powerful, informed network of well-organized women's groups has produced very little dramatic confrontation of such organizations with white power (the established economic, political, and social forces of San Francisco) is based on several realities in Hunter's Point. One important reason (but by no means the only one) is the fact of this female dominance itself. Men here by and large cannot, and will not, join an organization dominated by women. Thus, almost no community action-type organizations have any local men in them except for ministers and an occasional cowed husband of one of these dominant women.

Since in such organizations older and middle-aged men are not involved and young men are unrepresented, those involved in (infrequent) organizational confrontation with whites are middle-aged women and their predominantly female followers. This is one of the most important reasons why white power, which is mostly male, simply doesn't take Hunter's Point seriously. Still, the powerlessness of local organization is not adequately explained simply by attributing it to matrifocality.

Another vital aspect of organizational impotence is the lack of a "feeling of community" in Hunter's Point. Its residents perceive their life there (accurately or not) as temporary and do not "identify" in any positive sense with their neighbors. This again reflects their desire not to be identified as poor — and thus as backward and stupid. Even so, some indigenous social organizations do exist, not a few of which have a political flavor. There are also some Hunter's Pointers determined to develop some sense of community, even if on the basis of "reaction to a common enemy." The meaning and operation of such organizations, however, can be very convoluted because of the entire social-cultural context in which such organizational attempts occur.

We have seen how the structural position of Hunter's Pointers, as blacks in a white-dominated society, combined with a family structure and socialization experience which has its roots directly in the experience of racism, has led to the development of a unique subculture. We have also seen how this subculture, isolated geographically and through racial prejudice from the mainstream of white American culture, nevertheless exhibits remarkable similarities to the dominant culture. Though similarities between the two cultures may well become very much greater indeed, nonetheless, formal relations between the subculture of Hunter's Point and the middle-class power structure of San Francisco remain clumsy, poorly developed, and uncertain.

The discernible reasons for such particular total failure in relations between the two groups are related to their respective perceptions of the situation. First of all, two relatively distinct cultures are involved. Despite all lip service to the contrary, Hunter's Pointers and white San Franciscans continue to think of themselves as separate groups. Regardless of extensive similarities between whites and blacks, the differences created by differential access to power, which is inherent in the basically racially discriminatory social structure of San Francisco, totally colors relationships between blacks and whites. This differential access to power creates two truly distinct subcultural groupings: dominant whites with power and subordinate blacks without power. The result of this difference in access to power means that both white and black San Franciscans respond to political and other groupings of Hunter's Point blacks in paradoxical and contradictory fashions, which are almost never consciously articulated. *First*, in conjunction with the ethic of equality, the demands of Hunter's Point blacks must be given as much weight as demands by any other group. At least strong, overt lip service must be given to this principle, or else the ethic of equality is openly denied. After all, we are all Americans, aren't we? *On the other hand*, the undeniable fact that whites are presently powerful and blacks are not means that white power responds to black power, whether consciously or unconsciously, either condescendingly or with outright contempt. Even when individuals in the white power structure seriously try to respond

171

on a person-to-person, equal-to-equal basis, their response always has the underlying quality of being perceived as a gift, an act of noblesse oblige, by black recipients.

The result of this is that blacks are understandably infuriated even when they are unable to pin down precisely just what the white power structure has done (or failed to do) that is unfair. One by-product of impotent rage is a tendency for some members of Hunter's Point power groups always to react intransigently and with a defensive aggressiveness toward the white power groups. What keeps the system of interaction between white and black power continually breaking down is that it doesn't matter how white power responds to this antagonism. When it responds by becoming more intransigent itself, it confirms Hunter's Pointers' opinions of the hopelessness of their differential power status and creates more hate and frustration (which of course in turn convinces white power of the moral propriety of dealing arbitrarily with such "unpleasant" people). When white power backs down, Hunter's Pointers are simply convinced that the concessions are being made condescendingly and that they (Hunter's Pointers) have somehow been gulled because they should have demanded more. The result is frustration, hate, and a determination to press harder — at least on those occasions when the Hunter's Pointer does not merely give up.

Inextricably intertwined with this major block to intergroup communication is the weakness of the indigenous organization in the community itself. Hunter's Pointers feel inadequate vis-à-vis whites, and even to organize against them is a difficult act of will. Because of the personal, familial, and social disorganization in Hunter's Point, indigenous organizations have a hard time holding together. The sense of personal strength and worth which is so badly eroded in the normal life of Hunter's Pointers makes it difficult for them to see themselves on a "winning team." Thus, the macropolitical reality of dominance by whites is further reinforced in the minds of whites and blacks alike. Both become convinced that Hunter's Point blacks are incapable of organizing for political power.

Exacerbating these difficulties is the existence of just enough "Uncle Tom" leaders (local blacks who implicitly or explicitly kowtow to white power for their own advantage or because they have internalized a very severe black self-hate) to weaken local organizations. Thus, even the most aggressive local leaders, the best of whom have at least some problems of personal identity, are faced with a reality of powerlessness which makes it very difficult for them to be taken seriously either by white power or by their own constituency — or, finally, by themselves.

If these were not problems enough, there is the additional fact that most men who are in positions of responsibility in local organizations in Hunter's Point are "outsiders." Furthermore, talented local leaders (as well as outsiders) are co-opted into the white power structure just as soon as it rears its head, as we shall see.

In the face of all these difficulties, organizations nevertheless do come into being, and some are actually effective. Their roots, their history, and their difficulties are all complexly interrelated, but basically organizational activity has been a response to the perception which Hunter's Pointers have of their position in the society at large. These perceptions are often sophisticated and realistic.

George, who has recently moved from Hunter's Point, had lived there for thirteen years, eleven of them employed as a bus driver. He suggests that the tremendous economic potential of Hunter's Point land, with its beautiful view, for high-rise apartment buildings has been obvious to everyone for a long time.

"Before the Housing Authority started kicking people out [it was necessary by 1970 to tear down the buildings through legal arrangements which had been made prior to that time] , you'd see big black Cadillacs come up to the hill on Sunday, and these fat old guys get out and look at the city, and then they'd smile like they were going to break their faces. It's no secret why the Housing Authority wants us out."

The consensus of opinion is that the Hunter's Point area has been described as an undesirable slum to disguise the fact that it has some of the most magnificent views, best weather, and generally excellent exclusive residential potential in the city. The argument then goes that in order for white power to cash in on this it is necessary for the people there be evicted, for their housing to be torn down, and then, as was done in the A-2 area of San Francisco, for low-cost housing to be replaced by high-cost, high-rise structures, with no regard for what happens to the dispossessed poor.

It is only recently that such views have become articulated by any number of people in Hunter's Point, and community organizations have begun to grow at least in part because of such beliefs. All this organization, however, has occurred in the context of the value system, the social system, and the familial situation that has existed in the past and which exists now. Thus, such organizations have unique dimensions and unique problems.

Probably the first social and quasi-political organization in Hunter's Point was the Crispus Attucks Club.[3] It was started around 1944 and gave way in a few years (1950) to the Bayview Community Center. Originally, Dr. Thompson, a minister, and Mrs. Neighbors were the informal leaders of the center and of whatever other quasi-political community organizations there were. Around the beginning of the '50s, the Bayview Community Center actively sought to prevent some of the evictions of "undesirables," but these attempts produced few victories that might have kindled a feeling of political strength.

The growth and development of this and similar organizations was occurring, moreover, against a background of changes in the community itself and in its relationship to the larger society.

It was during the early 1950s that the first serious confrontations (mostly symbolic) of whites and blacks occurred in San Francisco. Some racial tensions were evident in the local high school, where incidents of racially tinged violence were reported. The reaction of the police was to try to keep Hunter's Point black youths "in line" by denying them access to the rest of the city, which only exacerbated tensions.

About this time also, probably at least partly because of this police pressure which made "turf" (local territory) boundaries even more important, "bopping gangs" were forming in Hunter's Point. These fighting gangs were a serious menace to both life and property and imposed a virtual reign of terror on the extreme east end of Hunter's Point just south of the naval shipyard. This area, with its few small stores and combination nightclub-bars, became a completely isolated, self-contained, totally black world. This is so even now, perhaps to a greater extent than in any other part of San Francisco or the Bay Area. While car traffic to the shipyards coming from the south may pass the area, none but its denizens stop there.

The existence of fighting gangs and other "gang trouble" provoked the police to adopt an even more aggressive "quarantine" procedure (of exceedingly doubtful legality), which in turn further enraged the inhabitants of the area against the "legitimate law and order" of the city. Under this quarantine procedure, black youths who were recognized as Hunter's Pointers and found in other areas of the city were rousted and sent back to Hunter's Point. In practice this meant that groups of young boys or girls who appeared anywhere west of Third Street — the "boundary" of Hunter's Point — were given the alternatives of going "back up on the Hill where you niggers belong" or being arrested on a variety of charges that police save for such situations.

The bitterness of many Hunter's Point residents about the arrest records they compiled for doing little or nothing more than being black in an area where a white policeman did not want them to be is immense. The Housing Authority, at that time working in close liaison with the police, simply evicted "troublemakers." However, this had the actual effect of undoing what the police were trying to do. The attempts to quarantine the black population in the Hunter's Point area came to naught when the Housing Authority, by evicting such "undesirables," simply dispersed them into the community at large.

Thus, increasing racial tensions, arbitrary police activities purportedly for the purpose of reducing such tensions, and the bitterness these tactics engendered set up a negative feedback system of racial antagonism out of which the first really effective and long-lasting political organizations in Hunter's Point were formed. Some of the residents (many of them the same matriarchs who now run Hunter's Point) first banded together to resist the arbitrary use of power by the Housing Authority. Out of these more or less unsuccessful struggles have come the present-day organizations and their leaders.

These organizations, however, had a broader perspective than simple reaction to interracial tension per se. Very soon they began to concern themselves with questions of housing and jobs and education. At some periods of time, essentially peripheral items such as juvenile delinquency have taken the center of the stage. However, little by little it began to be clear that the primary function which the Bayview Community Center was serving was to direct, educate, and support emerging local political leaders.

This became especially clear when in the beginning of the 1960s, as a result of a shooting incident, the Housing Authority decided to evict five families. This case was only another in a long series of such evictions, but for some reason Mrs. Neighbors this time successfully organized the community to protest this action, and the Hunter's Point residents finally tasted victory: the Housing Authority gave way, and the families stayed on. Mrs. Neighbors's popularity in the area soared, as did her power.

This incident marked the beginning of the unusual expansion of

175

political and social organization in Hunter's Point. Coinciding with the beginning of John F. Kennedy's presidential term, it was a period marked by a growing and enthusiastic optimism regarding possible change in Hunter's Point. From spasmodic organizational activity with long periods of quiesence, Hunter's Point went to a point of abundant local organization. To put the matter in perspective, it should be re-marked that whereas until 1960 there was but one organization in Hunter's Point of any social-political significance, the Bayview Community Center, by 1967 there were at least five major community organizations, about ten lesser ones (all of which, however, were important enough to get press coverage for events they organized, and at least two local and one national "outreach" organizations (ones dedicated to bringing people who are outside the economic structure into it) — all in addition to the offices of the local and state welfare agencies and voluntary groups organized through local colleges and universities for specific training programs.

Along with this organizational expansion, however, have come a series of problems. Competition among indigenous and superimposed power groups, difficulties with "disinterested and objective" help organizations, the co-opting of local leadership out of the community, and the ubiquitous matriarchal domination have all reduced the effectiveness of local organization.

One of the most serious problems has been the competition between local and superimposed organizations. In the early 1960s, for example, the San Francisco Committee on Youth announced plans to open a Youth Opportunity Center in Hunter's Point for the purpose of offsetting delinquency by training Hunter's Point youths for jobs. In the process, the Bayview Community Center, the only meaningful community organization up to that time, was neither consulted nor included in the plans. The reason the Committee on Youth chose to ignore the Bayview Community Center, the committee claimed, was that the Bayview Center's activities simply did not seem relevant to those of the youth center, even though at the time the former was already conducting a program of youth education. The more probable reason, and almost certainly the only real reason in the eyes of Hunter's Point blacks, involved the indigenous black character of the Bayview Community Center, and especially its leadership: the Committee on Youth, according to this view, was directed mostly by "downtown," white interests who had no particular interest in allowing Hunter's Point blacks to have a hand in controlling the committee's programs — even though these programs would help shape the destiny of those same Hunter's Point blacks. (This was years before "community control" of such organizations was even a rallying cry, much less a fact.)

Mrs. Neighbors, acting from her position of power in the community, sought consideration for appointment as director of the Youth Opportunity Center. Community sentiment seemed to feel that since she was already coleader of the Bayview Community Center, the only truly representative organization in Hunter's Point, it stood to reason that both centers could profit from a pooling of resources and leadership. The Committee on Youth turned down her application.

Hunter's Point residents retaliated by picketing the meetings concerned with opening the San Francisco Committee on Youth, hoping thereby to influence the Ford Foundation, which was funding the youth center. In this they were successful. Hunter's Point residents believe that the Ford Foundation pressured the Committee on Youth into formulating a plan that would not provoke picketing — on pain of having their funds withheld. The Committee on Youth then decided to bring the Bayview Community Center into their plans, for suddenly — and miraculously, it seemed, they discovered that the Bayview Community Center did indeed have a youth constituency.

Such superimposition, plain and simple, presents one sort of problem. Another, subtler problem is presented by the powerful "disinterested and objective" institution which provides "help." Because there are supposedly altruistic motives behind, for example, the University of California's programs for change in Hunter's Point, such organizations justify extremely arbitrary and authoritarian actions on the grounds that they are simply "doing what's best" and have "no axe to grind." It is in its relationships with these institutions that the inner workings of the community's own power structure are revealed most clearly.

One example of this kind of interaction occurred when in 1965 a group headed by Albert Peale (a black sociology student), under the auspices of the Criminology Department of the University of California (Berkeley), was sent to organize the Hunter's Point area (again, with funds from the Ford Foundation) for a two-pronged attack on community problems. First, Peale was to supervise the organization of the community into blocks of politically conscious persons. Secondly — and this was a much vaguer aim — Peale was to set up a community group involving itself in crime prevention and the organization of youth. The entire scheme had been started by the director of the Youth Opportunity Center who had proposed the funding (from the Ford Foundation once again since it was the original funding group for the Youth Opportunity Center through the San Francisco Committee on Youth).

Before the inception of Peale's mission, Youth for Service, a multi-branched citywide organization, had been founded. Its personnel, recruited from former street gang members, were to serve as a liaison between the police and youth gangs in the city, especially in such predominantly nonwhite areas as the Mission district, Chinatown, the Fillmore district, and Hunter's Point. Youth for Service prided itself, and got a great deal of press coverage, for supposedly being able to head off gang fights before they got started. Nobody had yet noticed that gang fighting activity in the early 1960s seemed to be disappearing all over the United States, whether the area was blessed with a Youth for Service group or not. (See Klein, 1967.) In Hunter's Point itself, gangs had become largely inactive by 1961. By 1965, there were no "bopping" gangs of any kind left in Hunter's Point, though there still remained organizations of young men who prided themselves on being members of titled gangs.

Thus, while it was clear that Youth for Service was concerned about the University of California group intruding in its jurisdiction, it also seems probable they feared that the university's intrusion and investigation would point out that there were no gangs which needed controlling in Hunter's Point.

The university group, meanwhile, expressed a wish to orient their efforts toward the Bayview Community Center and to help this indigenous organization. The Bayview Community Center, however, rejected this proferred help. In part, this was due to the center's interlocking organizational structures with Youth for Service. The director of Youth for Service also sat on the board of directors of the Bayview Community Center, and the directors of the two organizations were friends. Furthermore, whereas the Bayview Community Center had claimed to be the only truly indigenous community organizer and mobilizer, the university group's actions now suggested that *it* could as well (or better) organize people in Hunter's Point. Furthermore, although the university group could abandon its youth work in order to avoid clashes with Youth for Service, it was compelled to maintain its adult organization efforts if it was to stay involved in the project. Something had to give.

Having failed to establish the Bayview Community Center as an affiliated base, Peale chose to build an independent nuclear center for the block club organizations. One of the outcomes of the unfortunate struggle among Peale, Mrs. Neighbors, and others in the community over control of these various programs and the patronage and political power which it was felt would flow from them was an alienation of many people in the community from the entire business of attempting to take some control of their own community through these help programs. As we have seen, this was reflected in Mrs. Neighbors' inability to obtain the directorship she so desired.

This state of affairs also began to expose another dynamic in Hunter's Point — the conflict between men and women over power — and further revealed the poverty of male leadership in the community when a young black man from an eastern university was hired as the director of the Youth Opportunity Center. He flew out on weekends to direct the center.

This unstable situation nearly came to a head when the directors of the Youth Opportunity Center, seeking to put pressure on the staff of the Bayview Community Center to oust Mrs. Neighbors as its director, managed to persuade her associate director to quit in order to become a director of the Youth Opportunity Center.

The Bayview Community Center continued to function in a state of questionable stability and is now (1967) organizationally in some difficulty; it has a large overhead and little steady income. Its one grant of funds from the Economic Opportunity Program was not renewed. Nor can the center's independence long take the strain of having their best people lured away by the huge salaries offered by the Ford Foundation, the city, and the Office of Economic Opportunity. But this is not only their problem: any indigenous independent leadership that shows any promise is co-opted almost immediately into government or government-assisted or -associated organizations. Such co-optation is yet another stumbling block in the way of effective community organization.

This co-optation of local talent does not appear to be purposeful sabotage of local organizations — as some believe, partly because the organizations that co-opt them are usually more powerful than those they come from and often view themselves as similarly oriented toward the "progress" of the inhabitants of Hunter's Point. Rather, recognized, available talented leaders are so few in number that co-optation is one of the few techniques left to directors of governmental and other organizations seeking indigenous involvement. Because co-optation functions to remove local leaders from indigenous organizational positions and often puts them into quasi-governmental organizations, however, it can be seen — and in fact is seen by many Hunter's Pointers — as one way of keeping community leaders from "getting out of line." Perhaps even more important, the level of responsible grassroots community leadership is kept low. Local male leaders, especially, are quickly co-opted into nonlocal organizations.[4]

But while the conflicts among power groups and would-be power groups continue in Hunter's Point, while confrontations still occur between dominant community power representatives and between local community organizations, a struggle of equal importance is being worked out within local organizations. The problem of male-female relationships is being reinacted and is finding new resolutions within the new indigenous and nonindigenous organizational structures.

Women still have many, if not most, of the power positions in the newer organizational structures, except perhaps in those groups organized under the Economic Opportunity Act.[5] The manner in which such power is being handled is itself interesting.

While on one level many of the matriarchs of Hunter's Point are deeply and sincerely concerned with what goes on there — with the problems of poverty, jobs, education, schooling, housing, and so on — it is also quite clear that many if not all of them personally stand to gain a great deal more by keeping the situation as it is, permitting only minor changes, than by initiating or even tolerating dramatic changes, for power would flow into male hands if dramatic structural changes occurred.[6] When organizational structures are superimposed on Hunter's Point but effect little in the way of radical change, the women who inevitably come to control these organizations continue to draw good salaries and maintain themselves in positions of power and leadership in the community, and need fear no interjection of indigenous male leadership arising to challenge them. Such confrontations as that between Ed Thorp and Mrs. Thompson resulting in a male victory (see footnote 5) are rare; in any event Mrs. Thompson still retains power.

Significantly, it appears that only with "outside" assistance can an indigenous black male attain power in Hunter's Point. In this mode of confrontation, older, established dominant matriarchs are replaced by younger male leadership, partly as a result of pressures directed by outsiders who control organizations located in the community and partly as a result of the competence and brilliance of the men involved.

On the other hand, there is another type of confrontation in which the older matriarchs who have established themselves in positions of authority — in the federal poverty program, the Bayview Community Center, Bay Area Neighborhood Development, Planned Parenthood, the Interblock Council, and various other organizations in the area — are thwarted by aggressive young men who simply outtalk them. In organizational meetings where programs are proposed and ideas kicked around, such younger men — such as John Peters and Henry Rivers, who are themselves prototypes of the newer male leaders in Hunter's Point (though neither is from Hunter's Point or a current resident of it) — often couch their proposals in complex sociological jargon using an unusually convoluted grammatical style. This has the effect of sufficiently confusing the middle-aged women in the audience and on the board of directors to keep them from understanding what has been proposed.[7] Ordinarily, rather than expose their own ignorance they will permit such proposals to pass unchallenged. When this happens, however, they inevitably demand some kind of payment for it — typically some executive responsibility in a new program and often an item veto over certain aspects of it. This veto power is an informal one, and the women almost never exercised it for fear of provoking a showdown in which they could lose control entirely.

However, this situation, which existed throughout 1965 and 1966, had changed significantly by 1967. The old matriarchs had themselves begun to learn sociological jargon and, to the shock and dismay of the young men, were capable of aggressive verbal assault with similar weapons whenever necessary. To consolidate their positions of power, they have accepted as coleaders the young black male outsiders, but still nothing has been done to encourage local male leadership. Thus, local social and political organization is yet unable to mobilize vast numbers of Hunter's Pointers.

A good example of the way in which some of the organizational problems we have discussed affect Hunter's Pointers can be seen in the block clubs. These groups are of particular interest because of their political potential and their essentially democratic character, which is unusual for the area. The University of California's operation in Hunter's Point (noted above) eventually settled down into block club organizations along the modified Sol Alinisky approach (approach power with power of your own). That is, it was decided that Hunter's Pointers needed determined conscious political organization. Clubs were then formed by Baker, the university's organizer, in natural grouping units, such as individual blocks of buildings, and have acted as educational arms, barometers of protest, and political consciousness-raising tools. There were in the summer of 1967 about fifteen organized clubs. (The "about" simply indicates the problem of determining the level of function.)

The clubs themselves are formed around natural friendship units. This is both their strength and their weakness. Because they are almost exclusively female-dominated, they tend to perpetuate the freezing out of males from relevant decision making. Most competent males work at full-time jobs and use this as an excuse to avoid "women's stuff" — although the head of the Interblock Council, the umbrella organization for the block clubs, Thorp, is a fully employed man.

The natural friendship units tend to be rigidly exclusive, and once a base of some half-dozen to a dozen is established, no further attempts are made by members to recruit new ones. Thus, recruitment and organization itself is seen as a responsibility of the organizer (Baker) and his staff. The organization was started from outside, depends on outside funds, and is thus weak. This reflects the general passive approach to governmental power which exists in the community. There are a limited number of individuals who view organization as a tool for attaining political power, and most are quite uncertain as to the immediate ends to be accomplished, let alone possible long-range goals.

One example of this is the Kirkwood Club, one of the block clubs. This club has been instrumental in forcing the Housing Authority to put pressure on the owner of the local laundromat to extend its hours, install a change machine in the police station across the street, and put larger lightbulbs in the laundromat. The owner's compliance with these minimal demands — even though the Housing Authority did not act on demands to staff the laundromat with someone till midnight and to deal with associated pressing needs in the neighborhood— inspired such gratitude that the Kirkwood Club at first considered sending a "thank you" note to the Housing Authority. When it was pointed out by an "outsider" that such compliance was not a gift, but had only been achieved through threat of picketing — that in fact it was the natural right of the citizens of Hunter's Point to have such demands met and that there were immense problems surrounding the operation of the laundromat that had yet to be dealt with — most members indicated that they did not really realize that their power had brought about the change, but merely had thought of the whole problem in terms of petitions for blessings and grace, not demands for rights.

The kind of inability of persons to perceive their political action potential exemplified by the attitude of the members of the Kirkwood Club is an inevitable result of the many problems existing in Hunter's Point social and political organization. But these problems do not mean that all such organizations must be, or even have been, ineffective. Some have had a significant impact on the city. About the time that Proposition 14 was being debated (1964),[8] some of the residents and established leaders in Hunter's Point, expressing concern with the housing problems that had resulted from the Area 2 redevelopment in San Francisco, founded a housing corporation, the Joint Housing Committee. The committee, established in part to force the Housing Authority to redevelop along lines more compatible with the interests of the project's current residents, contained representatives from many groups in Hunter's Point. Fortunately, the impact of the "War on Poverty," a new concern with city development, and the organizational power which the Hunter's Point community had been developing all combined to elicit promises (at first vague) from the director of redevelopment. Then, as more and more organizations and block clubs came into the committee, definite commitments were elicited and, finally, apparent capitulation was made to the demands of the residents.

With the present potential inherent in the "Demonstration Cities" concept (in which federal funds are to be made available for precisely what the Hunter's Point residents want from the San Francisco Housing Authority), there seems less doubt of some ultimate success for this group. One measure of the power which Hunter's Point residents now possess but have not fully begun to realize is that the director of the Redevelopment Association in San Francisco now frequently attends community meetings in Hunter's Point to explain in detail what he is doing and how he is carrying out the wishes of the organizations in Hunter's Point, in return receiving further "instructions" (expressions of local wishes), which by and large he carries out.

As I have suggested before, these organizational entities, some of which are very new, provide a battleground for the working out of some of the dynamics of the Hunter's Point community in addition to being oriented toward such tasks as solving housing and job problems. The ability of some young black men to elicit respect and aquiescence from older women, partially through outside organizational help and structure and partially through the manipulation of complex verbage, has resulted in a movement, however slight, away from matriarchal domination of the Hunter's Point society. Such a structural change may have both positive and negative aspects.

Lest it be felt that the significance of this movement is being exaggerated, it must be remembered that the matriarchy of Hunter's Point stands to lose the most from progressive change, increasingly grassroots democracy, or increasing numbers of jobs for men, and at present this particular group thus represents a real obstruction to any possible progress in Hunter's Point.[9] At the same time, it also represents the only real grassroots organizational power in Hunter's Point. Thus, any dimunition in its power is a dimunition in the power of the whole community.

On the more negative side, as a result of the novelty and complexity of many organizational structures in Hunter's Point, an unusual cleavage has developed between leaders and followers in such organizations. As leaders move into well paying jobs, that is, different posts in different federally funded organizations, these moves are not seen as an expression of legitimate aspiration by competent individuals so much as they are seen as "abandonment" of as yet unfulfilled commitments to earlier programs. In some cases these upwardly mobile individuals leave the community, while in other cases they simply do other jobs in the same community. In any event, their one-time followers, who tend very often to be oriented to a specific program, tend to become increasingly cynical. Viewing the new affluence of their leaders, many Hunter's Pointers are convinced that these leaders are either pulling some gigantic "ripoff" on the whites or planning some new and subtle "sellout." A minimal amount of patronage exists as a result of federal, state, and local programs — just enough to convince many Hunter's Pointers that a "hustle" is underway, yet not enough to dramatically benefit the community. It is not the fact of the suspected "hustle" which disturbs Hunter's Pointers, however, but the fear that either whites or their leaders or both are using them. Inevitably, this breeds distrust, widening the gap between leaders and followers. Whether this cleavage can be easily repaired by continual organizational and structural changes or by increases in educational and job opportunities is not immediately clear at this point. Whether this cleavage is even significant depends on the future course of certain organizational structural factors.[10]

NOTES

[1]A common complaint of SFHA personnel is that when two or more sisters live near one another they take turns babysitting for one another's children and that this practice leads to child neglect. It is not clear on what evidence they base this assumption, since this does not seem to be the case.

[2]The block clubs, discussed below.

[3]Named after the first black killed in the hostilities preceding the Revolutionary War.

[4]A few of the cases may give a clearer idea of this procedure.

Ben Wexler was director of the Bayview Community Center (an indigenous organization) for only six months before being hired by the Youth Opportunity Center (a citywide organization) as an associate director.

Albert Peale, who was the University of California's director of the block organizing effort (which is what he changed the original program into) — a local activity with only minimal ties to the university, became the local federal poverty program director in Hunter's Point.

Paul Thorne, another director of the Bayview Community Center, was also hired to serve in the federal poverty program after about a year.

Ed Maypole, who was important in the ad hoc organizing group of the South East City Alliance, (the most recent of Hunter's Point's indigenous organizations), was also hired by the poverty program. There are numerous other examples.

[5]Again, some examples might be illuminating.

Bessie Thompson, the former chairwoman of the Interblock Council and also chairwoman of the Christian Welfare Society, which came into Albert Peale's block club organization as a group, is a prototype of the middle-aged matriarch of Hunter's Point. She ran the Interblock Council (the executive committee of the block clubs) with an iron hand and viewed "outsiders" in the community as dangerous threats to her power. To maintain that power, she prevented the Interblock Council from adopting any bylaws — thus making it nearly impossible to remove her from office, since most members of the council were afraid to confront her directly.

Since Peale was no longer associated with the project which had created the Interblock Council since having become an official in the poverty program the university brought in a new organizer, Abel Baker. After ascertaining the situation, Baker suggested that the council adopt bylaws, which it did, and then he manipulated the group into replacing Mrs. Thompson with Ed Thorp. (He was able to do this because the university still had some control over the organization through the salaries it paid organizers.) Mrs. Thompson, not to be shoved aside, then succeeded in being elected new codirector of the Bayview Community Center, thus managing to land on her feet and maintain her power in the community.

Ruby Tan has for a long time been concerned with Hunter's Point problems and, as a resident there, has been instrumental, as has Mrs. Neighbors, in starting many successful activities there. She is reputed to be the local Burton organizer — Phil Burton is the local congressman and his brother John the local state assemblyman — and it is believed locally that she gets the vote out well enough to be paid a retainer for her efforts. Hired onto the federal poverty program staff, she eventually moved to a well-paying job with Bay Area Neighborhood Development, an organization concerned with consumer education which grew out of the cooperative movement. She is also head of the Housing Corporation, an indigenous organization which is working as equal partners with the City Redevelopment Agency.

Mrs. Plainfield and Mrs. Black, both placed on the advisory board of the Youth Opportunity Center because they had been vocal and aggressive critics of its policies, were hired originally by Albert Peale as organizers to help with his block club organization. They supported Peale in his campaign to be appointed director of the local branch of the federal poverty program, and after he became director he returned the favor by hiring them to work for the program.

Tina Roberts, the director of Planned Parenthood, was instrumental along with Joe Washington and Mrs. Pingora in getting the food cooperative started. Her articulateness was immediately recognized and she was hired as the director.

[6]I am not suggesting this is a conscious attitude, but some of the actions of the matriarchs do seem deliberate attempts to freeze men out.

[7]Interestingly, this technique has a cultural prototype in the convoluted, "high falutin'" grammatical styles of black preachers in the area. Thus, as well as having an instrumental aspect, it validates and is validated by an already existing cultural pattern.

[8]The passage of Proposition 14 in the 1964 California elections effected repeal of the Rumford Fair Housing Act. The act had outlawed racial discrimination in the sale of housing, and thus the proposition to repeal it was viewed by both its opponents and supporters as an attempt to reduce the ability of blacks to avoid being victimized by restrictive covenants on housing.

[9]A final evaluation in mid-1967 suggests that the matriarchy is now even more firmly entrenched. There has been a systematic leakage of male leadership either to school or to high-status jobs outside any community organization. The matriarchs remain, even more highly trained by virtue of their now successful relations with the white power structure.

[10]This introduces a theme that will be developed in greater detail in the next chapter. In fact, very little of what Hunter's Pointers do is finally effective in changing their lot. Thus, in many cases questions of cleavage between leaders and followers are primarily academic. Such concerns will cease to be academic only when Hunter's Point organizations develop the kind of power they do not now have.

9

RELATIONS
WITH WHITES

AS the foregoing makes clear, real personal or even political confrontation between whites and Hunter's Point blacks is rare. In Hunter's Point itself only a very limited and highly specialized kind of black-white interaction takes place.

Numerous representatives of federal, state, and local service agencies, a small number of local Housing Authority personnel, street cleaners (most of whom are white even though the unemployment rate in Hunter's Point is very high, perhaps one-quarter of all males being unemployed), some of the Housing Authority police (called "Mickey Mouse cops" because of their obvious lack of real police status), the regular municipal police from the Potrero Hill station who very occasionally patrol the area (or, more likely, answer an emergency call), occasional salesmen, and an increasing number of social scientists from the local colleges and universities more or less exhaust the categories of whites who ever visit Hunter's Point.

In passing, it might be noted that the Housing Authority personnel in Hunter's Point are, for the most part, hired from the local population, which provides, as a top-level executive in the Housing Authority suggested, some sort of "transmission belt" for the grievances of the tenants against the Authority as well as increased employment opportunities. On the local Housing Authority staff, however, as elsewhere in the world of work, there are more jobs available for black women than for black men. Regarding the transmission of grievances, the tenants have organized themselves (see below) into a much more effective, direct-confrontation group for dealing with both the Housing Authority and the Redevelopment Agency of San Francisco.

In actual practice, the Housing Authority personnel in Hunter's Point serve more as a "transmission belt" for Authority directives to the tenants. Even this function is somewhat curtailed by the increasing political and social consciousness of the alternate power structures being developed by the local tenants themselves. The main function of the Housing Authority office in Hunter's Point appears to be to add people to the employment roles.

To cross check my intuitive perception that few whites outside the categories I have indicated have ever been in Hunter's Point, I asked some eighteen residents of the Bayview area, no more than four blocks from Third Street, to suggest a reasonable if arbitrary dividing line used to determine Hunter's Point occupancy. Only two respondents had ever been in Hunter's Point. Both of these were men who had been employed at the naval shipyard.

Consciousness of Hunter's Point among white residents in the rest of the city appears to be at an even lower level. Until the "riots" of the fall of 1966, a substantial number of whites living in such middle-class neighborhoods as the Sunset district (on the western edge of the city facing the Pacific Ocean) were not even sure where Hunter's Point is. Some had heard it was a black neighborhood, though very few evidenced any understanding of conditions there. Those who had opinions tended to hold to a generalized belief that conditions in Hunter's Point were "bad."

Because of this lack of communication, there is little overt hostility shown toward whites by Hunter's Point blacks. This pattern continued even throughout the "riots" (see Chapter 10). In fact, the "riots" merely permitted the police to reintroduce the pattern, which had been temporarily abandoned, of isolating Hunter's Point residents.

Young men and women and older teenagers spend very little time in Hunter's Point proper. There is nothing to do there. Aside from a gymnasium in the school and the schoolyard itself, there are no places in Hunter's Point that can conceivably be thought of as entertainment

188

centers. This is especially true for anyone over twenty years of age. Most of the time the young people of Hunter's Point (and most of the time their elders as well) go "down to Third Street" to the bars, restaurants, fried chicken or barbecue stands, and record shops which dot the area. Some ten to fifteen years ago, as we have noted, black youths who came down "off the hill" at night were met by police who would roust them and send them back to Hunter's Point. The police theory at the time, as explained by older police officers and as fully understood by the Hunter's Point residents, was that it was better to keep them "niggers in their place" — their place obviously being on the "hill."

Both Housing Authority "cops" and the local municipal police concurred in this judgment and overall had some degree of success in keeping Hunter's Point youth in Hunter's Point, which again reduced the possibilities of interracial contact for the Hunter's Pointers. This, as I have suggested, was probably one of the contributing factors in the rise and importance in the "bopping gangs" in Hunter's Point.

That is, the Hunter's Point youth, prevented by this quarantine from releasing their energies by exploring the city, thrown together into the game of fighting for status, and having no way to relieve their frustrations (let alone normal youthful aggressiveness) except in fighting each other, turned to "bopping." Bopping gangs are, of course, fighting gangs, and this period up until approximately 1962 was characterized by the existence of organized predatory gangs in Hunter's Point. There was an extremely high level of general reputed violence, though local police are extremely reluctant to discuss relative crime frequencies in the area.

At the present time organized youth gangs have all but disappeared. There are no doubt several factors contributing to this. Although the population of "the hill" is greatly reduced from that of the Korean war and post-Korean war periods,[1] the expansion of the black community past Third Street into the Bayview area has made it meaningless to try to "keep 'em on the hill." Local police attitudes, at least at the highest levels of policy making, have changed dramatically (even though many Hunter's Point residents feel the chief of police of the city is a racist and that the average patrolman is no better). Additionally, the general change in the mood of black communities throughout the United States from one of passive resignation and self-hate, with the concomitant violence directed toward other blacks, has changed in the face of civil rights revolutions and general attitudes of whites.

The extent to which either these general factors or the reduced pressure on Hunter's Point youth to "stay in their place" have been instrumental in the disappearance of the gangs is not clear. More research needs to be done to determine this.[2] One other possible factor is the Housing Authority itself, which until 1966 had arbitrarily "kicked out" any tenants whose families had a "bad character." Obviously, the most spirited and aggressive blacks and their children were the natural targets for such action. In any event, it is now a neighborhood of relative safety for visitors. Relationships with whites at Hunter's Point are still seen as being with "the man" or his representatives and are rarely satisfactory for those inhabitants.

It might be proposed as well that this concern with "the man" (as any white in a position of power — or whites in authority collectively — is called) is a further reflection of the recognition that the structural situation of the blacks in Hunter's Point has made him feel that masculinity, with its prerogatives of power and independence, are available only to whites. The unavailability of such prerogatives to Hunter's Point blacks must inevitably lead them to make insidious and unflattering comparisons of themselves vis-à-vis whites. In such a situation, relationships with whites can hardly be friendly.

The Youth Opportunity Center, a clearing house for service organization currently under the direction of the State Employment Service, is one of the best examples of a self-conscious contact agency between the larger (white) and smaller (black) societies. Its purpose is supposedly to bring youth to jobs and jobs to youth, to act as a center for job preparation and training, and to advise on school matters and those related to the development of saleable skills. Its most important function is supposedly that of an outreach organization.

On the first day of my investigation in the area, I was accosted at the door of the Youth Opportunity Center by a small group of black male teenagers.

Myself: Is this the Youth Opportunity Center headquarters?
Youth: Yeah, man. Hey, you come to be our teacher?
Myself: What?
Youth: We supposed to get some guy volunteered to teach us. You a teacher?
Myself: Yes.
Youth: You teach us square roots?

Myself: Why?

Youth: We got to know square roots to pass the tests to be apprenticed carpenters. It's got square roots in the test.

Myself: This is the Youth Opportunity Center — won't they teach you here how to do square roots to pass the test here? This is where they're giving the test, isn't it?

Youth: They say they ain't got nobody to do it with. Besides, they don't teach you nothin' here.

Myself: Okay, come here and I'll show you some square roots.

The boys were correct in their evaluation of the Youth Opportunity Center. It is no particular exaggeration to say that the "opportunity center" teaches little and offers few opportunities. On paper, there were always many "courses" listed leading to salable skills. (Apart from the fact that most handicraft-type skills are rapidly becoming obsolete, and that such training only trains individuals into obsolescence, the idea of having lower-class youth trained only for "lower-class" jobs tends to recreate a "ghetto" atmosphere in the minds of everyone concerned.) The "courses" actually available, however, seemed mostly to be for girls. There were only two courses for boys, one for gardeners and the other for office boys, neither being given at the time and both having had a high dropout rate while they were being given. One of the staff directors (white) explained, "We just can't set up classes for boys, there is no one to teach them useful skills. Besides, it's hard to get jobs for them, especially if they have records, and so many of them do, you know. Girls we can always place."

Thus, the very service which is supposed to create economic power for blacks by expanding job skills, and thus perhaps help "normalize" the family structure in such a community, tends to teach little to boys and to perpetuate matridominance by training mainly girls. The training facilities are so inadequate that to prepare for a test which might get them a "good-payin' job," young black males on the very doorstep of the Youth Opportunity Center had to ask a complete stranger to teach them square roots so that they could pass the test that day.

Willy, one of the boys involved, was not at all impressed with the possibilities of getting a job, regardless of whether he passed the test or not.

"Man, they send you down to the place, the man tell you he ain't got no jobs. Now how come they don't know they ain't got no jobs before he get you there? They [the center personnel] tells you this guy just called askin' for some guy. You go right down, twenty minutes later, they ain't got no job. They ain't nobody wants to hire us, I don't care how many fuckin' square roots you know."

If one level of confrontation between whites and Hunter's Point blacks involves the unsuccessful job applicant, another involves the inability of certain kinds of staff members in service agencies to understand the people they are dealing with.

Willy, four days after the above incident, led a sit-in at the Youth Opportunity Center demanding that he and his friends be given jobs. The community's police liaison man for youth talked them out of it after the staff director (at this point a white) of the center proved totally inadequate to the situation. Angered by this affront, the staff director refused to talk to the strikers. In retaliation for what was perceived as a calculated insult, the participants in the sit-in turned on the fire extinguisher in the building. They were dissuaded from violence by the police liaison man, who calmed the tempers that had been aroused by the abrupt, distant, and patronizing manner of the staff director himself.

The staff director did not lack insight into his difficulty, and was concerned with his inability to deal in a personal manner with the people of the community in which he had been placed.

"I just don't like them. I can't help it. I wish I was at some nice middle-class office. You see, I can't stand the trashy music they listen to on their transistors. Now, I know they have a right to listen to the kind of music they like, and I am broadminded about the fact that they do, but I can't help not liking it. I'm a KKHI person [KKHI is a local "classical" music station] and no matter how hard I try I just can't understand them."

The essential desire of many service agency personnel to run an effective office and to serve this community is thus buried beneath the glacierlike movement of bureaucratic adaptation, lack of understanding, fear, and powerlessness to change even so simple a thing as the hiring habits of San Francisco employers.

Many more such examples could be cited, the limiting factor being only the limited number of organized contact points between the dominant and subordinate communities.

192

THE POLICE AND SOCIAL CONTROL

About the only major representative of the white community that the average Hunter's Point resident comes into more or less continuous contact with is the policeman. Technically, the Hunter's Point resident police are only Housing Authority police. They do not belong to the San Francisco Police Department and, being essentially private police in charge of guarding property, they are theoretically unable to enforce municipal laws. Though their captain is a municipal police force inspector assigned to the Potrero Hill station, San Francisco police rarely enter Hunter's Point.[3]

The Housing Authority police in Hunter's Point function as a buffer between Hunter's Point residents and adequate police protection. That is, the residents of Hunter's Point complain bitterly not of the brutality of the racially integrated Housing Authority police (though there are complaints about their generally unpleasant disposition), but of their refusal to give meaningful police protection. The anger of the tenants is especially directed at the fact that the main job of the police seems to be to let people into their houses (after they have inadvertently locked themselves out) for a five-dollar fee.

"Them kids come into the halls shootin' them craps and turnin' over the fire extinguishers, and you call the cops and they tell you, 'Don't worry, they's just kids.' I used to walk from the bus stop in 1946, and up to 1950, but I haven't for a long time now, sometimes they come and grab your purse and they insult you and throw things. The cops, they never come when you call."

"I called them when these boys throwed rocks through my window. That policeman, he say, 'What do you expect me to do about it?'"

"They don't care, you know they don't, long as no one gets killed, they don't even interfere in fights. They just drives by like they don't see nothin'."

The observations of the Hunter's Point residents are that the police tend to avoid any conflict situations, offer very little in the way of protection, and actually by their presence keep the Housing Authority area from being adequately patrolled. Moreover, these police have a "bad attitude" toward the tenants. This "bad attitude" in the tenants' terms consists of "looking down on" tenants, verbally abusing them, and in general making their distaste for the tenants obvious. This "bad attitude" reflects, according to the tenants, the attitude of the city government in general and the Housing Authority in particular.

The inspector in charge of the Hunter's Point police, the liaison to the Potrero Hill station, admits that the Housing Authority police rarely request help from the Potrero Hill station except in extreme cases such as murder (which he claims is no more frequent here than in the rest of the city, though there is a real reluctance on the part of the Housing Authority police to discuss crime rates in Hunter's Point). On the other hand, the inspector says it is a quiet place with nice folks and "just like any other middle-class area of the city."[4]

After delivering himself of these opinions he went on to reminisce about the "good old days," when there was a lot more fighting in the city.

"Everybody used to fight a lot then; there was a lot of fight clubs. Everybody knew how to box and you could have some real good fights on Saturday night. We didn't care as much about fighting then as we do now, people I guess just get more nervous about simple little fights than we used to. It used to be lots of fun. People shouldn't get so upset by a little fighting nowadays, but I guess things have changed a lot. It's the same with all this talk about Bay pollution. Heck, we used to swim right near the sewer outlets, if you's see a big one [a piece of human excrement] you'd just yell and duck."

The inspector was of course suggesting that though the general opinion of Hunter's Point is that it's a dangerous place with a great deal of fighting, the fighting there is not significantly different from the fighting he remembers as a boy in the then predominantly Irish Mission district. More important, his suggestion (here and in other statements to me) that there is no unusual crime or nuisance problem in Hunter's Point obviously serves to take him off the hook — and the Hunter's Point and city police as well — in terms of their responsibility in policing the area.

The patrolmen themselves have a somewhat different attitude.

194

"I been here twelve years and I could tell you some hair-raising stories about these people. Some of 'em — not all, mind you, 'cause there's some good ones — but some of 'em are no better'n animals. Yeah, you could find a lot of trouble if you go looking for it, but I don't. No sir, I don't go looking for trouble — let 'em knock their own heads together."

Thus, although there is a difference in the two interpretations — the inspector's normal-neighborhood perception and the patrolman's perception of an unusual amount of trouble — they are both used to rationalize a low level of police activity within Hunter's Point.

Most citizens expect the police, whether Housing Authority or city police, to prevent crime, to intervene when crimes are taking place, and to solve crimes and apprehend criminals. In fact, however, there are values and expectations of behavior on the part of both the police and tenants in Hunter's Point which make it impossible to perform these functions. For example, many of the phone complaints which the Housing Authority police receive from tenants concern noisy parties, loud behavior on the streets, gambling in the halls and on the stairways of apartment buildings, general rowdyism, and similarly offensive, but not necessarily criminal, behavior. Given this wide range of possible "violations" of law in the eyes of the complainer, the police obviously must make some decisions as to which situations demand their intervention.

What constitutes "crime" to be stopped while taking place? While many complainants classify loud, boisterous behavior or dancing down the sidewalk playing a transistor radio full blast as "disturbing the peace," the police under most circumstances do not consider this to be a police matter. Unless the complaints persist, loud parties or loud street behavior seem to fit into the same category. This stems from certain perceptions and has certain effects. The police feel that, after all, "this is not a normal neighborhood" (despite the above-quoted comments of the inspector to the contrary) and that the police should not try too strictly to enforce codes of conduct and morality in this neighborhood which might be appropriate to some others. (The whole idea that police are enforcers of moral codes and mores reflects an interesting notion in itself, but it is too involved to go into here.)

This is based on the commonsense observation that behavior is different in this neighborhood than it is in some others, and that it would only irritate and unnecessarily harass the population (and concurrently make police work that much harder) to police it strictly. While this observation is a somewhat sophisticated recognition of subcultural differences, it also implies to many residents a paternalistic and racist attitude on the part of the police. Some tenants are infuriated by the implication that borderline public disturbances or loud behavior are to be tolerated because the people in Hunter's Point "don't know no better." On the other hand, many of these same people are just as infuriated by attempts to codify and enforce middle-class morality.

In this "damned if you do and damned if you don't" situation neither side can possibly be happy with the other, and it is important to remember that both the police and the tenants see themselves as mutually antagonistic and not cooperative except through necessity. If "middle-class" standards (as interpreted by the police) were enforced insofar as public behavior is concerned, many residents would see this as the latest in a series of attempts to crush black individualism and mold it along "white" lines. Yet the police's very failure, in effect, to do this is equally infuriating, at least in part because the tenants (correctly) observe the racial prejudice and (partly sophisticated) cultural bias which largely underlie such police behavior.[5]

The same kinds of perceptions operate with regard to the police function of preventing crime and solving crime. A typical technique for preventing crime in lower-class neighborhoods is simply to "roust" and harass "suspicious-looking" people or those who are known to have criminal records or who associate with known criminals. However, many of the outward signs that policemen in other neighborhoods would associate with a "suspicious person" simply cannot be reasonably applied in Hunter's Point. Where the majority of the youth affect clothing which would be considered bizarre by white middle-class standards (though the "hippie" revolution in clothing is narrowing this difference), clothing does not serve to indicate "suspicious persons" — or, put another way, to the police, clothing indicates only too well the degree of "suspiciousness" of Hunter's Point youth.

Unpleasant demeanor and attempts to intimidate the police by insulting words and gestures are so common that police simply do not respond to them any more, although they certainly add to police-community tensions.

Furthermore, in other parts of town automatic suspicion tends to fall on poor, young, male blacks of "sullen" disposition and aggressive temperament, so that they are differentially rousted and harassed compared to whites in the same area (not meaning, incidentally, to imply that these relatively normal criteria for "suspiciousness" are either proper or correct, but merely to identify them as existing police techniques). At any rate, in a neighborhood such as Hunter's Point, where most of the young may fit this description and where there may be no visible opposing "majority" code to judge deviations by, such criteria are largely irrelevant.

Thus, patrolmen in Hunter's Point, who have already decided that normal standards of acceptable behavior in white middle-class neighborhoods are not applicable in this neighborhood, must decide further that what they would usually term "suspicious behavior" is also inadequate here as a criterion of potential criminality. This leaves them with only informants or their own observations and knowledge of who has been previously involved in criminal activities as means of determining whom to keep an eye on. But in a neighborhood where police informing is despised more than in most neighborhoods, and where nascent motives of black solidarity against whites operate, few reliable informants exist. Furthermore, the criterion of prior criminality loses much of its value in Hunter's Point where a large percentage of the youth have some form of criminal record and many others do not only because of the leniency of the police or a refusal to prosecute.

Besides facing these obstacles to the prevention of and intervention in crime, the Housing Authority police are often frustrated in their attempts to solve crimes. The most common complaints requiring police action are personal assaults and theft (including burglary), the latter being far the more common of the two. Few families in Hunter's Point have not had something of value stolen from them, from wash hanging on a line (no woman in her right mind allows wash to dry on the line in her absence) to the contents of an entire apartment. Indeed, "babysitters" are commonly hired for furniture, since anyone absent from his Hunter's Point apartment for two or three days faces the real possibility of having his furniture stolen – or at least his television, radios, and/or stereo. But since theft is so common and disposal of stolen merchandise apparently so easy, the possibility of solving cases of petty theft or burglary is so remote that police typically do not even try; in many cases, they do not even respond to residents' reports of theft.

A final factor contributing to the relatively low level of police activity in Hunter's Point is that most police, whether Housing Authority or city, perceive (correctly) the largely racial overtones of the police-tenant

relationship and dread the possibility of some chance encounter explod-
ing into a massive racial incident. To reduce the possibility of such
encounters to the bare minimum, therefore, they intercede in the community as police only as a last alternative. No matter how well inten-
tioned their caution, however, their apparent — in fact, real — lack of
concern and avoidance of responsibility is obvious.

Police behavior may swing to the other extreme as a result of this
situation, however. Frustration among the police engendered by their
general feelings of impotence, recognition of their reduced importance,
and avoidance of traditional police roles may lead to periodic outbursts
of truly excessive police brutality. There is apparently a limit to the
number of times most policemen can fail to catch teenage thieves escap-
ing on foot before they lose their control and act in a vicious, brutal,
and excessively destructive way (which in part was the genesis of the
"riot").

Hunter's Point residents respond to both too little and too much
police action. While excessive use of police power currently receives
more coverage in the media, the response to underpolicing is more important to this study, as it predates and influences the violent responses
and counterresponses that characterized the "riot."

First of all, inadequate police protection is seen by Hunter's Pointers
as one more reflection of the (white) general public's disinterest in and
contempt for their community and its problems. Their (often correct)
assumption is that police think of them merely as "animals" and don't
care what they do to each other so long as they stay on "the hill." Secondly, police indifference and refusal to get involved is sometimes seen
as a result of police "fear" of the strength, power, and manliness of
black Hunter's Point males: since this agrees with the community's
value-judgment of blacks as stronger, more skilled in fighting, and hyper-
sexed (i.e., as "superspades," compared with effeminate whites), it is a
highly acceptable interpretation for Hunter's Pointers. And as usual with
such perceptions, it partially reflects reality. The reality it reflects, however, is not the actual power and hypersexuality of black males, but a
generalized belief and fear in the minds of the police that such power
exists.

Since these fears and values and part-distorted, part-accurate perceptions exist among both police and tenants in Hunter's Point, each group
succeeds in interpreting the attitudes of the other with only partial
validity. This leads not to the supposed fruits of greater understanding —

i.e., tolerance – but to increasingly more unbearable tensions and aggravating incidents which appear at least now to require periodic release among both groups in the form of outbursts of aggression.

To return again to the issue of black male power and strength, I have said that being a "bad motherfucker" is probably valued more highly than, or at least as highly as, any other image in Hunter's Point. Regardless of the reality, all the young men there like to view themselves as "mean" and "bad." Apart from the obvious indications of psychic stress indicated by terming oneself a "motherfucker" (which is at least suggestive of poorly resolved Oedipal concerns and which I believe reflects the matrifocal situation),[6] to value "mean" and "bad" as personal appellations is to indicate the necessity of defending the ego against the feelings of impotence and powerlessness easily fostered by the structural situation of the black male. If, as I have suggested, the most common psychic defense in Hunter's Point is denial of reality, it becomes clearer why the weak, emasculated, personally powerless, poor, and – in his own eyes – backward black male in Hunter's Point would grasp the opportunity to picture himself as effective. If nothing else, he is "bad" (able and willing to impose himself physically on others).

But I might also suggest that such designations are infantile. Words such as *bad* and *mean* connote childish behavior in the absence of parental norms, or small and petty malfeasance. It might well be that Hunter's Point males for all their bravado do not even fool themselves, that even in the process of denial of their impotence they must use words suggestive of an infant's status. It seems, however, that this is not a conscious attitude.

I am more confirmed in this belief in view of the responses to racial violence on the part of the inhabitants of Hunter's Point. Commenting at length on the infamous "Watts riots" in Los Angeles, which antedated the Hunter's Point "riot," Hunter's Point residents saw it as a tremendous expression of black strength, though in fact nearly all the victims of the riot were black. "We really showed them gray [i.e., white] bastards," seems somehow incongruous in the face of the fact that very little violence was directed against "grays," with the exception of absent owners of retail establishments. Black "rioters" in Watts did not leave Watts to attack whites in their own neighborhoods. They simply did what blacks have traditionally done – introjected the violence and turned it as much on themselves as on others. This was to be an even clearer pattern in San Francisco.

Thus, fantasized aggression against police is used in place of actual aggression more often than not. The police, however, aware of this hostility, are as concerned about symbolic as real aggression. Insofar as frustration and prejudice can combine to provoke explosive actions by the police, they even more strongly provoke black males — and not all such aggressiveness is symbolic. While "being a man" is extremely important to the young black male, and while his friends and others continuously confirm this image by addressing him as "man," the police have a tendency not to treat him at all like a man. He is called "punk," "stupe," and a variety of other insulting epithets. These threats hit too close to home for many teenage black males. Many arrests and charges of "resisting arrest" or "assaulting an officer" have as their genesis unbearable tongue-lashings by police which are seen as demeaning by young black males.

Police-resident relationships, then, are predictably unpredictable and unsatisfactory. Both police action and police inaction provoke negative response among the residents. The former is seen as racially oppressive, the latter as stemming from indifference or fear; and, as I have discussed, both perceptions are accurate enough to receive support from each new confrontation. In this circularly negative situation, the police cannot be expected to enforce general social sanctions in such a way that the community accepts them.

INDIGENOUS COMMUNITY SOCIAL CONTROL

Much of the social control in Hunter's Point, therefore, can be exercised only by force of community opinion, but problems inherent in the structure of the ghetto — or perhaps more accurately, "plantation" system (as Eddington suggested to me in 1967) — make this method of enforcing laws and mores as ineffectual as those the police currently apply. "Community opinion" is likely to have the greatest effect in Hunter's Point on those younger than teen age and over fifty. Teenagers and people in their twenties — those most likely to be involved in gambling, heavy drinking, fighting, and theft — are least likely to be affected by the types of personal social sanctions which are brought to bear upon them in Hunter's Point. This is true for several reasons. First, Hunter's Point is not truly a community in the sense that its residents have a conscious self-identification with, and pride in, their neighbors. It is merely a place to live — or more accurately, to sleep. For young men and women, since they spend little time there, it does not represent "home" in some secure sense.

But more importantly, the social sanctions represented by the complaints of middle-aged women can be ignored with a certain degree of impunity, especially by young males. Since this is one of the few ways of exhibiting independence and superiority over women by young men, they do it willingly and happily. On the other hand, it is well to remember that many of the complaints registered by older blacks against promiscuity and drinking (which in some senses are not legal problems at all in that they are "crimes without victims"), and against gambling, fighting, and thievery are motivated by a generational and subcultural value shock.

Many of the older blacks exhibit the "Uncle Tom" pattern of the handkerchief-headed, shuffling "good nigger"; they are industrious, thrifty, concerned with what "folk" (including whites) will think of "all this carryin' on", and are intensely religious churchgoers. It is these people who are the complainants against other Hunter's Pointers. The rather rigid attitudes they express reflect an antisex, antidrinking, antipleasure ethic based on fundamentalist Southern Protestant religious tradition, all of which conflicts (at least superficially) with both the "cool" pattern of adaptation which stresses a detached and cynical non-involvement and with the rowdy pattern of black male exhibitionism, not to mention the newer, pro-Third World supranational black militancy.[7] In Hunter's Point there was by the summer of 1967 little of the "black militancy" which many whites and many older blacks both fear and despise. But the "rowdy" pattern and the even more reprehensible (from the churchgoers's point of view) "cool" pattern involving emotional detachment, occasional drug use, and a rejection of middle-class white values were prevalent. Community sanctions applied by such "traditionally oriented" blacks as remain in Hunter's Point can only fail to affect these quite disparate life styles.

As I pointed out earlier, the final major sanctioning agency in Hunter's Point is the Housing Authority itself, but its main power, that of simply evicting tenants (sometimes arbitrarily), is rapidly being reduced. In the absence of any other effective form of social control, then, what sanctions and control as exist have become related more directly to the values of the young. And what this has come to mean is a greater consciousness of the antagonisms between white and black society and a growing acceptance of the belief that whatever behavior hurts a white man, regardless of its middle-class moral status, is justifiable on that account alone.

This violent distortion of relations between the races here — ultimately attributable to the racist attitudes of whites, the personal pathologies resulting from the typical family pattern among blacks, and the black adult's powerlessness in relation to whites — inevitably led to a confrontation (the "riots") in which the entire scenario of white-black relationships was played out in microcosm.

NOTES

[1]Both a drop in the number of shipyard jobs and the opening up of the rest of the city to blacks have contributed to this, as has the increasing sophistication and urbanization of this originally "Southern black" enclave.

[2]Personal communications from various social scientists in other urban areas also suggest the decrease in the phenomenon of the bopping gangs. See discussion in *Transaction* 4, 1967, pp. 79-80.

[3]This has become less true since the "riot."

[4]The inspector was openly distrustful of "reporter types" with what he considered good justification. He felt irresponsible statements about Hunter's Point were inflammatory and created more difficulties than they solved. Having been "burned" (exploited) by such types in the past, he was noticeably reluctant to discuss certain things with me. His patrolmen had no such reservations.

[5]This is merely one aspect of the larger problems which such issues suggest, including the core problem of the meaning and technique of law enforcement in an urban context with heterogeneous populations and a heritage of individual freedom. See Kenneth Rexroth, "The Fuzz," *Playboy,* July 1967, p. 76 ff.

[6]Even though such terms have become culturally sanctioned expressions, I believe that they continue to express dominant modes of emotional expression. That they have become more common in the dominant culture reflects less some abstract "cultural borrowing" and more significant changes in the social and family structure of the dominant culture, an issue we cannot discuss at length here.

[7]Lipset and Bendix (1959) argue that this particular pattern of Uncle Tomism is a reflection of lower-class status-"transvaluation" religion which teaches that the good rather than the rich will be rewarded in the afterlife and of a high degree of child-centeredness that encourages parents to seek satisfaction in high aspirations for their children even though their own personal goals have not been achieved.

Yinger (1965), on the other hand, observes that the militant Black Muslim movement "strengthens the family, encourages thrift, honesty and discipline on the job. . . . It furnishes symbolic outlets for hostility."

This form of revitalization had not occurred in Hunter's Point.

10

THE "RIOT"

THE specific precipitating factor in the "rioting" which began on Tuesday, September 27, 1966, was a shooting incident. When Matthew Johnson, a sixteen-year-old black, fled on foot from a white San Francisco police patrolman, Alvin Johnson, despite the latter's commands to halt for questioning, the patrolman shot and killed the youth in a lot off of Navy Road, which runs through Hunter's Point. Patrolman Johnson, new to the beat, believed that young Johnson and two other youths were fleeing from a stolen car which they had abandoned at his approach.

The police account of this incident and the events growing out of it was published as a pamphlet entitled "128 Hours"[1] (the total length of the disturbance), which details events in strict chronological form. The report implies that the San Francisco police handled the situation in an orderly and dignified fashion, at no time misread the situation, and overall displayed professional competence.

As might be expected, the police report is at variance in several serious respects with descriptions of some participating police officers (none of whom I can name at this time without prejudicing their positions), with certain reports in the public media, and with the reports of many civilians who were present and/or arrested. Clearly those who are involved in a confrontation situation with the police and whose relations with the police are less than friendly even under "normal" circumstances cannot be expected to side with the police account of such an affair, nor necessarily even to be objective. On the other hand, the police themselves have an obvious vested interest in seeing their actions vindicated. One uncontested fact, however, is that police action in subsequent events did *not* result in any deaths after that of Matthew Johnson.

Immediately following the shooting a large, angry crowd gathered around the spot where the boy had been killed, breaking up only after two hours (by about four in the afternoon). Fearing the eruption of violence as an aftermath, as had happened in preceding year's Watts riots, the police attempted to head off trouble by enlisting the cooperation of black members of the city's Human Rights Commission, whom the police considered to be community leaders.

The fact of this lack of police killings is about the only thing everyone agrees upon concerning these events. The following account of these events is based upon some of my own eyewitness experiences, the comments and ex post facto reconstructions of a number of people (both Hunter's Point residents and police), and material from the public media. What follows, apart from any analysis of its meaning, is as close to an accurate account of the events as I am able to give.

Thus, a conference was arranged in the Economic Opportunity Center on Third Street, just outside the Hunter's Point housing site, between the "responsible community leaders" and seventy or so local black youths. Predictably, the black middle-class "community leaders" made absolutely no impression on the local young men except to further inflame their emotions. The young men of the community who had come together for this meeting expressed an interest in only one thing — that Patrolman Johnson be punished for "murder." In the light of our discussion of police community-relations in the Hunter's Point area, this reaction was understandable — although apparently not to the police.

The dynamics were simple. Young black men, emboldened by the action of blacks in Watts and thoroughly out of joint with their own passivity in the face of whites, aware of their economic deprivation and frustrated by the interpenetration of all of these factors, were making every attempt to assert themselves in the face of this traditionally feared element of the white community (the police). They had also learned to despise "Uncle Toms" (which they had come to view as including essentially all successful middle-class blacks) — a term that acts as a focal point for rejecting the passive responses with which Harriet Beecher

204

Stowe's character has been popularly (though somewhat mistakenly) identified. The assumption is made in Hunter's Point that "the man" owns the world so completely that "soul folk" can get ahead only by shuffling and saying "yassuh." Thus, achieving success in the white world is de facto evidence that one has been "Tomming."

The police, either realizing their mistake or simply attempting a new tack, turned to the head of Youth for Service, an organization of ex-gang youths which supposedly operated as a liaison between the police and the fighting gangs. This, too, of course, was doomed to failure, for the police, having failed to recognize that such gangs in Hunter's Point were no longer a focus of fighting activity or in fact of any organizational strength, were totally mistaken in believing that the Youth for Service leader exerted any significant community influence.

These two tactical errors were only the first ones committed by the city government. Later that evening Mayor Shelley of San Francisco addressed an "unruly crowd" at Third Street near the Bayview Community Center and indicated that Patrolman Johnson had been suspended pending an investigation of the incident. This move also backfired, for the individuals who by this time had begun to think in terms of "making their own little Watts" regarded the mayor's appearance on the scene as irrelevant, and even those who were not so minded were incensed by the mayor's apparent belief that the shooting was the sole incident causing the "riot," an attitude reflecting his basic inability to understand the roots and meaning of discontent in Hunter's Point. The promise of a mere suspension of one policeman had become insignificant.

For their part, Shelley and other civic leaders, taking refuge on the dignity of their offices, failed to understand that their "refusal to be moved by violence" was interpreted by Hunter's Point residents as an indication of their indifference and hate.

As one of the "rioters" said some days later:

"Shit, man, that the first time the white motherfucker ever come down here to Hunter's Point. Fuck, man, we should riot every week — that get something out of that motherfucker."

In fact, the desire to move "the man" by violence, which could also serve to offset feelings of personal inadequacy, was a core element of the situation.

Misperceptions involving the intervention of the black middle-class "leadership" were even more pitiful. The major error in judgment, of course, was thinking that their presence could do any good at all, which itself was based on a series of misperceptions — i.e., that they were in any sense leaders of Hunter's Point or even respected there, that they even understood what the disturbance was about at its core, and, finally, that they had any real power to change the social situation that underlay the disorders. Many of these "leaders" later expressed a view which went something like this: "If they [the Hunter's Pointers] only realized what is being done for them and what we're all trying to do, they wouldn't riot." It was apparent that these "leaders" did not see that "what was being done for them" was itself part of the whole complex package of frustrations of the sort leading to the disturbance.

The most eminent "Negro political leader" in the city, the only black on the city Board of Supervisors (Mayor Shelley had appointed him) and a man with a record as a leader in the NAACP and as a defense lawyer in civil rights cases in the city, was also part of the entourage which accompanied the mayor to Hunter's Point to address the "rioters" and to try to calm them. If anything, he was greeted with even greater hostility and violence than was the mayor.

Rocks were thrown at the entourage, some of them narrowly missing both the mayor and the black supervisor. The supervisor was completely unable to make himself heard. As one Hunter's Pointer put it:

"That cocksucker forget he's black, but when we put them fuckers on the run, they sure let him know at City Hall right away. Sheeit, man, who the fuck he think he's foolin'?"

By which the speaker meant that co-optation into the "white power structure" had turned the supervisor into a "white nigger." The speaker assumed that the supervisor was "trying to be white" and that the white power structure was abetting him in this fiction — until they needed him to suppress discontent among "his" people. At that point, the Hunter's Point logic followed, he was forced to "pay his dues" to the white power structure. The Hunter's Pointers felt that they more realistically perceived the situation than the supervisor, who was "fooling" himself into believing that he was really accepted as an equal. They thought of him as a hired overseer.

Thus, the situation passed the stage of seeking compromise and negotiation and reached the stage of total confrontation, at least partly

due to the original attempts of the police and the city fathers to calm
the situation. Their inaccurate perception of the leadership structure of
the community and their misconceptions concerning what would mollify
it only increased tensions and led to the degeneration of the situation
into more heightened confrontation.

After a night of sporadic looting, rock-throwing, and acts of petty
arson, an expanded group of "community leaders" (self-selected ones
as well as those chosen by the police and the mayor, but still having no
power to alter the real underlying problems in the community) were
unable (not surprisingly) to calm the situation. They were then given a
deadline ultimatum by the police: if by a certain time on Wednesday
afternoon they had not brought events under control, the police would
enter in force to do so. The "community leaders" — many of them part
of the middle-aged matriarchy and/or their ministerial allies, and others
who were ministerial and poverty workers not part of this structure —
got no further than before, and for a simple reason: *there was nothing
that they were empowered to offer the "rioters" to induce them to
stop "rioting" that was even half as rewarding as the "rioting" itself.*[2]
The feelings of manhood and power — especially the power to reverse
the roles of underdog and top dog relative to the police, who stand for
the white community — could not be compensated for by vague
promises.

Later Wednesday afternoon, the police asked for the assistance of the
National Guard and units of the Highway Patrol. Shortly before six an
incident occurred which inflamed the tempers of Hunter's Point residents
to a pitch that insured the "riot's" prolongation. Interestingly, the
police report notes this incident only in passing in the narrative section,
and in the official police log of activities it is not noted at all.[3] Police,
in response to alleged gunfire directed at them from the Bayview Community Center, began to open fire on the center. This unnecessary police
shooting occurred as a result of panic (again confirmed by reports from
individual policemen). Just before the shooting at the Bayview Community Center a policeman was hit on his forehead by a rock, which opened
a small cut. The rumor quickly spread: "They got one of our guys."
(Only later was it established that there were no police casualties by
shooting.) It was then that an unnamed sergeant gave the order to fire
at the center. Many officers apparently did so in panic. After literally
riddling this frame-structure building with every caliber bullet available
to them, police entered it only to find no gunmen, no weapons, no evi-

dence that any shooting had originated from inside the building, and several huddled, cowering children of preteen age.

The inhabitants of the community reacted to this incident in a predictable way and with a certain degree of realism in their analysis. The attack on the center confirmed their belief that the police were merely seeking excuses to kill them and that they could expect no mercy from the police. (As we have noted, the police in fact did not kill any of the "rioters.")

The accuracy of the community's perception is supported not only by reliable reports of overt antiblack attitudes expressed by the police, but also by strong evidence that police supposedly shooting into the Bayview Community Center engaged in willful property destruction. A careful examination of the center and surrounding buildings later revealed firearms damage on nearby buildings in places that offered no apparent reason for firing at — high up on the wall of a windowless concrete building, for example. One building in particular was clearly out of the line of fire of the center and more than a hundred feet beyond it. Yet there were as many bullet marks found on this building as there were on the center. Since the Bayview Community Center is a rather large target (a three-story building approximately 60 feet long and 40 feet wide) and since the police are trained marksmen and, it was established, *not* themselves under fire, there is little reason to believe that these misses were accidental. In fact, the pattern of bullet damage made some observers speculate that there was a competition among several policemen to see who could hit the gutterspouting on another building, a contention later supported by statements from policemen themselves.

That this panic and unnecessary shooting occurred is extremely important in evaluating the relationships between the white and black communities in San Francisco. White people in San Francisco continue to have the stereotyped notions of black dangerousness. This is a stereotype shared by most policemen, though there has been little evidence of other than juvenile attacks by blacks on whites in San Francisco. This stereotype, resultant in part from whites' projection of their racial hatred onto its object and guilt over the mistreatment of blacks, has continued in full force — even among police, who should actually be the most aware of the fact that black aggressiveness is almost always directed against other blacks.

After the shooting incident at the Bayview Community Center, the disturbances took the form of pure and simple race confrontation. Prior to this time, even though many people were angry there was still a "holiday mood" and confrontations were essentially verbal. Essentially the police, concerned and frightened, were in no position to make discriminations between "good" (law-abiding) blacks and "bad" (nonlaw-abiding) blacks. Thus, in the eyes of the police all blacks became automatically suspect — even members of the police force itself. Some black policemen (especially those in plain clothes and even after identifying themselves) were mistreated, manhandled, and racially insulted, as were (from their own reports) any of a number of inoffensive black middle-class people whose primary "sin" was that they happened to be the wrong color at the wrong time (such as those who came to "sightsee" the events, which proved a particular problem to one black informant who was arrested and subsequently dismissed from his job even though he was not convicted).

That the ultimate character of the confrontation would be racial should have been clear from the very start. For example, virtually no use was made of the police Community Relations Unit, the arm of the police force established specifically to deal with minority groups and whose head enjoys an excellent reputation even among some of the most incorrigible criminals in the Hunter's Point area. According to its members, no one from this unit, with the exception of the officer permanently assigned to the area, was called in. Some on the police force, both in and outside the unit, believe that failure to employ the unit was because of a rather thoroughgoing racism in the department which manifested itself as a distrust in the use of "soft tactics" in dealing with "rioters."

However, the core of the problem was perhaps what may be termed the "polarity dilemma" of racial disturbances. The police response was to consider residents riotous and dangerous long before they had actually become so; furthermore, they misunderstood the activities of the "rioters" and failed to comprehend what it would take to calm the situation. This perception of the blacks in Hunter's Point as essentially dangerous, while based (I believe) on an unreal perception, nonetheless determined the actions of the police — and consequently the actions of the "rioters." Just as the police may tend unconsciously to support a black's symbolic or fantasized aggressiveness or dangerousness and thus feed back the desired stereotype to be amplified and enlarged in day-to-day encounters in Hunter's Point, in a situation such as the "riot" this circular process of judgment and response is greatly accelerated. When such a process is in motion, once a "riot" has begun the police have no easy techniques for identifying friend or foe, and skin color then becomes the sole criterion: black skin = "rioter," white skin = "friend."

When responses are based on such an arbitrary characteristic as skin color, there is little opportunity for further, more sophisticated perceptions to develop. Response then is motivated almost entirely by past perceptions, regardless of how unrealistic they may be.

The next three days (Thursday, Friday, and Saturday, September 29-October 1), saw the "riot" continue with a decreasing incidence of violence, and then finally peter out. The property damage (several hundred thousand dollars) compared with riots in comparably sized cities was minimal, as were the casualties (ten civilians reported victims of gunshot wounds, no casualties among the police or other antiriot personnel).

This is in part why I have continued to set the word "rioters" in quotation marks; not only was the actual violence and destruction low in amount, but the character of the riot itself was quite significant.[4] Like its counterparts in Watts, it consisted with few exceptions of attacks on the property of whites (but also of nonwhites), shows of bravado calculated to frighten and cow police, and enough running around and breaking windows to give the participants a feeling of real potency while actually not confronting white power in any significant way.[5]

Perhaps the best indication of both the essentially passive character of the response of black males in Hunter's Point and the unreasonable magnitude of white fears is the fact that, aside from long-range brick throwing, less than a half a dozen assaults by blacks against whites were recorded in the course of five days of "rioting." (Throwing bricks from a distance at policemen, breaking store windows, and looting can hardly be considered acts of physical violence of the same order as the mayhem perpetrated against persons daily in every large metropolitan area.) Also, the fact that "riots" took place in all parts of the city with sizeable black populations (the Mission district, the Potrero Hill area, the huge Fillmore district) and yet resulted in so few injuries indicates the presence of some restraining factor other than the police. I suggest it was the black "rioters'" internalized fear of whites, so difficult to break down, coupled with a "holiday mood." Thus, these "riots" have to be seen as attempts to strengthen personal self-image at least as much as direct expressions of hatred and dissatisfaction with whites. The two are deeply intermingled.

The response of the police was itself interesting in terms of the history of Hunter's Point. We have noted above that traditionally until the beginning of the sixties the police had dealt with black youths from Hunter's Point essentially by isolating them there. One officer described his customary way of dealing with blacks "out of bounds" as saying:

"Get back up on the hill where you belong, nigger. If I see your black ass down here again, I'll shoot it off."

At the outbreak of the riots, though they were more or less citywide, the same tactic was once again utilized. Blacks, no matter who they were or what their reason for being in the area of Third Street, were either arrested or herded back up "the hill."

This strategy used by city and state forces in isolating the "rioters" meant that very seldom did any officers themselves attempt to go up on the hill. Thus, the hill became a staging area for those "rioters" old enough to remember that "they're doing to us again what they used to do."[6] The agitation that moved the "rioters" then had a focal point in time and space as well as in the general conditions under which the people lived.

However, not all responses by either whites or blacks were negative. The official police report (Long and Trueb, n.d.) notes that by Thursday black youth peace patrols had begun forming. These were the result of actions by some of the young men in Hunter's Point, among them the few truly effective community leaders, who were aided as best they could be by the severely hampered head of the police Community Relations Unit attached to the Hunter's Point area. Unfortunately, while the police at the highest levels officially approved these honest efforts to reestablish peace in the community (for example, members of the peace patrol wore distinctive armbands to that end), the actions of the police rank and file on the scene were a great deal less than enthusiastic: here the polarity dilemma was given a new dimension by the introduction of the implied issue of "professional competence" — although the underlying issue was really racial antagonism.

Many police officers viewed positive police responses to these attempts as "coddling," as granting official approval to what they viewed as illegitimate black youth organizations — in their minds, an undifferentiated amalgam of the (nonexistent) "bopping gangs," various poverty workers, and other local political activists. Such an attitude was, of course, inevitable in the face of the developments which had caused the "riot" polarity. If all individuals who had black skin were to be considered enemies and potential "rioters," then empowering these very "enemies" to do what the police had clearly not so far done could only antagonize the more prejudiced members of the police force.[7]

While the aftermath of the "riot" cannot be easily evaluated in a systematic fashion, its effects on the community were clearly massive and far-reaching. There has been a noticeably greater distrust of whites – any whites – in the Hunter's Point community, and while this might be expected, its implications go beyond the statement of fact. Immediately after the "riot," many residents of Hunter's Point clearly harbored the hope that the events of the fall would lead to a greater solidarity among community groups. There was the anticipation that many of the young men who had distinguished themselves in peace-making activities would gain prestige and power in the community.

Not only did these hopes fail to materialize, but the opposite occurred: even greater community disintegration resulted. The general beliefs that "nobody cares" and that "it's too late to do anything" became widespread. Many of the most personally secure individuals in Hunter's Point have now come to believe that what they had perceived as a real "opening" for dialogue with the white community was mere white hypocrisy and double-dealing. Finally, the impact of the appearance and use of automatic weapons, portable artillery, and United States troops, which residents perceived as a full-scale war directed against them because of their skin color, can hardly be exaggerated.[8]

For some the "riot" inspired grandiose plans of "war" against white society, for less adventurous souls at least the purchase of small arms to "take some of them with us." Others perceived such orientations as essentially self-deluding and have simply given up hope and withdrawn. Overall there seems to be a general acceptance of the massive power which the white community did, can, and will bring to bear against them.

Since the white community apparently agreed that skin color was ultimately the only useful criterion that police could use in deciding whether or not to "rough you up," blacks have found it very difficult to initiate or continue dialogues with whites in Hunter's Point. Thus, this channel for the resolution of problems has dried up.

In addition, very few community organizations continued functioning in Hunter's Point after the "riots." Even the long-existing Bayview Community Center now counts many pessimistic and cynical "time servers" among its staff, and the general feeling is that it will soon close.

Interestingly, there was by 1967 very little discussion of the "riots" by Hunter's Pointers. It was in fact difficult to elicit responses from anyone there concerning them. One pseudopositive effect has been an increased belief on the part of teenaged and young adult males that they are now perceived as truly dangerous. Myths have grown up locally about the bravery, audacity, and "badness" of many young men, which further reduces their reality orientations. This so desperately wanted recognition of themselves as meaningful and potent has done little to remedy the underlying causes of these inadequacy feelings.

The white community has also utilized denial of reality as a technique for coping with this problem. Immediately after the "riots," a consortium of local business leaders offered "two thousand jobs" for Hunter's Point youths to try to alleviate the severe unemployment problem. These promises of steady full-time or part-time work were made in October 1966. Such jobs were to be channeled through the Youth Opportunity Center. As of June 1967, nineteen job openings had actually materialized.

As one of the staff at the Youth Opportunity Center indicated:

"It is no longer possible to get the kids here to be enthusiastic about going for jobs — or waiting for all those jobs to come through. They just don't believe it will happen. They are right! After the first big rush of kids coming here for jobs after the riots, when no jobs happened, they just stopped coming. It's just as well, we don't have anything for them."

Demoralization and generalized fear or hopelessness on the one hand, or unrealistic bravado on the other, now tend to characterize the attitudes a large number of Hunter's Point residents.

NOTES

[1]"128 Hours: A Report on the Disturbance in the City and County of San Francisco," compiled and prepared by Sgt. F. Long and R. Trueb (San Francisco: San Francisco Police Department, n.d.).

[2]This point is discussed in greater detail in Hippler (1970a, 1970b, 1970c).

[3]Nevertheless, it is the one incident every police officer involved in the riot remembered clearly and the one all Hunter's Point residents recall.

[4]A few fires were set, some windows broken, some looting along Third Street but primarily just movement of large numbers of "uncontrolled" blacks along the streets, made up the character of the "riot."

[5]It must be remembered that San Francisco was early in the pattern of summer riots in major cities in the United States and that the increasing ferocity of such

riots can be attributed to growing feelings of potency and an awareness among black youths that they must do something "real bad" to "whitey" to make themselves feel more powerful. It also goes without saying that this attitude on the part of blacks reflects their recognition of the increasing antagonism of the dominant majority toward the legitimate claims of the black community in the United States and the increasing belief that the only way to deal with the problem is through the use of massive armed force. Unfortunately, it is easy to predict that the use of such force will lead to an intensification of the "polarity dilemma" of riot control in which the only essential criteria used either for arrests or killing is skin color and in which individual race hatreds on the part of participating whites are allowed almost punishment-free release. This in turn can only lead (at this stage of increasing personal awareness of their personal pathology and inadequate social position on the part of blacks) to a development of increasingly more sophisticated techniques of guerilla warfare and increasingly more acceptability of the polarity dilemma itself. That this can only lead to social catastrophe if the self-fulfilling prophecy aspects and the spiraling reactions are not stopped seems about as clear as any statement of social fact can be. A prediction which includes the possibility of total race war and concentration camps is not beyond possibility, nor even extreme, under these circumstances.

[6]Even "moderately responsible" black adults expressed the direct fear that blacks were being herded into Hunter's Point so that they could be systematically bombarded by naval vessels in the bay. This feeling was exacerbated by the coincidental movement of an aircraft carrier in the bay which was then passing Hunter's Point. Panic, fear, and a sense of total isolation from the United States as a social system typified the feelings of many residents.

> "When I was a boy in the army, I mean, man they was bringing in ninety-millimeter recoilless rifles against us. I was scared. Man, that was what we was trained to use against the enemy. And that's what I was now — the enemy. I was just waiting for that carrier to send over planes and bomb us like they do in Vietnam."

[7]Reports of various officers indicate that this was a further precipitating factor in the development of a strong cadre of John Birch Society members among the San Francisco police force. Antagonism to the police Community Relations Unit and the concept of indigenous community leadership as potential police power in the ghetto areas has, from the reports of various officers, burgeoned through this confrontation and the inadequacy of the various techniques used to solve it. All this, however, is matter for another study.

[8]Even those individuals characterized as "Uncle Toms" and old "grannies" notorious for their prowhite attitude have begun stating that they see whites as racists.

Conclusions

IN the Introduction, I suggested that this investigation is an attempt to relate social and cultural realities to their coexistent individual psychological dimensions in a black ghetto in San Francisco. I suggested further that this study in part attempts to discover whether there have been any substantial changes from the findings of previous scholars who have studied black Americans. I have further attempted to show the manner of integration of the social situation in which black Americans find themselves, their economic and political position, and the family structure common in the black American family households in large urban areas. Based on these observations, I also attempted to clarify the attitudes, values, and behaviors inevitably following from this interpenetration of the social and personal.

It appears reasonably clear that there is a complex feedback network among the social structure, individual psychological dynamics, and family structure of the black American subculture. A structural situation in which men are less economically potent than women may elicit from the former certain concerns about their potencies in other areas. One of the defenses against these feelings is physical or at least emotional abandonment of the family. Families which are raised in the absence of the father and are dominated by the mother tend to produce cross-sex identity in young males as well as difficulties in the proper psychosexual development of females. When these facts act in conjunction within a social-cultural context where the black American is despised, seen as inferior (and treated as such by and large), given an inadequate education by individuals who feel that he could not make use of a better one, and put into a situation where his inability to handle the types of jobs which are available becomes a self-fulfilling prophecy, certain results inevitably occur.

217

Interaction between Hunter's Pointers' perception of social sex role and the reality of the social-structural position they occupy leads to a socialization experience unconsciously designed to help replicate the conditions which produced it. The dimensions of this interaction stand out most clearly when the relationship between the themes of sexuality, aggression, nurturance, expressive activity, and achievement as they are perceived by Hunter's Point residents are elucidated.

In general, Thematic Apperception Test (TAT) responses concerning sexual themes indicated that many see sex as an instrumental as well as an expressive activity. The quality of these responses indicates sexual activity is perceived as dangerous by males and as an opportunity for manipulation by women. Struggles for dominance between men and women are a continuous theme. This seems to be related to the ambivalence which men show about dependency. But even more striking is the joyless dangerousness surrounding sex for men. In contrast to the defensive hypersexuality myth, so necessary to black males — faced as they are with the reality of their economically subordinate position to women and to whites in general — is the reality of their deep concern about their sexual identity and potency.

The need for sexual manuevering and posturing and the early sexual awakening and disappointments we have noted all seem to be reflected in the TAT records. Relations between the sexes in Hunter's Point might be summarized as being distrustful, manipulative, and essentially destructive. For women there is the expectation of abandonment and nonsupport, fully borne out by the reality which their expectations at least partially help to create. For men, there is the recognition of social impotence and the fear of sexual impotence, occasioned by cross-sex anxiety produced by the entire socialization and life experiences. Defensive aggression against women and abandonment of them due to fear of involvement and eventual passive resignation to the feared (and unconsciously desired) supremacy of women characterizes the modal behavior of men with respect to women.

Additionally, nurturance and sexuality are equated by both men and women, and both use it defensively and manipulatively. That is, men are, by and large, unable to face their needs for nurturance and unable to be nurtured in a trusting way. The complex fear-love relation with the mother has prevented many from being able to view such needs as other than dangerous.

All this seems clear from the ethnographic observations and is well

218

supported by the TAT evidence. There are implications involving the relationships of such values as those surrounding achievement and expressive needs, however, that are not as immediately evident. Some of these implications are important as well in discussing the probable future of individuals, and by extension of groups of like individuals.

The achievement themes shown in the TAT responses of the Hunter's Pointers were sparse and often highly unrealistic; in fact, a significant proportion of the time achievement was rejected as unattainable or undesirable. Often, even where achievement was seen as attainable, the processes leading to it were either ignored or magically fantasized. Often achievement was seen as the simple result of wishing. Processes which might bring achievement-oriented values into conflict with expressive values were both overtly and covertly rejected. Hunter's Pointers simply did not find any positive expressive content in achievement except through magical thinking.

All this, too, is not unexpected. In detail any one of these points might very well have been clear from the ethnographic observations. The TATs and the ethnographic observations taken together, however, present a remarkably uniform and coherent picture of life in Hunter's Point which appears to be very stable indeed.

Keeping in mind Wallace's (1952) warnings about the inadequacies of the "unimodal personality" approach to any population, I still feel that general statements about the "typical" Hunter's Point resident are justified.

In Hunter's Point, children are raised in an essentially absent-father, matrifocal family. The distrust of males by females and the cross-sexuality this engenders in males are never overcome. The family, being black, is in a subordinate and despised position in the larger and dominant society. At the same time, the child is learning to respond to his defensive needs in the area of male-female relations with aggression, dominance, and manipulation. He is learning, by means of a host of subtle and not-so-subtle clues, that he is considered inadequate vis-à-vis whites.

From his (or her) parents, he has already learned there is little use to try to achieve, since achievement is denied you by whites. He is also learning, though he tries to deny it, that he is perceived to be inferior. His perception of his inadequate social position and that of his peers and other blacks is empirical evidence that he is not sophisticated enough to successfully challenge the status quo, for which he at least in part accepts a racist explanation. His schoolteachers expect little from him

219

and thus lay the foundation for a negative performance, fulfilling in that way both his own and the teacher's expectations.

By this time, the young man or woman has begun to have the kind of disappointments in his relations with the opposite sex which characterize his adult life. Jobs are not easily available to men without education, which is hard to come by both because of the educational system and the values inculcated in him. Without a job he becomes increasingly powerless to control the destinies of his woman and child, whom he often abandons. He can save face neither with them nor within society at large except by accepting a set of values which denigrates the experiences he is unable to have, or by lying about his status, or by self-deception.

Women, pregnant at an early age, certain of abandonment by their men, and usually more capable of self-support (through ADC) than their husbands or lovers, soon become the core of a family. The stability of the mother-child bond is enhanced by government aid programs that penalize those families in which a man is present in the home. The mother inculcates her children with values of immediate gratification — her daughters with distrust of men, her sons with a fear and hatred of women — and the cycle is complete.

Individual blacks in Hunter's Point develop attitudes of self-depreciation, a low level of realistic achievement orientation, and defensively expressive life styles at variance with the type of life styles which might be more suitably oriented toward the macrosociety, and thus they continue the process of their own individual and group isolation.

These are not new observations. Scholars have noted these in the past. If there have been any significant changes from the type of findings of previous scholars such as Kardiner and Ovesey (1951), they are not apparent in Hunter's Point. Hunter's Point is a society selected, by virtue of the poverty of its members, for people who actually fill the role of being socially depressed. Now, this may seem a tautology: these are the depressed because they are the depressed. A careful examination of the life histories of those individuals interviewed in Hunter's Point, however, suggests that although all of them came from families which were structurally or personally disorganized, not all these families were necessarily on "relief" or public wards. This disorganization is modal and, according to Moynihan (1965a), increasing among black American families.

It is well to remember that while some Hunter's Point families have been long-time public housing residents, not all of them have been. There appears to be a large floating population in the black urban community which moves in and out of public housing depending on the level of its income, and this income itself fluctuates from time to time (because of obvious structural reasons). I am suggesting, then, that the quality of the experience of Hunter's Point inhabitants is not one which is bizarre or unfamiliar to most black Americans.

Personally inadequate defense systems such as those I have noted among Hunter's Point residents develop, it must be obvious, neither genetically nor in a social vacuum. The integration of defense systems is at least as dependent on social-structural situations as it is on inherent "ego strength" levels. The deleterious and destructive aspects (in my view) of the kind of matrifocality I have described will not easily be altered in short order. As long as the current structural situation of black Americans remains unchanged, so will the seemingly stable family structure and its negative effects.

EPILOGUE

FOLLOWING my initial field work (1966-67), I returned twice to the Hunter's Point area (in 1969 and 1970) for one- or two-day visits, during which times I attempted to look up families I had known there and generally observe conditions. Some things had changed, others had remained the same. More housing units had been destroyed in the process of a city redevelopment scheme; some additional units of the older housing had been abandoned. There was much greater evidence of Afro hairstyles and "dapping" handshakes and greetings. African-influenced clothing styles had become much more widespread, and much more militant graffiti decorated the abandoned houses.

Local residents complained that the local level of violence was much higher and expressed concern with endemic hard-drug use in the neighborhood. It was generally believed that the level of police protection had dropped to an all-time low. Many local organizations had disappeared and been replaced by (I assume) equally evanescent ones with much more militant names or programs.

Several of the families I had known had disappeared: in some cases their housing had been destroyed, in other cases they had moved more or less of their own accord, as many Americans do in our transient society.

Babalona had had another baby and was as cheerful as ever. Mango

had quit his job to become a "community activist," though no one
seemed to know just where he was or what he was doing.

The general sense of déjà vu which I felt during these return visits
prompted me to review both the meaning and nature of my original
field work and its underlying assumptions, and how these had changed
through my experiences.

I first entered Hunter's Point as a liberal-activist graduate student
concerned with and involved in what at that time was termed rather
loosely the "civil rights movement." My ideological stance at that time
was, I believe, characteristic of the many young white liberals of the
early and middle 1960s. It was my unshaken belief that the condition
(which I believed intolerable) of America's "Negroes" (*black* was a
term of opprobrium at the time) was entirely due to white racism. Following from these basic beliefs were several assumedly logical corollary
beliefs. I believed that blacks and whites were the same in any significant
sense. I believed that the socioeconomic condition of black Americans
was due entirely, ultimately, and effectively to structural factors in
American society as a whole. I further believed that all that was necessary to achieve a golden age of American interracial justice and cooperation was to remove these structural barriers.

I believed, in short, that passage of the proper legislation, perhaps
in response to militant (even if at times illegal) social action, would suf-
fice to remove barriers of discrimination and would consequently permit blacks to achieve full social, political, and economic equality in the
United States — and all within my own lifetime.

Such statements now appear to me painfully naïve. Within two years
— i.e., by the time I had completed field work and analyzed the data I
had collected — many of my perceptions had measurably changed.

The most crucial change in my thinking came about as a result of my
growing awareness of the importance of human emotional organization
in determining behavior. Emotional organization, created in part by
certain social-structural factors and in part by fundamental human
needs and feelings, becomes inextricably intertwined with and supportive of social-cultural phenomena. Eventually such unconscious attitudes
and behavioral sets come to have a dynamic of their own, stable and
long lasting, resistant to changes in the environment in which they are
expressed.

The basis for such theoretical assumptions is far too complex to deal

223

with here in other than a brief fashion. We have discussed it elsewhere (DeVos and Hippler, 1969; Hippler, Boyer, and Boyer, 1973; Hippler, 1973). Essentially, however, I have come to believe that cognition and perception, and even behaviors easily explained by reference to some "commonsense" psychology, are in fact motivated, informed, and deeply colored by unconscious emotional organization and defenses which are developed to deal with such unconscious feelings.

In short, I have come to believe that whatever may be the ultimate causes that have operated to produce the present "cultural personality" of a group, once established, that "cultural personality" has a persistence far greater than has usually been admitted. One of the most striking examples of this is the effect, which I believe to have demonstrated, of the matrifocal family in modern black urban culture.

In the discipline of physics there is a concept called entropy, which very simply defined is the tendency for all systems to lose energy. That is, everything in the universe has a natural tendency to run down. Life, then, may be seen to be an antientropic force, accumulating and concentrating energy.

It may be that there is such a thing as social entropy. I believe that great amounts of effort — energy, if you will — must be put into a social system to establish relatively equal adult sex roles and stable expectations. When such a system is disrupted, it "drops" to a lower energy level of the most fundamental and irreducible social unit, that of mother and child. I have noted in the text some of the very great emotional strains produced by such a family form. It is my belief that to overcome the inertia of such a system demands the expenditure of tremendous energy, and that that expenditure is demanded precisely of those who, because of the kinds of defenses they have had to develop to deal with these strains, are the least capable of mobilizing that energy.

It is for these reasons that I now believe that simple changes, such as legislative orders for equality, in social systems are inadequate to change the fundamental emotional organization of the members of a given group in any short period of time. That is, the social sex-role expectations (at the very least) and the general emotional organization and lifeview that result from a specific form of socialization will change over a number of generations, not within a few years. This would be so even if social-structural changes were easy to accomplish, and for many reasons they are not. Jacques (1957) has pointed out that even when social systems change, the way in which individuals perceive their position in the structure and the unconscious attitudes they bring with them may make changes appear more real than they are. He also points out that, conversely, the meaning of an unchanged social system can change if the attitude and unconscious feelings of the role players in it differ greatly from previous actors.

Viewing with this perspective the many overt changes in interracial relationships and in the "self-image" of black Americans over the past decade, it appears to me that much of what has passed for dramatic change has an underlying core of overriding stability. Supposed changes in the attitudes of white Americans reflect, I believe, not a fundamental shift in underlying perceptions, but a defensive adaptation to the seeming winds of change — a defensiveness that continues to generate anxiety in both blacks and whites. Growing demands for separation of the races for some "temporary period," I believe, reflect a thinly disguised acknowledgment of the unchanging fact of this separation which has existed since the first blacks were brought to the colonies as indentured servants in 1619. Though there are positive elements in the desire of many black Americans to glorify their blackness and their African roots and to consider the black experience as both unique and potentially creative, my own observations of this phenomenon have led me to believe it is in large part (understandably) defensive.

Change occurs. It occurs, however, much more slowly than Americans like to believe. Part of the active, pragmatic ethos of American culture insists that there are no insoluble problems. Part of that same ethos, expressed so dramatically in Henry Ford's observation that "history is bunk," ignores the power of the past to influence the present and believes that what is desired badly enough can be accomplished instantly.

It is my belief that changes which have occurred in interracial relations in the United States recently are part of a very slow, long-term trend. Within the scope of these changes individuals uniquely predisposed to take advantage of openings in the social system have increasingly greater opportunities to do so. For those most deeply imbedded in the pathic substructures of black American life, these changes will come about, if at all, with much more agonizing slowness.

I have in my analysis deliberately avoided any discussion of current controversies over "innate" intelligence as measured by I.Q.'s, etc. I neither feel qualified to comment on these issues nor believe that they are fundamentally relevant to the present study. People of fairly minimal intelligence (whatever that is) have the capacity to respond creatively and maturely to the world: a mature emotional organization is not beyond the reach of many "below-average" individuals. Conversely, a high level of intelligence does not alone predispose one to achievement or emotional maturity. While these issues of emotional adequacy versus intellectual capacity may be related, they are not necessarily so. The burden of my work has been to suggest the stability of a pattern of emotional organization which I believe to be the dominant influence in the subculture of lower-class urban blacks in the community which I observed.

APPENDIX

Rents and Incomes of Households
in Hunter's Point, San Francisco, 1967.

Adapted from Joint Report of Hunter's Point
Joint Housing Committee and San Francisco
Redevelopment Agency Survey, February 21, 1967.

Total Households Interviewed, by Race

Race	Households	
	Number	Percentage
Black	775	91.1
Other nonwhite	43	5.1
White	32	3.8
Total	850	100.0

Rents Paid by Tenants

Monthly Rent	Household	
	Number	Percentage
Under $49	33	3.9
$50-59	584	68.7
$60-69	200	23.5
$70-79	19	2.2
$80-85	2	0.3
Refused to answer	12	1.4
Total	850	100.0

Gross Income per Month in Temporary Housing Units (the More "Well-to-Do")

Income*	Percentage of Families
Under $200	16.2
$200-349	19.9
$350-499	27.7
$500 and over	30.3
Not reported	5.9
Total	100.0

*Many of the "above-poverty" incomes were in double-wage earner families.

Percent Distribution of Gross Monthly Income by Type of Household

Income	Under $200	$200-349	$350-499	$500 and Over
Single persons	47.2	23.5	18.4	10.9
Husband-Wife households	4.6	18.5	34.2	42.7
Other male head	13.9	13.9	36.1	36.1
Other female head	27.9	31.7	24.0	16.4

BIBLIOGRAPHY

Abrahams, Roger. 1962. Playing the dozens. *Amer. J. Folklore* 75:209-20.

Barnouw, Victor. 1963. *Culture and personality.* Homewood, Ill.: Dorsey Press.

Bettelheim, Bruno. 1962. *Symbolic wounds: Puberty rites and the envious male.* New York: Collier Books.

Bettelheim, Bruno, and Morris Janowitz. 1964. *Social change and prejudice.* London: Free Press of Glencoe, Collier-Macmillan.

Boyer, Ruth M. 1964. The matrifocal family among the Mescalero: Additional data. *Amer. Anthropologist* 66:593-602.

Brody, Eugene B. 1963. Color and identify conflict in young boys: Observations of Negro mothers and sons in urban Baltimore. *Psychiatry* 24:246-337.

Brown, Claude. 1965. *Manchild in the promised land.* New York: Macmillan.

Burton, R. V., and J. W. M. Whiting. 1961. The absent father and cross sex identity. *Merrill Palmer Q.* 7:85-95.

_____. 1960. The absent father: Effects on the developing child. Paper presented at APA meeting, Sept. 1960.

Cohen, Yehudi. 1955. Adolescent conflict in a Jamaican community. *J. Intl. Psa. Inst.* 9:139-72.

Dai, Bingham. 1948. Some problems of personality development among Negro children. In *Personality in nature, society, and culture,* ed. Clyde Kluckhohn, Henry A. Murray, and David Schneider, pp. 545-66. New York: Alfred A. Knopf.

Davis, Allison, and R. J. Havighurst. 1948. Social class and color differences in child rearing. In *Personality in nature, society, and culture,* ed. Clyde Kluckhohn, Henry A. Murray, and David S. Schneider, pp. 308-20. New York: Alfred A. Knopf.

DeVos, George A., and Arthur E. Hippler. 1969. Cultural psychology: Comparative studies of human behavior. In *Handbook of social psychology,* ed. Gardner Lindzey and Elliot Aronson, pp. 323-417. 2nd ed. vol. 4. Reading, Mass.: Addison Wesley.

Eddington, Neil A. 1968. The pimp as culture hero: The ethnography of the toast. Paper presented at the American Anthropological Association meeting, Nov. 1968, Seattle.

Elkins, Stanley. 1959. *Slavery.* Chicago: University of Chicago Press.

_____. 1961. Slavery and personality. In *Studying personality cross-culturally,* ed. Bert Kaplan, pp. 243-67. Evanston, Ill.: Row, Peterson.

Ellison, Ralph. 1952. *The invisible man.* New York: Random House.

Festinger, Leon. 1962. Cognitive dissonance. *Scient. Amer.* 207:93-102.

Frazier, E. Franklyn. 1957. *The Negro in the United States.* New York: Macmillan.

Galbraith, John Kenneth. 1958. *The affluent society.* Boston: Houghton Mifflin.

Grier, William H., and Price M. Cobbs. 1968. *Black rage.* New York: Basic Books.

Hendin, Herbert. 1969. *Black suicide.* New York: Basic Books.

Hippler, Arthur E. 1970*a*. The dangerous Negro: A defensive self perception in American Negro life. *Transcultural Psychiat. Research Rev.* 7:68-73.

_____. 1970*b*. The game of black and white at Hunter's Point. *Trans-Action* 7:56-63.

_____. 1970*c*. A microcosm of the American game of black and white: Race conflict in a San Francisco neighborhood. In *Social problems today,* ed. Clifford D. Bryant, pp. 136-154. New York: J. B. Lippincott.

_____. 1973. The Athabascans of interior Alaska: A culture and personality perspective. *Amer. Anthropologist,* Nov. 1973.

Hippler, Arthur E., L. Bryce Boyer, and Ruth M. Boyer. 1973. The psychocultural significance of the Alaska Athabascan potlatch system. *Psychoanalytic Study of the Child* 28.

Jacques, Elliott. 1957. Social systems as a defense against persecutory and depressive anxiety. In *New directions in psychoanalysis,* ed. Melanie Klein, Paula Heinmann, and R. E. Money Kyrle, pp. 487-97. New York: Basic Books.

Kardiner, Abram, and Lionel Ovesey. 1951. *The mark of oppression: Explorations in the personality of the American Negro.* (2nd ed. 1962). New York: Meridian Books, World Publishing Co.

Karon, Bertram. 1958. *The Negro personality.* New York: Springer Publishing Co.

Katz, Irwin, and Patricia Gurin, eds. 1969. *Race and the social sciences.* New York: Basic Books.

Klein, M. W. 1967. Street gang theory. *Trans-Action* 4,8:79-80.

Kluckhohn, Florence. 1951. *Dominant and variant value orientations.* Evanston, Ill.: Row, Peterson.

Kluckhohn, Florence, and F. L. Strodtbeck. 1961. *Variations in value orientations.* Evanston, Ill.: Row, Peterson.

Leighton, Dorothea, J. S. Harding, D. B. Macklin, A. M. MacMillan, and A. H. Leighton. 1963. *The character of danger: Psychiatric symptoms in selected communities: The Stirling County study of psychiatric disorders and sociocultural environment.* vol 3. New York: Basic Books.

Lewis, Oscar. 1961. *Children of Sanchez.* New York: Random House.

BIBLIOGRAPHY

_____. 1959. *Five families.* New York: Basic Books.

Liebow, Elliot. 1967. *Tally's Corner.* Boston: Little, Brown.

Lipset, Seymour Martin, and Reinhard Bendix. 1959. *Social mobility in industrial societies.* Berkeley: University of California Press.

Long, E., and R. Trueb. n.d. 128 hours: A report on the disturbance in the city and county of San Francisco. San Francisco: San Francisco Police Department.

McClelland, D.C. 1961. *The achieving society.* New York: Van Nostrand.

McClelland, D. C., V. W. Atkinson, R. A. Clark, and E. L. Lowell. 1953. *The achievement motive.* New York: Appleton-Century-Crofts.

Michel, W. 1961. Father absence and delay of gratification: Cross cultural comparisons. *J. Abnorm. and Soc. Psych.* 63:166-227.

Miller, Elizabeth W. 1966. *The Negro in America: A bibliography.* Cambridge: Harvard University Press.

Moynihan, Daniel Patrick, ed. 1965*a. The Negro family.* Washington, D.C.: Office of Policy Planning and Research, U.S. Dept. of Labor.

_____. 1965*b.* Employment income and the ordeal of the Negro family. *Daedalus* 94:745-70.

Murray, Henry A. 1950. Uses of the Thematic Apperception Test, in *Handbook of projective techniques.* Bernard I. Murstein (ed.). New York: Basic Books.

Mussen, Paul, and Luther Distler. 1959. Masculinity, identification, and father-son relationships. *J. Abnor. and Soc. Psych.* 59: 350-56.

Parsons, Talcott. 1964. *Social structure and personality.* New York: Free Press.

Pettigrew, Thomas. 1964. *A profile of the American Negro.* New York: D. Van Nostrand.

Radin, Norma, and Constance K. Kamii. 1965. The child rearing attitudes of disadvantaged Negro mothers and some educational implications. *J. Negro Ed.* 34:138-46.

Rexroth, Kenneth. 1967. The fuzz. *Playboy* 14:76.

Riesman, David, Nathan Glazer, and Reuel Denney. 1953. *The lonely crowd: A study of the changing American character.* New York: Doubleday Anchor Books.

Rosenthal, Robert, and Lenore F. Jacobson. 1968. Teacher expectations for the disadvantaged. *Scientific American* 218,4:19-23.

Schwartz, M. 1965. Northern United States Negro matriarchy: Status vs. authority. *Phylon* 26:18-24.

Smith, Howard P., and Marcia Abramson. 1962. Racial and family experience correlates of mobility aspirations. *J. Negro Ed.* 31:117-24.

Smith, Raymond T. 1956. *The Negro family in British Guiana.* New York: Grove Press.

Srole, Leo, T. S. Langner, S. T. Michael, M. K. Opler, and T. A. C. Rennie. 1962. *Mental health in the metropolis: The midtown Manhattan study.* Vol. 1. New York: McGraw-Hill.

Strodtbeck, F. L. 1964. The poverty dependency syndrome of the A.D.C. female based Negro American family. *Amer. J. Orthopsychiat.* 34:216-17.

Wallace, A. F. C. 1952. The modal personality of the Tuscarora Indians as revealed by the Rorschach test. Bulletin 150. Washington, D.C.: American Bureau of Ethnology.

Yinger, J. Milton. 1965. *A minority group in American society.* New York: McGraw-Hill Social Problems Series.

Young, Michael, and Peter Wilmott. 1957. *Family and kinship in East London.* Baltimore: Penguin Books.

INDEX

235

DATE DUE